STREET SPANISH SLANG DICTIONARY & THESAURUS

STREET SPANISH SLANG DICTIONARY & THESAURUS

David Burke

John Wiley & Sons, Inc.

New York • Chichester • Weinheim • Brisbane • Singapore • Toronto

Design and Production: David Burke
Front Cover Illustration: Ty Semaka
Inside Illustrations: Ty Semaka

This book is printed on acid-free paper ♾

Published by John Wiley & Sons, Inc.
Published simultaneously in Canada.

ISBN 0-471-16834-3

Printed in the United States of America
10 9 8 7 6 5 4 3 2

This book is dedicated to my wonderful friend Joseph DiMaggio...
No, not *that* one!

ACKNOWLEDGMENTS

It was a stroke of luck finding an artist as gifted as Ty Semaka who consistently provides illustrations that are distinctive, clever, and downright hilarious.

One of the absolute best parts of writing this book was working with immensely talented people like Chris Jackson, my editor at John Wiley & Sons. I'm so grateful for his guidance, enthusiasm, professionalism, unparalleled wit, and most important, his friendship.

A tremendous and warm thanks goes to Diane who was always supportive, encouraging, and available. She made the final phases of this book truly enjoyable.

CONTENTS

INTRODUCTION

Slang, idioms, and colloquialisms are all an active part of the living Spanish language. These nonstandard terms and expressions are used in movies, television and radio shows, news broadcasts, books, newspapers, magazines, and business writing, making it difficult for a nonnative speaker to feel like an "insider."

The **Street Spanish Slang Dictionary & Thesaurus** will lead the reader through many of the most popular and colorful terms and expressions rarely, if ever, taught in school.

This unique book is divided into two primary parts:

- **The Street Spanish Dictionary *(Part 1)***

  This section presents the reader with more than 2,000 popular Spanish terms, including slang, idioms, colloquialisms, vulgarities, proverbs, special notes, synonyms, antonyms, variations, plus an array of hilarious illustrations. In addition, usage examples are offered throughout this section to give the reader a clear understanding of the weight of a given entry.

- **The Street Spanish Thesaurus *(Part 2)***

  This unique thesaurus explores some of the most common expletives and obscenities used through the many Spanish-speaking countries. These pages allow the reader to look up a word in English and find an assortment of colorful, and often shocking, synonyms for each entry.

IMPORTANT: Slang must be used with discretion since it is an extremely casual "language" and certainly should not be practiced with formal dignitaries or employers that you are trying to impress! Most important, since a nonnative speaker of Spanish may tend to sound forced or artificial using slang, your first goal should be to recognize and understand these types of words. Once you have a firm grasp on the usage of the slang words and expressions presented in this book, try using some in your conversations for extra color!

Welcome to the expressive and "colorful" world of Spanish slang!

Legend

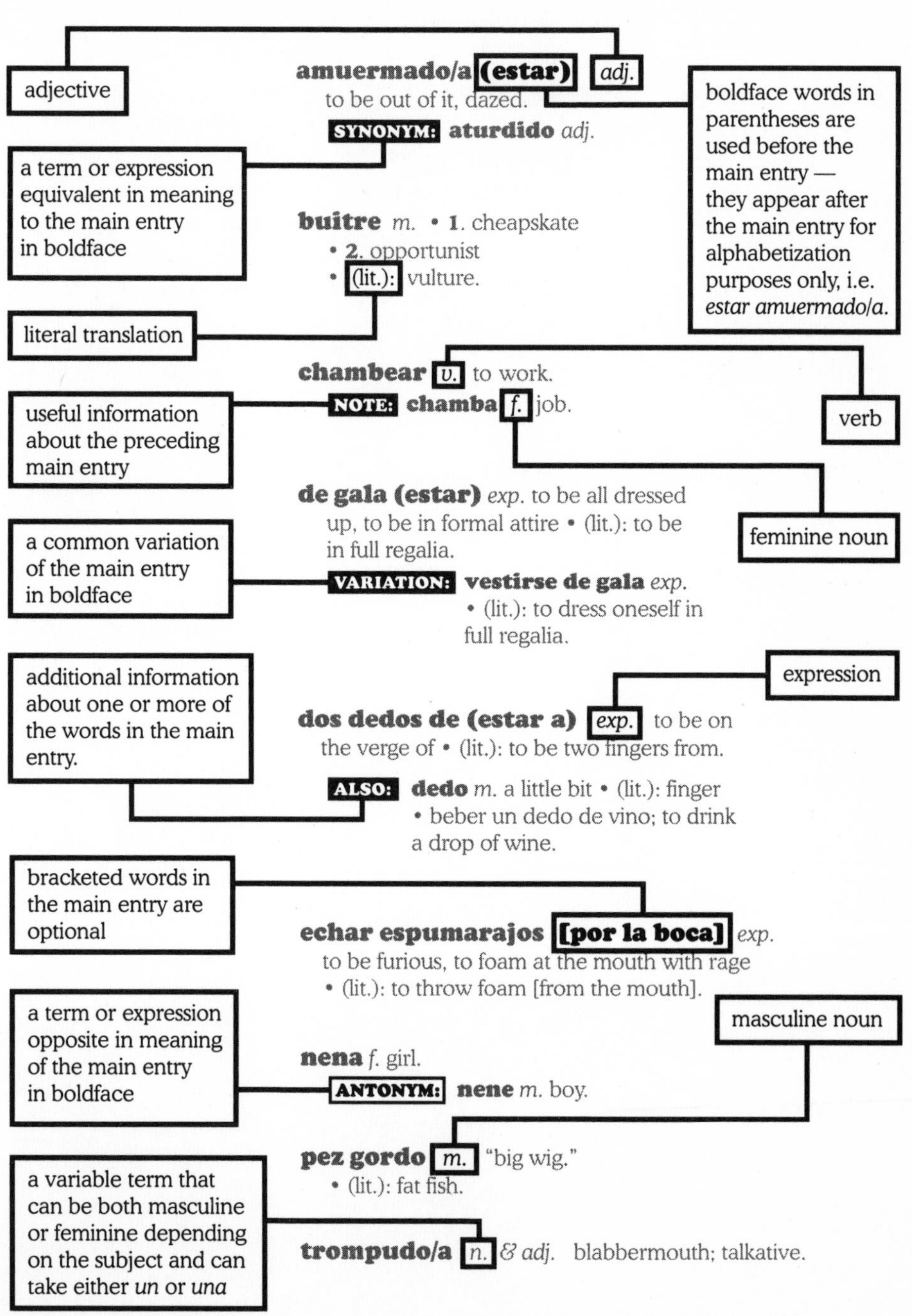

adjective
amuermado/a (estar) adj.
to be out of it, dazed.
SYNONYM: aturdido adj.
boldface words in parentheses are used before the main entry — they appear after the main entry for alphabetization purposes only, i.e. estar amuermado/a.
a term or expression equivalent in meaning to the main entry in boldface
buitre m. • 1. cheapskate
• 2. opportunist
• (lit.): vulture.
literal translation
chambear v. to work.
NOTE: chamba f. job.
useful information about the preceding main entry
verb
de gala (estar) exp. to be all dressed up, to be in formal attire • (lit.): to be in full regalia.
feminine noun
a common variation of the main entry in boldface
VARIATION: vestirse de gala exp.
• (lit.): to dress oneself in full regalia.
additional information about one or more of the words in the main entry.
expression
dos dedos de (estar a) exp. to be on the verge of • (lit.): to be two fingers from.
ALSO: dedo m. a little bit • (lit.): finger
• beber un dedo de vino; to drink a drop of wine.
bracketed words in the main entry are optional
echar espumarajos [por la boca] exp.
to be furious, to foam at the mouth with rage
• (lit.): to throw foam [from the mouth].
masculine noun
a term or expression opposite in meaning of the main entry in boldface
nena f. girl.
ANTONYM: nene m. boy.
pez gordo m. "big wig."
• (lit.): fat fish.
a variable term that can be both masculine or feminine depending on the subject and can take either un or una
trompudo/a n. & adj. blabbermouth; talkative.

STREET SPANISH DICTIONARY

Part 1

(Popular Spanish Terms Including Slang, Idioms, Colloquialisms, Vulgarities, Proverbs, Special Notes, Synonyms, Antonyms, & Variations)

a cuatro patas *exp.* on all fours (also used to describe a sexual position: "doggie-style") • (lit.): on all four paws.

a decir verdad *exp.* to tell you the truth • (lit.): to tell truth.

example:
A decir verdad, no me gusta nada esto.

translation:
To tell you the truth, I don't like this at all.

a despecho de *exp.* in spite of • (lit.): to spite of.

example:
Bueno **a despecho de** lo que pasó espero que sigamos siendo amigos.

translation:
Well, **in spite of** what happened I hope we are still friends.

a dos dedos de (estar) *exp.* to be on the verge of • (lit.): to be two fingers from.

example:
Estoy **a dos dedos de** comprar una casa.

translation:
I'm **on the verge of** buying a house.

a dos pasos de aquí *exp.* nearby, a hop, skip, and a jump from here • (lit.): two steps from here.

example:
La casa de Jorge está **a dos pasos de** aquí.

translation:
George's house is **a hop, skip, and a jump** from here.

ANTONYM -1:
en el quinto pino *exp.* very far away • (lit.): in the fifth pine tree.

ANTONYM -2:
en la loma del diablo *exp.* very far away • (lit.): in the hill of the devil.

ANTONYM -3:
en la loma del pepino *exp.* very far away • (lit.): in the hill of the cucumber.

a escondidas *exp.* secretly, on the sly • (lit.): on the hiding [from the verb *esconder* meaning "to hide"].

example:
Pablo y Sonia fueron al cine **a escondidas**.

translation:
Pablo and Sonia went to the movies **secretly**.

a fin de *exp.* in order to • (lit.): to end of.

example:
Voy a comer menos **a fin de** perder peso.

translation:
I'm going to eat less **in order to** lose weight.

SYNONYM:
con el fin de *exp.* • (lit.): with the end of.

¡A la chingada! *exp.* Fuck it!

¡A la puñeta! *interj. (Cuba)* Go to hell! • (lit.): Go to masturbation!

example:
La próxima vez que me insulte Olivia, ¡la voy a mandar **a la puñeta**!

translation:
The next time Olivia insults me, I'm going to tell her **to go to hell**!

¡A la verga! *intjer.* Damn! • (lit.): To the penis!

example:
¡**A la verga**! Este trabajo es demasiado difícil.

translation:
Damn! This job is too difficult.

SYNONYMS:
SEE – **penis**, *p. 243*.

a lo largo y a lo ancho *exp.* throughout • (lit.): lengthwise and sideways.

example:
Manuel siempre ha tenido mucha suerte **a lo largo y a lo ancho** de su vida.

translation:
Manuel's always been very lucky **throughout** his life.

a lo perro *adv.* (used to describe a sexual act) doggie-style • (lit.): in the style of a dog.

a pedir de boca *exp.* smoothly • (lit.): to taste from the mouth.

example:
Esta presentación me ha salido **a pedir de boca**.

translation:
This presentation **went smoothly**.

NOTE:
This popular expression can also be used in the culinary world when a dish has been prepared to perfection meaning "delicious" or "perfect" • *Esta langosta está a pedir de boca;* This lobster is delicious.

a primera vista *exp.* at first glance • (lit.): at first look.

example:
A primera vista, Manolo parece buena persona.

translation:
At first glance, Manolo seems like a nice guy.

a puerta cerrada *exp.* behind closed doors • (lit.): at closed door.

example:
Los ejecutivos de la empresa tuvieron una reunión **a puerta cerrada**.

translation:
The company's executives had a meeting **behind closed doors**.

SYNONYM -1:
en clausura *exp.* • (lit.): in confinement (said of life in a monastery).

SYNONYM -2:
en privado *exp.* • (lit.): in private.

ANTONYM:
a puerta abierta *exp.* with opened doors • (lit.): at opened door.

a punto de *exp.* on the point of, on the verge of, about to • (lit.): at point of.

example:
Estuve **a punto de** decirle lo que pienso de él.

translation:
I was **on the verge of** telling him what I think about him.

a que *exp.* I'll bet • (lit.): to that.

example:
A que llueve el día de mi cumpleaños.

translation:
I'll bet it rains on my birthday.

a toda prisa *exp.* at full speed, as quickly as possible • (lit.): at all speed.

example:
Voy a la escuela **a toda prisa** porque me levanté tarde.

translation:
I'm going to school **at full speed** because I woke up late.

SYNONYM -1:
a toda vela *exp.* • (lit.): at all sail.

SYNONYM -2:
a todo meter *exp. (Southern Spain)* • (lit.): at all putting.

SYNONYM -3:
en un abrir y cerrar de ojos *exp.* in the twinkling of an eye • (lit.): in the opening and closing of an eye.

SYNONYM -4:
en un avemaría *exp.* • (lit.): in one Hail Mary.

SYNONYM -5:
en un chiflido *exp.* • (lit.): in one whistle.

SYNONYM -6:
en un credo *exp.* • (lit.): in one creed.

SYNONYM -7:
en un decir Jesús *exp.* • (lit.): in one saying of Jesus.

SYNONYM -8:
en un dos por tres *exp.* • (lit.): in a two by three.

SYNONYM -9:
en un improviso *exp. (Colombia, Mexico, Venezuela)* • (lit.): in one sudden action.

SYNONYM -10:
en un menos de lo que canta un gallo *exp.* • (lit.): in less time that it takes a rooster to sing (or crow).

SYNONYM -11:
en un salto *exp.* • (lit.): in one leap.

SYNONYM -12:
en un soplo *exp.* • (lit.): in a gust or blow.

a todas luces *exp.* any way you look at it, clearly • (lit.): by all lights.

example:
Se ve que tiene dinero **a todas luces**.

translation:
You can **clearly** tell he's got money.

SYNONYM:
a toda luz *exp.* • (lit.): by all light.

abadesa *f. (Mexico)* pimp • (lit.): head of the house.

abriles (tener) *exp.* to be _____ years old • (lit.): to have _____ Aprils.

example:
Lola es muy joven. Sólo **tiene 20 abriles**.

translation:
Lola is very young. She's only **20 years old**.

ALSO -1:
tener muchas millas *exp.* to be very old • (lit.): to have many miles.

NOTE:
This expression is usually used in reference to an old woman.

ALSO -2:
tener___ años y muchos meses *exp.* to be old • (lit.): to be ___ years old and many months more.

ALSO -3:
una mujer que ha tenido mucho sexo *exp.* said of an old woman • (lit.): a woman who has had a lot of sex.

SYNONYM:
primaveras (tener _____) *exp. (Mexico)* • (lit.): to have _____ springtimes.

acabar *v. (Argentina)* to ejaculate, to have an orgasm • (lit.): to finish.

example:
¡Estoy por **acabar**!

translation:
I'm going to **ejaculate**!

acariciar *v.* • (lit.): to caress, touch lightly.

example:
Durante la película, ¡José empezó a **acariciarme** el cuello!

translation:
During the movie, José started **to caress me** on my neck!

acariciarse *v.* to masturbate • (lit.): to fondle oneself.

SYNONYMS:
SEE – **masturbate**, *p. 239*.

aceite *n. & adj. (Cuba)* tightwad; stingy • (lit.): oil.

example:
Eres tan **aceite**. Nunca te ofreces a pagar la cena.

translation:
You're so **stingy**. You never offer to pay for dinner.

acostarse con rosemaria *exp. (Mexico)* to smoke marijuana • (lit.): to go to bed with Rosemary.

example:
Manuel se comporta tan raro todo el tiempo. Creo que **se acuesta con rosemaria**.

translation:
Manuel acts so strange all the time. I think he smokes **marijuana**.

¿Adónde coño vas? *exp.* Where the hell are you going?

NOTE:
¿Adónde carajo vas? *exp. (Argentina, Mexico)*.

adoquín *m. (Cuba)* idiot • (lit.): **paving** stone.

example:
El hombre con quien salí resultó ser un **adoquin**.

translation:
The guy I went out with turned out to be a **jerk**.

SYNONYM -1:
boludo *m. (Argentina)*.

SYNONYM -2:
bruto/a *adj.* • (lit.): stupid, crude.

SYNONYM -3:
caballo *m. (Puerto Rico)*.

SYNONYM -4:
cabezota *n.*

NOTE:
This comes from the feminine noun *cabeza* meaning "head." The suffix *-ota* is commonly used to modify the meaning of a noun – in this case, changing it to "big head."

SYNONYM -5:
cateto/a *adj. (Spain).*

SYNONYM -6:
chorlito *m.* • (lit.): golden plover (which is a type of bird).

SYNONYM -7:
goma *f. (Argentina)* • (lit.): rubber, glue.

SYNONYM -8:
lolo/a *adj. (Spain)* silly, foolish.

SYNONYM -9:
matado/a *n. (Spain)* idiot or nerd.

SYNONYM -10:
menso/a *n. (Mexico).*

SYNONYM -11:
pendejo *m. (Argentina)* • **1.** idiot, imbecile • **2.** coward • 3. immature • (lit.): pubic hair.

SYNONYM -12:
soquete *m. (Cuba).*

SYNONYM -13:
tarado/a *adj. (Argentina).*

SYNONYM -14:
tosco/a *adj.* • (lit.): coarse, crude, unrefined.

SYNONYM -15:
zopenco/a *adj.* • (lit.): dull, stupid.

ANTONYM -1:
avispado/a *adj.* • (lit.): clever, sharp.

NOTE:
This comes from the term *avispa* meaning "wasp."

ANTONYM -2:
despabilado/a *adj.* • (lit.): awakened.

NOTE:
This comes from the verb *despavilar* meaning "to wake up."

ANTONYM -3:
despejado/a *adj.* • (lit.): confident, assured (in behavior), clear (as in a cloudless sky).

ANTONYM -4:
listillo/a *adj.* • (lit.): a small clever person.

NOTE:
This comes from the adjective *listo/a* meaning "ready" or "clever."

ANTONYM -5:
pillo *adj.* • (lit.): roguish, mischievous (used especially in reference to children).

NOTE:
This adjective is always used in the masculine form. Interestingly enough, the feminine form, *pilla*, is rarely ever seen.

ANTONYM -6:
vivo/a *adj.* • (lit.): alive.

aduana *f. (Mexico)* whorehouse • (lit.): Customs.

example:
Hoy ví a Felipe entrar a una **aduana**. ¿Qué le pasaría si su esposa lo supiera?

translation:
Today I saw Felipe go into a **whorehouse**! What would happen to him if his wife found out?

afeminado *m.* homosexual • (lit.): an effeminate [man].

afuera de sí (estar) *exp.* beside oneself • (lit.): out of oneself.

example:
Alberto parece **estar afuera de sí**. ¿Qué pasó?

translation:
Alberto seems **to be beside himself**. What happened?

SYNONYM:
fuera de sí *exp.* • (lit.): out of oneself.

agarraderas *f.pl. (Mexico)* breasts, "tits" • (lit.): grabbers (from the verb *agarrar* meaning "to take" or "to grab").

example:
Esperanza nunca será un manequín. ¡Ella no tiene **agarraderas**!

translation:
Esperanza will never become a model. She doesn't have any **breasts**!

agarrado/a *n. & adj.* tightwad; stingy • (lit.): held.

example:
Antonio es muy **agarrado**. Nunca le compra regalos a nadie.

translation:
Antonio is very **stingy**. He never buys anyone gifts.

agarrar con las manos en la masa *exp.* to catch [someone] red-handed, to catch [someone] in the act • (lit.): to catch [someone] with the hands in the dough.

example:
A Luis lo **agarraron con las manos en la masa** cuando pretendía robar un carro.

translation:
Luis was **caught red-handed** when he was trying to steal a car.

SYNONYM -1:
coger con las manos en la masa *exp. (Spain)* • (lit.): to catch [someone] with his/her hands in the dough.

SYNONYM -2:
coger/agarrar/atrapar en el acto *exp.* • (lit.): to catch [someone] in the act.

SYNONYM -3:
coger/agarrar/atrapar en plena acción *exp.* • (lit.): to catch [someone] right in the action.

NOTE:
In these types of expressions, the verb *coger* is used primarily in Spain. In the rest of the Spanish-speaking world, *agarrar* and *atrapar* are most commonly used.

agotado/a (estar) *adj.* to be exhausted, completely tired out • (lit.): to be emptied or drained.

example:
He trabajado toda la noche. Estoy **agotado**.

translation:
I worked all night long. I'm **pooped**.

SYNONYM -1:
como un trapo viejo (estar/sentirse) *exp.* • (lit.): to be/to feel like an old rag.

SYNONYM -2:
hecho polvo (estar) *exp.* • (lit.): to be made of dust.

SYNONYM -3:
muerto/a (estar) *adj.* • (lit.): to be dead.

SYNONYM -4:
rendido/a (estar) *adj.* • (lit.): to be rendered (all off one's energy).

SYNONYM -5:
reventado/a (estar) *adj.* • (lit.): to be burst (like a balloon whose air has been suddenly let out).

aguacates *m.pl. (Mexico)* testicles • (lit.): little avocados.

aguafiestas *m.* party-pooper, stick in the mud, kill-joy • (lit.): water-festival (referring to someone who "throws water on a festival" as one would throw on a fire to extinguish it).

example:
A mi novio no le gusta ir a bailar. ¡Es un verdadero **aguafiestas**!

translation:
My boyfriend never likes to go out dancing. He's such a **stick in the mud**!

SYNONYM -1:
aguado/a *n. (Mexico).*

SYNONYM -2:
chocante *m. (Mexico).*

SYNONYM -3:
embolante *m. (Argentina).*

ahogarse en un vaso de agua *exp.* to get all worked up about something, to make a mountain out of a molehill • (lit.): to drown in a glass of water.

example:
Antonio se preocupa demasiado de todo. Siempre **se ahoga en un vaso de agua**.

translation:
Antonio worries too much about everything. He always **makes a mountain out of a molehill**.

SYNONYM:
ahogarse en poca agua *exp.* • (lit.): to drown (oneself) in little water.

al fin y al cabo *exp.* after all, when the dust clears • (lit.): to the end and to the end.

example:
Al fin y al cabo todo salió bien.
translation:
When all was said and done, everything turned out okay.

albondigas *f.pl. (Mexico)* testicles • (lit.): meatballs.

alcahuete *m.* • **1.** pimp • **2.** gossiper (lit.): wild artichoke.

alcaucil *m.* pimp • (lit.): wild artichoke.

alforjas *m.pl.* testicles • (lit.): saddlebags.

algo por el estilo *exp.* something like that, similar. • (lit.): something of the same style.
example:
Esa casa es **algo por el estilo** paresida a la mía.
translation:
That house **is similar** to mine.

SYNONYM:
cosas por el estilo *exp.* • (lit.): things of the same style.

alimentos *m.pl. (Mexico)* "tits" • (lit.): **1.** food allowance • **2.** alimony.

allá (estar tan) *exp.* to be very far away • (lit.): to be so there.
example:
¡Yo no sabía que Chicago **estaba tan allá**!
translation:
I didn't know Chicago was **so far away**!

ALSO:
muy allá *exp.* very far away • (lit.): very there.

almeja *f.* an extremely vulgar term for "vagina" • (lit.): clam.

VARIATION:
almejilla *f.* • (lit.): small clam.

NOTE:
The term *almeja* literally means "clam" but is used in slang to mean "vagina," so be careful how you use it! For example:

Voy a la playa a buscar almejas.

Common Translation #1:
I go to the beach to look for **clams**.
Common Translation #2:
I go to the beach to look for **vagina**.

SYNONYMS:
SEE – **vagina**, *p. 263*.

alucinar *v.* to amaze, to astonish, to hallucinate.

example:
Me quedé **alucinado** cuando te presentaste en la fiesta en bikini.

translation:
You **astonished** me when you showed up at the party wearing a bikini.

SYNONYM -1:
eslembar *v. (Cuba, Puerto Rico).*

SYNONYM -2:
flipar *v. (Spain).*

alzado/a *n. & adj.* snob; stuck up • (lit.): from the verb *alzar* meaning "to lift" which refers to a snobby person's nose in the air.

example:
¡Diana es tan **alzada**! Sólo va a restaurantes caros.

translation:
Diana is so **snobby**! She only goes to expensive restaurants.

amaricado • **1.** *m.* homosexual • **2.** *adj.* effeminate.

amaricarse *v.* to become homosexual (from the masculine noun *maricón* which is derogatory for "homosexual").

amiguete *m. (Spain)* pal, buddy, friend.

example:
Felipe es mi **amiguete**. Siempre puedo contar con él.

translation:
Felipe is my **pal**. I can always count on him.

VARIATION:
amigote *m.*

ALSO:
amiguete del alma *exp.* bosom buddy, close friend • (lit.): buddy of the soul.

SYNONYM -1:
amigo/a del alma *n.* best friend, soul mate • (lit.): friend of the soul.

SYNONYM -2:
colega *m. (Spain)* • (lit.): colleague.

SYNONYM -3:
cuate *m. (Mexico)* pal, buddy.

amor a primera vista *exp.* love at first sight • (lit.): [same].

example:
Cuando se conocieron mis padres, fue **amor a primera vista**.

translation:
When my parents met each other, it was **love at first sight**.

ampuloso/a *n. & adj.* snob; stuck up • (lit.): verbose, pompous.

example:
Laura es una **ampulosa**. Sólo invita a gente rica a sus fiestas.

translation:
Laura is a **snob**. She only invites rich people to her parties.

amuermado/a (estar) *adj.* to be out of it, dazed.

example:
Parece que Luis no durmió bien anoche. Hoy está **amuermado**.

translation:
It looks like Luis didn't sleep well last night. He's **out of it** today.

SYNONYM -1:
aplantanado/a *adj.*

SYNONYM -2:
aturdido/a *adj.*

SYNONYM -3:
volando/a *adj. (Argentina).*

andar con el estómago flojo *exp. (Mexico)* to have diarrhea • (lit.): to walk around with a loose stomach.

example:
No puedo ir contigo al cine; **ando con el estómago flojo** (or: **ando un poco flojo del estómago**).

translation:
I can't go with you to the movies. **I have diarrhea**.

andar con mal tapón *exp. (Mexico)* to have diarrhea • (lit.): to walk around with a defective cork.

example:
No me encuentro bien. **Ando con mal tapón**.

translation:
I don't feel well. **I have diarrhea**.

andar con otra *exp.* to have more then one girlfriend • (lit.): to walk with another female.

example:
Sé que te gusta Juan, pero ten cuidado. **Anda con otra**.

translation:
I know you like Juan, but be careful. **He has more than one girlfriend**.

SYNONYM:
andar con más de una *exp.* • (lit.): to be going with more than one female.

andar con otro *exp.* to have more than one boyfriend • (lit.): to walk with another male.

example:
Iba a pedirle a Berta que se casara conmigo, pero me acabo de enterar de que ¡**anda con otro**!

translation:
I was going to ask Berta to marry me, but I just found out she's **going with someone else**!

SYNONYM:
andar con más de uno *exp.* • (lit.): to be going with more than one male.

andar con rodeos *exp.* to beat around the bush • (lit.): to walk with detours.

example:
Alfredo siempre **anda con rodeos** cuando quiere explicar sus opiniones.

translation:
Alfredo always **beats around the bush** when he wants to explain his opinions.

SYNONYM -1:
andarse por las ramas *exp.* • (lit.): to stroll/walk by the branches.

SYNONYM -2:
emborrachar la perdiz *exp. (Chile)* • (lit.): to get the partridge drunk.

andar de boca en boca *exp.* to be generally known, to be in everyone's lips, to have everyone talking about it • (lit.): to walk from mouth to mouth.

example:
Es cuento **anda de boca en boca**.

translation:
Everyone's talking about what happened.

SYNONYM:
andar en boca de las gentes *exp.* • (lit.): to walk on people's mouths.

ALSO:
andar en boca de todos *exp.* • to have a bad reputation (lit.): to walk in everyone's mouth.

ángel custodio *m. (Mexico)* condom, rubber • (lit.): guardian angel.

example:
Si va a tener sexo hoy en día, ¡debe usar un **ángel custodio**!

translation:
If you're going to have sex these days, you must wear a **condom**!

ángel de la guardia *m. (Mexico)* condom, rubber • (lit.): guardian angel.

example:
Los **ángeles de la guardia** no son siempre efectivos contra el embarago.

translation:
Condoms aren't always effective against pregnancy.

antenas *f.pl. (Spain)* ears • (lit.): antennas.

example:
Manolo tiene las **antenas** tan grandes que parece un elefante.

translation:
Manolo has such **big ears** he looks like an elephant.

NOTE:
orejudo/a *adj.* big-eared (from the feminine noun *oreja* meaning "ear").

SYNONYM:
guatacas *f.pl. (Cuba)*.

aparato *m. (Mexico)* penis • (lit.): apparatus.

example:
No puedes llevar ese traje de baño a la playa. ¡Se puede ver tu **aparato**!

translation:
You can't wear that bathing suit to the beach. People can see your **member**!

SYNONYMS:
SEE – **penis**, *p. 243*.

aparecer a tiempo *exp.* to arrive on time • (lit.): to appear on time.

example:
Mi maestro de matemáticas siempre **aparece a tiempo**.

translation:
My math teacher always **shows up on time**.

SYNONYM:
llagar a tiempo *exp.* • (lit.): to arrive on time.

apestar *v.* to stink • (lit.): to infect with the plague.

example:
Verdaderamente **apesta** aquí. Me pregunto si hay una mofeta cerca.

translation:
It really **stinks** here. I wonder if there's a skunk nearby.

VARIATION:
apestar a muertos *exp.* to stink to high heaven • (lit.): to stink to death.

ALSO:
peste *f.* • **1.** stink, foul smell • *¡Qué peste!;* What a horrible smell! • **2.** pain in the neck • *¡Qué peste es este tipo!;* What a pain in the neck this guy is! • (lit.): plague, epidemic disease

apestar la boca *exp.* to have bad breath • (lit.): to stink from the mouth.

example:
Yo creo que Ernie nunca se lava los dientes. ¡Siempre le **apesta la boca**!

translation:
I don't think Ernie ever brushes his teeth. He always has **horrible breath**!

aplomado/a *n. & adj.* lazy bum; lazy • (lit.): serious, solemn.

example:
Miguel nunca se ofrecerá a ayudarte. Es demasiado **aplomado**.

translation:
Miguel will never volunteer to help you. He's so **lazy**.

apretado/a *n. & adj. (Mexico)* tightwad; stingy • (lit.): squashed, tightly packed.

example:
Ana solía ser muy **apretada**. Pero desde que le ha tocado la lotería, se ha vuelto muy generosa.
translation:
Ana used to be very **stingy**. But now that she won the lottery, she's become very generous.

aracata *f. (Mexico)* marijuana.
example:
En los estados unidos, es ilegal cultivar **aracata**.
translation:
In the United States, it's illegal to grow **marijuana**.

ardilla *adj.* said of someone who moves fast • (lit.): squirrel.
example:
Alfredo se mueve tan rápido como una **ardilla**.

translation:
Alfredo moves as fast as a **squirrel**.

SYNONYM -1:
águila *m. (Cuba)* • (lit.): eagle.

SYNONYM -2:
zorra *f. (Puerto Rico)* • (lit.): fox.

argolla *f.* vagina • (lit.): ring, hoop, band.

SYNONYMS:
SEE – **vagina**, *p. 263*.

argolluda de mierda *n.* an insult for a woman • (lit.): big ring of shit (referring to her anus).

arma *f.* penis • (lit.): weapon.

armado (estar) *adj.* to get an erection • (lit.): to be armed.

SYNONYMS:
SEE – **penis**, *p. 243*.

arrastrado/a *n. & adj.* lazy bum; lazy • (lit.): wretched, miserable.
example:
Angela y yo hicimos una gran fiesta, pero no me ayudó nada. ¡Es tan **arrastrada**!
translation:
Angela and I threw a big party, but she didn't help me at all. She's so **lazy**!

arrecho *adj. (Peru, Ecuador)* horny • (lit.): sexually excited.

arreglarse *v.* to fix oneself up, to make oneself look attractive • (lit.): to fix oneself up (from the verb *arreglar* meaning "to repair something").

example:
María está guapísima cuando **se arregla.**

translation:
Maria is beautiful when she **fixes herself up**.

ALSO -1:
arreglarse con *exp.* to conform to, to agree with, to come to an agreement with.

ALSO -2:
arreglárselas *v.* to manage.

SYNONYM -1:
empaquetarse *v. (Puerto Rico)* • (lit.): to pack up oneself.

SYNONYM -2:
pintarse *v.* to put on makeup • (lit.): to paint oneself.

arreglárselas para *exp.* to manage to • (lit.): to arrange oneself by.

example:
No puedo **arreglármelas para** levantar esta caja. ¿Me puedes ayudar?

translation:
I can't **manage to** lift this heavy box. Can you help me?

arrimarse *v.* to get married, to tie the knot • (lit.): to shelve oneself (and be in circulation no longer).

example:
¡Enhorabuena! He oído que ¡**se van a arrimar** la semana que viene!

translation:
Congratulations! I heard that **you're going to tie the knot** next week!

ascuas (estar en) *exp.* to be on pins and needles.

example:
Estoy completamente **en ascuas**. ¡No sé nada de lo que está pasando!

translation:
I'm **on pins and needles**. I don't know what's going on!

SYNONYM -1:
bolas (estar en) *exp. (Argentina)* • (lit.): to be in balls (perhaps since one's hands may be clenched during times of great anticipation).

SYNONYM -2:
loco/a por saber algo (estar) *exp. (Cuba)* • (lit.): to be crazy to know something.

asentaderas *f.pl.* seat, buttocks • (lit.): from the verb *asentar* meaning "to seat."

example:
¡Pon las **asentaderas** en esta silla y no te muevas hasta que yo vuelva!

translation:
Put your **butt** on that chair and don't move until I get back!

así, así *exp.* so, so • (lit.): such, such.

example:
– ¿Te gustan las películas de miedo?
– **Así, así**.

translation:
– Do you like horror movies?
– **So, so**.

asqueroso/a *n. & adj.* jerk, disgusting person; jerky • (lit.): filthy.

example:
John es un **asqueroso**; no me gusta nada.

translation:
John is such a **jerk**. I really don't like him.

atar el nudo *exp.* to get married, to tie the knot • (lit.): to tie the knot.

example:
Después de diez años, Rodolfo y Julia finalmente van a **atar el nudo**.

translation:
After ten years, Rodolfo and Julia are finally going **to tie the knot**.

atizar coliflor tostada *exp. (Mexico)* to smoke marijuana • (lit.): to smoke toasted cauliflower.

example:
¡Creo que alguien está **atizando coliflor tostada** cerca de aquí!

translation:
I think someone is **smoking pot** near here!

atizar mota *exp. (Mexico)* to smoke marijuana • (lit.): to stir powder.

¡Ay que la chingada! *interj.* Oh, shit!

example:
¡**Ay que la chingada**! ¡Me he dejado las llaves dentro del coche!

translation: **Oh, shit**! I locked my keys in the car!

ayotes *m.pl. (Mexico)* testicles • (lit.): pumpkins.

azotea *f.* head • (lit.): flat or terraced roof.

example:
¡Caramba! Parece que este tío está mal de la **azotea.**

translation:
Geez! I think this guy is **crazy**.

SYNONYMS:
SEE – **coco**, *p. 41*.

baboso/a *n. & adj.* • idiot; stupid • (lit.): one who dribbles a lot.

example:
Victor llegó tarde su primer día de trabajo porque se le olvidó la dirección. ¡Qué **baboso**!
translation:
Victor was late his first day on the job because he forgot the address. What an **idiot**!

bacalao *m. (Mexico)* vagina • (lit.): codfish.

SYNONYMS:
SEE – **vagina**, *p. 263.*

bacán *m. (Argentina, Uruguay)* lazy bum.
example:
¡Eres un **bacán**! ¡Levántate del sofá y ponte a trabajar!
translation:
You're such a **lazy bum**! Get off the couch and start working!

bailón *m. (Spain)* dancer (usually applies to a Spanish folk dancer).
example:
Andrés conoce a muchas chicas porque es un **bailón** excelente y siempre va a las discotecas.
translation:
Andrés knows a lot of girls because he's a great **dancer** and goes to discos al the time.

NOTE:
This comes from the verb *bailar* meaning "to dance."

SYNONYM:
bailador/a *n. (Spain).*

bajar al pozo *exp. (Cuba)* to perform oral sex with a woman • (lit.): to go down to the well.

bandera roja *f.* menstruation • (lit.): red flag.

barbas *m.* bearded man.
example:
Augusto siempre ha sido un **barbas**. Parece que no le gusta afeitarse.
translation:
Augusto has always been a **bearded man**. It seems like he doesn't like to shave.

SYNONYM -1:
barbado *m. (Puerto Rico).*

SYNONYM -2:
barbón *m.*

SYNONYM -3:
barbudo *m.*

NOTE:
These synonyms come from the feminine noun *barba* meaning "beard."

SYNONYM -4:
fulano *m.* • **1.** *(Mexico)* bearded man • **2.** *(Argentina)* nobody • *Es un fulano cualquiera;* He's a nobody.

barrigón/ona de mierda *n. (Argentina)* an insult said of someone who is very fat, fatso • (lit.): potbelly of shit.

example:
¡Qué **barrigón de mierda**! Él debe ponerse a dieta.

translation:
What a **fatso**! He should go on a diet!

basuco *m. (Mexico, Central and South America)* crack cocaine.

example:
¿Has oído las noticias? Detuvieron a Ricardo por poseer **basuco**!

translation:
Did you hear the news? Ricardo got arrested for possession of **cocaine**!

bebido/a (estar) *adj.* to be drunk, "wasted," inebriated.

example:
Creo que Pedro está **bebido** porque no se puede mantener en pie.

translation:
I think Pedro is **wasted** because he can't even stand.

SYNONYM -1:
alegre (estar) *adj.* • (lit.): to be happy.

SYNONYM -2:
borrachín (estar) *adj.*

NOTE:
This comes from the adjective *borracho/a* meaning "drunk."

SYNONYM -3:
cuba (estar) *adj.*

SYNONYM -4:
en pedo *adj. (Argentina)* • (lit.): in fart.

SYNONYM -5:
pellejo (estar) *adj.* • (lit.): to be skin (as in chicken skin) • *No me guastaría estar en su pellejo;* I wouldn't like to be in his shoes.

SYNONYM -6:
piripi (estar) *adj.*

SYNONYM -7:
tomado/a (estar) *adj.* • (lit.): to be drunk/taken.

bereco/a *n. & adj. (El Savador)* idiot; stupid.

example:
Angélica es tan **bereca**. Echó sal en el café pensando que era azúcar.

translation:
Angelica is so **stupid**. She put salt in her coffee thinking it was sugar.

berenjenal *f.* penis • (lit.): eggplant.

SYNONYMS:
SEE – **penis**, *p. 243*.

berreadero *m. (Mexico)* whorehouse • (lit.): a place where one can listen to animals bleat.

example:
Todos los vecinos son enojados porque hay un **berreadero** en su calle.
translation:
All the neighbors are angry because there's a **whorehouse** on their street.

besa mi culo *exp.* kiss my ass.
example:
Si el jefe quiere que trabaje hasta tarde hoy también, va a tener que **besarme el culo**.
translation:
If the boss wants me to work late again, he can **kiss my ass**.
VARIATION:
bésame el culo *exp.*

besar con la lengua *exp.* to give a French kiss • (lit.): to kiss with the tongue.
example:
¡Rafael trató de **besarme con la lengua** en nuestra primera cita!
translation:
Rafael tried to give me a **rench kiss** on our first date!

beso francés *m.* French kiss • (lit.): [same].

besugo *m.* idiot, fool, harebrained person, scatterbrain • (lit.): sea bream (which is a kind of fish).
example:
Jorge es un **besugo**. Siempre comete errores.
translation:
Jorge is an **idiot**. He's always making mistakes.
SYNONYMS:
SEE – **adoquín**, *p. 6.*

biberón *m.* penis • (lit.): baby bottle, feeding bottle.
example:
Este gatito es claramente varón. Puedo ver su **biberón**.
translation:
That kitten is definitely male. I can see his **peepee**.
SYNONYMS:
SEE – **penis**, *p. 243.*

bicho *m.* penis • (lit.): bug.
NOTE:
The term *bicho* literally means "bug" but is used in slang to mean "penis," so be careful how you use it! For example:

uan o eo un bicho lo pisoteo.

Common Translation #1:
Whenever I see a **bug**, I squash it.
Common Translation #2:
Whenever I see a **penis**, I squash it.
SYNONYMS:
SEE – **penis**, *p. 243.*

bien conservado/a (estar) *adj.* to be in good shape for one's age • (lit.): to be well-preserved.

example:
Mi abuelo está muy **bien conservado** para su edad.

translation:
My grandfather is **well-preserved** for his age.

SYNONYM:
buena forma (estar en) *exp.* • (lit.): to be in good form.

bigote *m.* vagina • (lit.): mustache.

SYNONYMS:
SEE – **vagina**, *p. 263*.

bijirita *f. (Cuba)* derogatory for "homosexual."

bizcocho *m.* vagina • (lit.): sweet bread or sponge cake.

SYNONYMS:
SEE – **vagina**, *p. 263*.

blando/a de corazón (ser) *exp.* to be softhearted • (lit.): to be soft of heart.

example:
Marcos es muy **blando de corazón**.

translation:
Marcos is very **softhearted**.

ANTONYM -1:
corazón de piedra (tener) *exp.* to be very hardhearted • (lit.): to have a heart made of stone.

ANTONYM -2:
duro/a de corazón (ser) *exp.* to be hardhearted • (lit.): to be hard of heart.

bobo/a *n.* idiot, fool.

example:
Carlos es un **bobo**. No sabe ni atarse los cordones de los zapatos.

translation:
Carlos is an **idiot**. He doesn't even know how to tie his shoes.

VARIATION:
bobo de capirote *exp.* a complete idiot • (lit.): stupid in the hat.

SYNONYM -1:
asno *adj.* • (lit.): donkey.

SYNONYM -2:
atontado/a *adj.* • (lit.): stupid person.

SYNONYM -3:
bobazo *m. (Argentina).*

SYNONYM -4:
burro *adj.* • (lit.): donkey • SEE – **burro**, *p. 28.*

SYNONYM -5:
ganso *adj.* • (lit.): goose.

SYNONYM -6:
mentecato/a *adj.* • (lit.): silly, foolish.

SYNONYM -7:
pasmarote *adj.* • (lit.): silly, foolish.

SYNONYM -8:
patoso/a *adj.* • (lit.): boring, dull.

SYNONYM -9:
tonto/a *adj.* • (lit.): stupid person.

SYNONYM -10:
zopenco/a *adj.* • (lit.): dull, stupid.

SYNONYM -11:
zoquete *adj.* • (lit.): chump, block (of wood).

ANTONYM -1:
listillo/a *adj. (Spain)* • (lit.): small clever person.

ANTONYM -2:
pillo *adj.* • (lit.): roguish, mischievous, rascally.

ANTONYM -3:
vivo/a *adj.* clever, smart • (lit.): alive.

bocaza *f.* mouth, big mouth.

example:
¡Ese tipo tiene una **bocaza** tan grande como la de un tiburón!

translation:
That guy's **mouth** is as big as a shark's!

SYNONYM:
bocacha *f.*

bocón/ona *n. & adj.* blabbermouth; gossipy • (lit.): big-mouthed.

example:
Estuve hablando por teléfono con Susana más de una hora. ¡Es una **bocona**!

translation:
I was on the telephone with Susana for an hour. She's such a **blabbermouth**!

NOTE:
This is from the feminine noun *boca* meaning "mouth."

SYNONYMS:
SEE – **blabbermouth**, *p. 208.*

bofa *n.* crazy woman *(Cuba).*

example:
Mira a esa **bofa**. Está hablando sola.

translation:
Look at that **crazy woman**. She's talking to herself.

NOTE:
This is from the verb *bofarse* meaning "to sag."

bolas *f.pl.* testicles • (lit.): balls.

bólido *m.* *(Spain)* car, automobile • (lit.): race car.

example:
Ana y yo vamos a dar una vuelta en mi **bólido** nuevo.

translation:
Ana and I are going for a ride in my new **car**.

NOTE -1:
In formal Spanish, this term usually refers to an impressive car, although it is occasionally used in a sarcastic way referring to a car that does not work properly.

NOTE -2:
In Argentina, *bólido* means "idiot" or "jerk."

SYNONYM -1:
autazo *m. (Argentina).*

SYNONYM -2:
auto *m. (Argentina).*

SYNONYM -3:
buga *f. (Spain).*

SYNONYM -4:
carrazo *m. (Cuba, Puerto Rico)* big car.

SYNONYM -5:
carro *m. (Mexico).*

SYNONYM -6:
cochazo *m.*

SYNONYM -7:
coche *m. (Argentina).*

SYNONYM -8:
máquina *f. (Cuba, Puerto Rico)* machine.

bolitas *f.pl.* testicles • (lit.): little balls.

bollaca *f.* a derogatory term for "lesbian."

bollera *f.* a derogatory term for "lesbian" • (lit.): baker.

bollo *m.* vagina • (lit.): a type of bread.

CAUTION:
In western Venezuela, the expression *tremendo bollo* means "nice vagina." However, in other parts of the same country, the expression would simply translate as "big mess" or "fine pickle."

NOTE:
The term *bollo* literally means "a type of bread" but is used in slang to mean "vagina," so be careful how you use it!
For example:

Este restaurante tiene los mejores bollos.

Common Translation:
This restaurant has the best **bread rolls**.

Translation in Cuba:
This restaurant has the best **vaginas**.

SYNONYMS:
SEE – **vagina**, *p. 263*.

bollo loco *m. (Cuba)* an easy lay • (lit.): crazy bread roll or bun.

example:
Ana se acuesta con un tipo diferente cada noche. Es un **bollo loco**.

translation:
Ana has sex with a different guy every night. She's a **real easy lay**.

NOTE:
In Cuba, *bollo* ("bread roll" or "bun") is used to refer to "vagina."

bolo *m. (El Salvador, Nicaragua)* drunkard • (lit.): skittle.

example:
Eduardo tiene un problema con la bebida. Creo que es un **bolo**.

translation:
Eduardo has a problem with alcohol. I think he's a **drunkard**.

bonachón/na *n. & adj.* sucker, simpleton; gullible • (lit.): someone who is too nice and good (from the adjective *bueno* meaning "good").

example:
Enrique se cree todo lo que le dices. ¡Es un **bonachón**!

translation:
Enrique believes everything you tell him. What a **sucker**!

borrachal *m.* drunkard (from the adjective *borracho/a* meaning "drunk").

example:
David no puede encontrar trabajo porque todo el mundo sabe que es un **borrachal**.

translation:
David can't get a job because everyone knows he's a **drunkard**.

borrachón/ona *f. & adj. (Argentina)* severe drunkard • (lit.): big drunkard.

example:
Como siempre, Marco bebió demasiado en mi fiesta. ¡Es un **borrachón**!

translation:
As usual, Marco had too much to drink at my party. He's such a **drunkard**!

bosta *f.* turd, cow dung • (lit.): cow dung.

example:
Cuidado por donde andas. El pasto está lleno de **bosta**.

translation:
Be careful where you walk. The grass is full of **turds**.

botarse la cantúa *exp. (Cuba)* to masturbate • (lit.): to throw the *cantúa* (a candy made of sweet potato, coconut, sesame, and sugar).

SYNONYMS:
SEE – **masturbate**, *p. 239*.

botarse la puñeta *exp.* *(Cuba)* to masturbate • (lit.): to throw the cuff.

SYNONYMS:
SEE – **masturbate**, *p. 239*.

botarse la yuca *exp. (Cuba)* to masturbate • (lit.): to throw the yucca plant.

SYNONYMS:
SEE – **masturbate**, *p. 239*.

botarse una paja *exp.* *(Cuba)* to masturbate • (lit.): to toss a straw.

SYNONYMS:
SEE – **masturbate**, *p. 239*.

botija *n. & adj.* fat slob; chunky, fat • (lit.): short-necked earthen jug.

example:
A mí me daría vergüenza salir con ese **botija**.

translation:
I would be embarrassed to go out with that **fat slob**.

bravo/a *adj.* upset, angry • (lit.): fierce, ferocious.

example:
Lucía está **brava** hoy porque no durmió bien anoche.

translation:
Lucia is **upset** today because she didn't sleep well last night.

ALSO:
¡Bravo! *interj.* Well done!

SYNONYM -1:
cabreado/a *adj. (Spain)*.

SYNONYM -2:
embolado/a *adj. (Argentina)*.

broca *f.* penis • (lit.): the bit of a drill.

SYNONYMS:
SEE – **penis**, *p. 243*.

bruja *f.* whore • (lit.): witch.

bruquena *f.* vagina.

SYNONYMS:
SEE – **vagina**, *p. 263*.

bruto/a de mierda *n.* *(Argentina)* idiot • (lit.): brute of shit.

example:
¡Qué **bruto de mierda**! ¡Mira cómo maneja!

translation:
What an **idiot**! Look at the way he's driving!

buche *n. & adj. (Cuba)* idiot; crazy • (lit.): mouthful.

example:
Si fuera tú, no me fiaría de él. Francamente, creo que está un poco **buche**.

translation:
I wouldn't trust him if I were you. Frankly, I think he's a little **crazy**.

buena onda *f.* good egg, good person • (lit.): good wave.

example:
Agustín es muy **buena onda**. Siempre está dispuesto a ayudar.

translation:
Agustín is a **good egg**. He's always willing to help.

SYNONYM -1:
buena gente *f.* good person • (lit.): good people.

NOTE:
The term *buena gente* is commonly used to refer to only one person, although the literal translation is indeed plural. However, when used to refer to a group of people, it is no longer considered slang rather academic Spanish.

SYNONYM -2:
buenas (estar de) *adj. (Puerto Rico).*

SYNONYM -3:
buen partido / buena partida *n. (Cuba).*

NOTE:
In Argentina, *un buen partido* means "a good catch." For example: *Mi madre quiere que me case con Fernando porque él es un buen partido;* My mother wants me to marry Fernando because he's a good catch.

SYNONYM -3:
tío enrollado *m. (Spain)* • (lit.): rolled up uncle (or a person rolled up into one great package).

NOTE:
tío *m. (Cuba/Spain)* man, "dude."

bueno/a • **1.** *adj.* well • **2.** *interj.* sure! • **3.** *adj.* bad, nasty • **4.** *adj.* considerable • **5.** *interj.* come off it! • **6.** *adj.* okay • (lit.): good.

example (1):
Bueno, resulta que Juan y Fiona se van de vacaciones a París.

translation:
Well, it so happens that Juan and Fiona are going on vacation to Paris.

example (2):
– ¿Quieres comer en ese restaurante?
– ¡**Bueno**!

translation:
– Do you want to eat in that restaurant?
– **Sure**!

example (3):
Me siento muy mal. Tengo un **buen** costipado.

translation:
I feel sick. I have a **bad** cold.

NOTE:
This could be compared to the American expression "to have a real good cold" where "real good" actually refers to something negative or unpleasant.

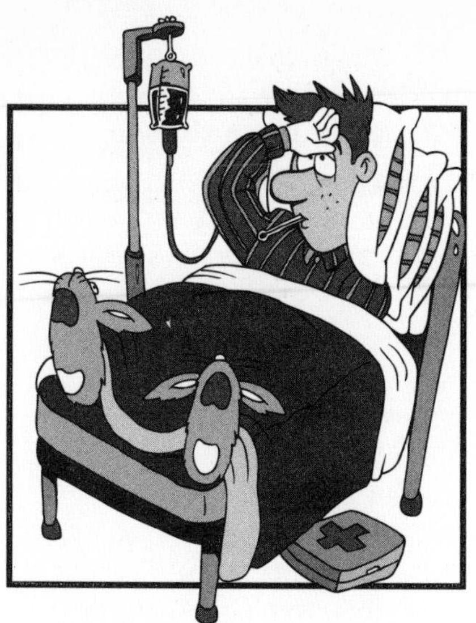

example (4):
Parece que José tiene una **buena** cantidad de dinero en el banco.

translation:
It seems that Jose has a **considerable** amount of money in the bank.

example (5):
– ¡Me acabo de enterar que mis antepasados eran nobles!
– ¡**Bueno**! Eso es un poco difícil de creer.

translation:
– I just found out that my ancestors are royalty!
– **Come off it**! That's a little hard to believe.

example (6):
– ¿Te gustó la película de anoche?
– **Bueno**. Me gustó más o menos.

translation:
– Did you like the movie last night?
– **Kind of**. It was okay.

NOTE:
In Mexico, using the interjection *bueno* is a common way of answering the telephone.

SYNONYM:
caramba *interj. (Puerto Rico)* • **1.** used as a synonym for definition **1.** • **2.** used as a response for example (1): *¡Caramba!*; Geez!

buenona *f. (Spain)* beautiful girl, hot chick.

example:
¿Has visto a esa **buenona** que sale con Juan? ¡Es preciosa!

translation:
Did you see the **hot chick** Juan is going out with? She's beautiful!

NOTE:
This is from the feminine adjective *buena* meaning "good."

SYNONYM -1:
buenachón *f. (Puerto Rico)*.

SYNONYM -2:
cuero *m.* • (lit.): skin.

SYNONYM -3:
diosa *f. (Argentina)* • (lit.): goddess.

SYNONYM -4:
potra *f. (Argentina)*.

SYNONYM -5:
tía buena *f. (Cuba, Spain)* • (lit.): aunt good.

buey *n. & adj.* idiot; stupid • (lit.): ox, bullock.

example:
A Juan se le olvidó ponerse los ones para salir. ¡Qué **buey**!

translation:
Juan forgot to put on his pants when he went outside. What a **geek**!

bufa *f.* • **1.** *(Cuba)* drunkard • **2.** fart.

example -1:
Yo no sabía que Antonio era un **bufa**. Ayer se presentó al trabajo con una botella de vino en la mano.

translation:
I didn't know Antonio was such a **drunkard**. Yesterday he showed up at work holding a wine bottle.

example -2:
¡Qué olor! Huele a **bufa**.

translation:
What a smell! It smells like a **fart**.

bufete *m.* buttocks, ass • (lit.): **1.** writing desk • **2.** lawyer's office.

bufo *m.* derogatory for "homosexual" • (lit.): clownish, comic.

buitre *m.* • **1.** cheapskate • **2.** opportunist • (lit.): vulture.

example (1):
Jorge es tan **buitre** que nunca desayuna para ahorrar dinero.

translation:
Jorge is such a **cheapskate** that he never eats breakfast just so that he can save money.

example (2):
Julio es un **buitre**. Cuando perdí mi trabajo, en vez de ayudarme, intentó conseguir mi trabado.

translation:
Julio is a real **opportunist**. When I lost my job, instead of helping me, he tried to get my old job.

SYNONYM:
amarrete *m. (Argentina)*.

bujarrón *m.* derogatory for "homosexual" • (lit.): sodomite.

burro/a *n. & adj.* jerk, fool, moron, simpleton, stupid person • (lit.): donkey.

example:
José es un **burro**. Nunca hace nada bien.

translation:
Jose is a **moron**. He never does anything right.

NOTE:
In Argentina and Mexico, the term **burro/a** is also used to mean "a bad student."

SYNONYMS:
SEE – **adoquín**, *p. 6.*

buscar flete *exp. (Cuba)* to look for some ass • (lit.): to look for freight, cargo.

buscarle tres pies al gato *exp.* to nitpick• (lit.): to look for three of the cat's feet.

example:
¡Relájate! No le **busques tres pies al gato**.

translation:
Relax! Don't **nitpick**.

SYNONYM -1:
buscarle cinco pies al gato *exp.* • (lit.): to look for five of the cat's feet.

SYNONYM -2:
buscarle mangas al chaleco *exp.* • (lit.): to look for sleeves in the vest.

NOTE:
buscarle los tres pies al gato *exp. (Cuba)* It's very interesting to note that in Cuba, the definite article *los* is used before *tres pies*.

buscona *f.* prostitute • (lit.): one who searches (from the verb *buscar* meaning "to search").

example:
Nunca vas a adivinar la carrera de Ramona. ¡Ella es una **buscona**!

translation:
You'll never guess what Ramona does as a career. She's a **prostitute**!

butifarra *f.* penis • (lit.): pork sausage.

SYNONYMS:
SEE – **penis**, *p. 243*.

caballo *m.* • **1.** tampon • **2.** heroin • (lit.): horse.

cabrón/ona *n. & adj.* asshole; jerky • (lit.): billy-goat.
example:
¡Ese **cabrón** me robó mi novia!
translation:
That **bastard** stole my girlfriend!

VARIATION:
re-cabrón *m. (Argentina)* a big asshole.

NOTE:
In Argentina, the prefix *re-* is commonly added to many words to add greater emphasis.

cachapera *f. (Puerto Rico, Venezuela)* a derogatory term for "lesbian."

NOTE -1:
This comes from the feminine term *cachapa* which is a thin pancake, usually served stacked. Therefore, a stack of *cachapas* conjures up the image of several vaginas stacked on top of the other.

NOTE -2:
cachapear *v.* to engage in lesbian sex • *Ellas se estaban cachapeando;* They're having lesbian sex.

cachar *v. (Peru)* to have sex, to fornicate • (lit.): to break into pieces.

cacharritos *m.pl.* rides in an amusement park • (lit.): small pieces of junk, small machines that don't work properly.
example:
Cuando fuimos al parque de atracciones David y Stefani se subieron en todos los **cacharritos**.
translation:
When we went to the amusement park, David and Stefani went on all the **rides**.

NOTE:
This is a very popular expression especially among kids.

cacharro *m.* • **1.** jalopy, old wreck • **2.** lemon (any piece of machinery that does not work properly).
example (1):
Este **cacharro** nunca quiere arrancar por las mañanas.
translation:
This **old wreck** never wants to start in the morning.
example (2):
Este lavaplatos no limpia los platos bien. Es un **cacharro**.
translation:
This dishwasher doesn't clean the dishes properly. It's a **piece of junk**.

SYNONYM:
porquería *f. (Argentina)* said of anything worthless.

cachas *m.* good-looking young man, a hunk.
example:
Sergio está haciendo mucho deporte últimamente. Se está convirtiendo en un **cachas**.

translation:
Sergio is doing a lot of exercise lately. He's becoming a real **hunk**.

SYNONYM:
langa *m. (Argentina).*

NOTE:
This is a reverse transformation of the word *galán* (lan-ga) meaning "gallant" or "handsome."

SYNONYM -3:
tío bueno *m. (Cuba, Spain)* • (lit.): uncle good.

SYNONYM -4:
tofete *m. (Puerto Rico).*

SYNONYM -5:
tremendo tipazo *m. (Cuba).*

cachetes *m.pl.* buttocks • (lit.): cheeks (of face).

cachetes del culo *m.pl.* buttocks • (lit.): cheeks of the ass.

cacho *m. (El Salvador)* penis • (lit.): chunk.

SYNONYMS:
SEE – **penis**, *p. 243.*

caérsele la baba por *exp.* to be wild about, to love someone • (lit.): to slobber for.

example:
A Marcos **se le cae la baba por** Patricia.

translation:
Marcos **is wild about** Patricia.

cafiche *m. (Chile)* pimp.

caficio *m. (Argentina)* pimp.

cagada *f.* shit (from the verb *cagar* meaning "to shit").

example:
Los fertilizantes están realmente hechos de **cagadas**.

translation:
Fertilizer is actually made of **shit**.

ALSO -1:
hacer una cagada a alguien *exp.* to do something nasty to someone.

ALSO -2:
cagada (una) *f. (Argentina)* said of something unpleasant or poorly done • (lit.): a shit • *Este trabajo es una cagada;* This work is a piece of shit.

cagadero *m.* bathroom, "shithouse" (from the verb *cagar* meaning "to shit").

example:
Antes de salir, tengo que ir al **cagadero**.

translation:
Before we leave, I need to go to the **shithouse**.

cagado/a (estar) *adj.* to be full of shit • (lit.): to be shit.

cagado/a de miedo (estar) *exp.* to be scared shitless • (lit.): to be shit with fear.

example:
¡Estaba **cagado de miedo** cuando vi al oso corriendo para mi!

translation:
I was **scared shitless** when I saw the bear running toward me!

cagar *v.* • **1.** to defecate • **2.** to make a mistake • (lit.): to shit.

example:
¡Ese niño está **cagando** en la acera!

translation:
That little kid is **shitting** on the sidewalk!

cagarse de gusto *exp.* to enjoy something very much • (lit.): to shit oneself with pleasure.

example:
Pasamos todo el día en el parque de atracciones. ¡**Me cagué de gusto**!

translation:
We spent the entire day at the amusement park. **I had a blast**!

cagarse en alguien o algo *exp.* to curse someone or something • (lit.): to shit on someone or something.

example:
¡Manuel me mentiró otra vez! !**Me cago en él**!

translation:
Manuel lied to me again! **I can't stand him**!

cagarse en los pantalones *exp.* to be scared shitless • (lit.): to shit in one's pants (due to fear).

example:
Miguel **se cagó en los pantalones** cuando fue a su escuela por primera vez.

translation:
Miguel was **scared shitless** when he went to his school for the first time.

cagarse por las patas abajas *exp.* to be scared to death • (lit.): to shit all the way down one's legs.

example:
Durante el robo, ¡**me cagaba por las patas abajas**!

translation:
During the robbery, I **was scared to death**!

cagitis (tener) *exp.* to have diarrhea • (lit.): to have the shits.

example:
El pescado que comía ayer no fue bueno. Yo **tenía cagitis** toda la noche.

translation:
The fish I ate yesterday wasn't fresh. I **had the shits** all night.

cagón/ona *n. & adj.* coward, scared • (lit.): one who is scared shitless.

example:
A Juan no le gusta acampar porque tiene miedo de la oscuridad. ¡Qué **cagón**!

translation:
Juan doesn't like to go camping because he's afraid of the dark. What a **scaredy-cat**!

cajeta *f. (Argentina)* vagina • (lit.): a small box.

SYNONYMS:
SEE –**vagina**, *p. 263*.

NOTE:
In Mexico the term *cajeta* is used to refer to a type of sweet pudding which looks like caramelized sweetened condensed milk. In Argentina, the same popular dessert is called *dulce de leche*. Be careful not to call this dessert *cajeta* in Argentina since this term is a crude way of saying "vagina!" For example:

¡Me gusta mucho la cajeta!

Common Translation:
I really like **sweet pudding dessert**!

Translation in Argentina:
I really like **vaginas**!

calabaza *m. (Mexico)* buttocks • (lit.): squash, pumpkin, marrow.

calcetín *m.* condom, rubber • (lit.): sock.

example:
Durante el acto sexual, siempre es imporante usar un **calcetín**.

translation:
During sex, it's always important to wear a **condom**.

calcetines con canicas *m.pl.* sagging breasts • (lit.): socks with marbles.

example:
Cuando sea vieja, ¡espero que los pechos míos no parecer dos **calcetines con canicas**!

translation:
When I get old, I hope my breasts don't look like **socks with marbles**!

calco *m.* bald • (lit.): tracing (drawing).

example:
¿Conoces a Ernesto? ¡Es **calco** y sólo tiene diecisiete años!

translation:
Do you know Ernesto? He's **bald** and he's only seventeen years old!

calentorro/a *adj.* horny.

NOTE:
This is a variation of the adjective *caliente* meaning "hot."

calienta-culos *f.* prostitute, hooker • (lit.): ass warmer.

example:
Cada día, Monica tiene sexo con un tipo diferente. Creo que trabaja como una **calienta culos**.

translation:
Every day, Monica has sex with a different guy. I think she makes her living as a **hooker**.

calientapollas *n. & adj.* *(Spain)* prick teaser • (lit.): one who makes a penis (*polla*, literally "young chicken") hot (*caliente*).

example:
Ana es una **calientapollas**.

translation:
Ana is such a **prick teaser**.

caliente *adj.* horny, sexually hot • (lit.): hot.

example:
¿David sale con Luisa? ¡Ella es bien **caliente**!

translation:
David is going out with Luisa? She's really **hot**!

calvito *n. & adj.* baldy; bald.

example:
Me temo que voy a ser **calvito**, porque mi padre perdió todo el pelo en su veintena.

translation:
I'm afraid I'm going to be **bald** because my father lost all of his hair when he was in his twenties.

NOTE:
This is from the adjective *calvo* meaning "bald."

¡Cállate! *interj.* Shut up! • (lit.): Shut yourself!

example:
¡**Cállate**! ¡Hablas demasiado!
translation:
Shut up! You talk too much!

¡Cállate/Cierra el hocico! *interj.* Shut up! • (lit.): Shut your mouth!
example:
¡**Cállate/Cierra el hocico**! ¡Es mentira!
translation:
Shut up! That's a lie!

NOTE:
hocico *m.* • (lit.): the mouth of an animal (and derogatory when used in reference to a person).

¡Cállate/Cierra el pico! *exp.* Shut your trap! • (lit.): Shut your beak!
example:
¡**Cállate/Cierra el pico**! ¡Lo que estás diciendo es mentira!
translation:
Shut your trap! What you're saying is a lie!

¡Cállate/Cierra la boca! *exp.* Shut your mouth! • (lit.): Close your mouth!
example:
¡**Cállate/Cierra la boca**! ¡Deja de hablar de ella de ese modo!
translation:
Shut your mouth! Stop talking about her that way!

callejear *v.* to take a walk (from the feminine noun *calle* meaning "street.")
example:
Cuando hace sol me gusta **callejear**.
translation:
When it's sunny outside, I enjoy going for a **walk**.

SYNONYM:
dar una vuelta *exp.* to go for a walk • (lit.): to give around.

callejera *f.* prostitute, hooker • (lit.): pertaining to the street.
example:
Esta vecinidad era muy agradable. Ahora hay **callejeras** por todos lados.
translation:
This neighborhood used to be so nice. Now there are **hookers** everywhere!

cambiarle el agua al canario *exp.* to urinate • (lit.): to change the canary's water.
example:
Antes de salir de viaje, tengo que **cambiarle el agua al canario**.
translation:
Before we leave on our trip, I need **to take a leak**.

camote *m.* penis • (lit.): sweet potato.

SYNONYMS:
SEE – **penis**, *p. 243*.

canario *m.* penis • (lit.): canary.

SYNONYMS:
SEE – **penis**, *p. 243*.

cáncamo *m. (Cuba)* ugly man • (lit.): louse.

example:
¡Qué **cáncamo**! Me pregunto cómo puede tener una hermana tan guapa.

translation:
What an **ugly man**! I wonder how he could have such a beautiful sister!

canijo/a *adj.* • **1.** very skinny person • **2.** feeble, frail, sickly.

example:
Ese tipo es un verdadero **canijo**. Parece que nunca come.

translation:
That guy is **really skinny**. It looks like he never eats.

SYNONYM -1:
esqueleto *m. (Cuba, Puerto Rico)* • (lit.): skeleton.

SYNONYM -2:
flacucho/a *adj. (Argentina)*.

cantarle las cuarenta *exp.* to tell someone off • (lit.): to sing the forty (truths about the person).

example:
¡Estoy harto! ¡Voy a **cantarle las cuarenta**!

translation:
I'm fed up! I'm going **to tell him off**!

cántaros *m.pl.* breasts • (lit.): pitcher.

example:
¿Viste a las enormas **cántaros** de esta mujer? ¿Crees que son naturales?

translation:
Did you see the huge **breasts** on that woman? Do you think they're real?

caoba *f. (Cuba)* penis • (lit.): mahogany tree.

SYNONYMS:
SEE – **penis**, *p. 243*.

capucha *f.* condom, rubber • (lit.): hood (of a garment).

example:
Mi hermana está embarazada aunque su esposo usaba una **capucha**.

translation:
My sister got pregnant even though her husband was using a **rubber**.

capuchón *m.* condom, rubber • (lit.): hood (of a garment).

example:
Si vas a tener sexo, no olvides traer un **capuchón**.

translation:
If you're going to have sex, don't forget to bring a **rubber**.

capullo *m.* bastard, asshole • (lit.): bud or head of the penis.

example:
Adolfo es un **capullo**. Siempre miente.

translation:
Adolfo is a **bastard**. He lies all the time.

SYNONYMS:
SEE – **penis**, *p. 243*.

cara a cara *exp.* **1.** right to a person's face • **2.** privately • (lit.): face to face.

example:
Me gustaría hablar con Jaime **cara a cara**.

translation:
I would like to talk to Jaime **privately**.

SYNONYM:
frente a frente *exp.* • (lit.): front to front.

caradura *f.* • **1.** arrogant • **2.** nervy, brazen • (lit.): hard face.

example (1):
Laura es una **caradura**. Se cree que es mejor que nadie.

translation:
Laura is so **arrogant**. She thinks she's better than anybody else.

example (2):
Jose Luis es tan **caradura** que siempre le pide dinero a sus amigos.

translation:
Jose Luis is so **nervy**. He's always asking his friends for money.

SYNONYM:
descarado/a *adj.* • (lit.): faceless (from the feminine noun *cara* meaning "face").

carajo *m.* penis • (lit.): penis.

NOTE:
This term is commonly used in Mexico as an expletive. For example: *¡Carajo!*; Damn!

SYNONYMS:
SEE – **penis**, *p. 243*.

carallo *m.* penis.

NOTE:
This is a variation of the masculine noun *carajo* meaning "penis."

SYNONYMS:
SEE – **penis**, *p. 243*.

caramba *interj*. geez, holy cow.

example:
¡**Caramba**!, no me puedo creer el calor que hace.

translation:
Geez! I can't believe how warm it is.

SYNONYMS:
SEE – **¡Hombre!**, *p. 111*.

caramelo *m*. beautiful woman, knockout, "fox" • (lit.): candy.

example:
Anabel es un verdadero **caramelo**. Se nota que se cuida.

translation:
Anabel is a real **fox**. You can tell she takes care of herself.

SYNONYMS:
SEE – **merengue**, *p. 138*.

carapedo *m*. stupid, fart-face • (lit.): fart-face.

example:
¡**Carapedo**! ¡Déjame en paz!

translation:
Stupid! Leave me alone!

caricia *f*. caress • (lit.): caress.

example:
Mi mamá me hizo una **caricia** en la cabeza cuando yo estaba enojado. Eso me tranquilizó en seguida.

translation:
My mother gave me a **caress** on my head when I was so upset. That calmed me down right away.

carne de gallina *exp*. goose bumps • (lit.): chicken meat.

example:
Se me puso **la carne de gallina** cuando oí las noticias.

translation:
I got **goose bumps** when I heard the news.

carroza *f*. elderly person, old relic • (lit.): carriage.

example:
Esa mujer es una **carroza**. Creo que tiene noventa años.

translation:
That woman is an **old relic**. I think she's ninety years old.

SYNONYM -1:
abuelo *m*. • (lit.): grandfather / **abuela** *f*. • (lit.): grandmother.

SYNONYM -2:
añoso *m*. • (lit.): from the masculine noun *año* meaning "year."

SYNONYM -3:
antañón *m*. • (lit.): from the masculine noun *antaño* meaning "long ago."

SYNONYM -4:
Más viejo que Matusalén *exp*. very old person • (lit.): older than Methuselah.

SYNONYM -5:
prehistórico *m.* • (lit.): prehistoric.

SYNONYM -6:
reliquia histórica *f. (Cuba)* • (lit.): historic relic.

SYNONYM -7:
vejestorio *m.* • (lit.): from the adjective *viejo* meaning "old."

SYNONYM -8:
vejete *m.* • (lit.): from the adjective *viejo* meaning "old."

casa de citas *f.* whorehouse • (lit.): a house where one can have a date.

example:
¡Ayer vi al jefe salir de una **casa de citas**! Me dicen que va allí todos los días durante el almuerzo.

translation:
Yesterday I saw the boss walk out of a **whorehouse**! I hear he goes there every day during lunch.

casa de putas *f.* whorehouse • (lit.): house of whores.

example:
Cuanda Ismael tenía doce años, su padre lo llevó a una **casa de putas**.

translation:
When Ismael was twelve years old, his father took him to a **casa de putas**.

casado con la viuda de los cinco hijos (estar) *exp. (Cuba)* to masturbate, to be married to Rosy Palm and her five sisters • (lit.): to be married to the widow of the five children.

example:
No quiero una novia. Me voy a quedar **casado con la viuda de los cinco hijos**.

translation:
I don't want a girlfriend. I'm going to **stay married to Rosy Palm and her five sisters**.

SYNONYMS:
SEE – **masturbate**, *p. 239*.

casco *m.* ugly woman • (lit.): helmet.

example:
Paula era un **casco**, pero despues de la cirujía estética, está guapísima.

translation:
Paula used to be a **real ugly woman**, but after her plastic surgery, she's beautiful.

casinadie *m.* a person of great integrity and influence, a very important person • (lit.): almost nobody.

example:
¡Mira! Por ahí viene el Señor Smith, es un **casinadie** en esta compañía.

translation:
Look! Here comes Mr. Smith. He's a **very important person** in this company.

ANTONYM:
donnadie *m.* loser • (lit.): Mr. Nobody • SEE – *p. 80.*

casita de paja *f. (Puerto Rico)* vagina • (lit.): small house of straw.

SYNONYMS:
SEE – **vagina**, *p. 263.*

casquete (echar un) *exp.* to have sex • (lit.): to throw a helmet.

castillo *m.* home, house • (lit.): castle.

example:
¿Te gusta mi **castillo** nuevo? Tiene cuatro dormitorios.

translation:
Do you like my new **house**? It has four bedrooms.

SYNONYM -1:
hogar *m.* • (lit.): home.

SYNONYM -2:
morada *f.* • (lit.): home.

SYNONYM -3:
nido *m.* • (lit.): nest.

cataplines *m.* testicles.

cebollín *m. (Cuba)* stupid person • (lit.): small onion.

example:
Me pregunto cómo un **cebollín** como Oscar ha podido sacar una A en el examen de matemáticas.

translation:
I wonder how an **idiot** like Oscar got an A on the math test.

cebollón *m. (Cuba)* stupid person • (lit.): large onion.

example:
Todo el mundo piensa que Marcelo es un **cebollón**, pero la verdad es que es un genio.

translation:
Everyone thinks that Marcelo is an **idiot**, but he's actually a genius.

cepillar *v.* to fornicate • (lit.): to brush.

VARIATION:
cepillarse a *v.*

cepillo *m.* vagina • (lit.): brush.

SYNONYMS:
SEE – **vagina**, *p. 263.*

cerote *m. (Nicaragua)* turd • (lit.): large zero.

example:
Algo huele mal. ¿Has pisado un **cerote**?

translation:
Something smells terrible. Did you step in a **turd**?

ciendango *m. Cuba)* derogatory for "homosexual."

cipote *m.* penis • (lit.): silly, foolish.

SYNONYMS:
SEE – **penis**, *p. 243*.

cita sorpresa *exp.* blind date • (lit.): surprised date.

example:
Estoy nervioso porque mañana tengo una **cita sorpresa**.

translation:
I'm nervous because I have a **blind date** tomorrow.

SYNONYM -1:
cita a ciegas *f. (Spain)* • (lit.): blind date.

SYNONYM -2:
cita amorosa *f. (Mexico)* • (lit.): love date.

clavar *v.* to fornicate • (lit.): to nail.

clavar los ojos a/en *exp.* to stare at, to fix one's eyes on, to check out • (lit.): to nail one's eyes on.

example:
No puedo dejar de **clavarle los ojos a** este cuadro. ¡Es precioso!

translation:
I can't stop **staring at** that painting. It's beautiful!

SYNONYM -1:
clavar la atención en *exp.* • (lit.): to fix one's attention on.

SYNONYM -2:
clavar la vista en *exp.* • (lit.): to nail the sight on.

SYNONYM -3:
hacer ojos *exp. (Colombia)* • (lit.): to make eyes.

cobo *m. (Puerto Rico)* old whore • (lit.): gigantic snail.

cochazo *m.* impressive car.

example:
Alvaro tiene un **cochazo**. No sé cómo se puede permitir ese lujo.

translation:
Alvaro has a **impressive car**. I don't know how he can afford it.

SYNONYMS:
SEE – **bólido**, *p. 23*.

cocho *m. (El Salvador, Mexico)* vagina • (lit.): dirty, filthy.

SYNONYMS:
SEE – **vagina**, *p. 263*.

cochón *m.* derogatory for "homosexual."

coco *m.* head • (lit.): coconut.

example:
¡Caramba! ¡Ese tipo tiene un **coco** enorme!

translation:
Geez! That guy has a huge **head**!

SYNONYM -1:
azotea *f. (Spain)* • (lit.): flat roof, terraced roof.

SYNONYM -2:
bocho *m. (Argentina)* said of a very intelligent person.

SYNONYM -3:
cachola *f.* • (lit.): hounds.

SYNONYM -4:
cholla *f.* • (lit.): mind, brain.

SYNONYM -5:
cráneo *m.* • (lit.): cranium, skull.

SYNONYM -6:
mate *m. (Argentina).*

NOTE:
estar mal del mate *exp.* to be cray • *Ese tipo está mal del mate;* That guy's crazy.

SYNONYM -7:
melón *m. (Argentina).*

SYNONYM -8:
molondra *f.*

SYNONYM -9:
sesera *f.* • (lit.): from the masculine noun *seso* meaning "brain."

SYNONYM -10:
terraza *f. (Argentina)* • (lit.): terraced roof.

SYNONYM -11:
testa *f.* • (lit.): from the Latin term *testa* meaning "head."

ALSO:
tener seco el coco *exp.* to be/to go crazy • (lit.): to have the dried coconut.

VARIATION:
secársele a uno el coco *exp.* • (lit.): to get one's coconut dried.

codo *m. & adj.* tightwad; stingy • (lit.): elbow.

example:
La razón por la que mi tío es tan rico es porque es un **codo**. Nunca gasta dinero en nada.

translation:
The reason my uncle is so rich is because he's a **tightwad**. He never spends money on anything.

ALSO -1:
hablar por los codos *exp.* to talk nonstop • (lit.): to speak by the elbows.

ALSO -2:
mentir por los codos *exp.* to lie a lot • (lit.): to lie by the elbows.

ALSO -3:
metido/a hasta los codos en (estar) *exp.* to be in a real jam • (lit.): to be put by the elbows.

codo empinado *m.* drunkard • (lit.): tilted elbow.

example:
¡Nunca me había dado cuenta de que Francisco era un **codo empinado**! ¿Has visto cuánto vino tomó durante la cena?

translation:
I never realized what a **drunkard** Francisco was! Did you see how much wine he drank during dinner?

coger *v.* to fornicate • (lit.): to get, to catch.

NOTE:
In Spain, the verb *coger* simply means "to catch." It would not be unusual for a Spaniard traveling to Argentina, Chile, or Mexico, and ask where he could "catch" the bus by using the phrase: *¿Donde puedo coger el autobús?* However, in these countries, the unsuspecting visitor may be shocked to discover that he/she has unintentionally asked: "Where can I fuck the bus?" In Argentina, Chile, and Mexico, these are the preferred ways to say, "Where can I catch the bus?"

- ¿Dónde puedo agarrar *(to grab, to seize)* el autobús?
- ¿Dónde puedo tomar *(to take)* el autobús?
- ¿Dónde puedo pillar *(to catch)* el autobús?
- ¿Dónde puedo recoger *(to pick up, to gather, to fetch)* el autobús?

coger una mierda *exp.* to get drunk, "shit-faced" • (lit.): to catch a shit.

example:
Había tanto cognac en la torta que María hizo anoche, que tenía miedo de **coger una mierda**.

translation:
There was so much brandy in the cake Maria made last night, I was afraid I was going to **get shit-faced**.

cogetuda *f. (Argentina)* an easy lay.

example:
Todo el mundo sabe que Laura es una **cogetuda**. Los hombres siempre quieren salir con ella.

translation:
Everyone knows that Laura's **an easy lay**. Guys always want to go out with her.

NOTE:
This is from the verb *coger* meaning (in many Spanish-speaking countries) "to fuck."

cojinetes *m.* testicles • (lit.): small cushions.

cojones *m.pl.* testicles, "balls" • (lit.): testicles.

NOTE:
The term *cojones* is commonly used in many different expressions and may also be used as an interjection of surprise, anger, or annoyance.

example -1:
¡No me importa dos **cojones**!

translation:
I don't give a **rat's ass**! • (literally – I don't care two balls, or testicles, about it).

example -2:
¡**Cojones**!

translation:
Bullshit!

example -3:
¡**Y un cojón**!

translation:
Like hell it is!

example -4:
Hace falta tener **cojones**.

translation:
You've got to have **balls** [i.e. "be brave"].

example -5
Es un tipo **sin cojones**.

translation:
That guy's a **coward** • (literally – That guy doesn't have balls, or "courage").

NOTE:
cojonear *v.* to act like a jerk.

cojudo/a *n. & adj.* idiot; stupid • (lit.): uncastrated.

example:
Clara es **cojuda**. Se cree todo lo que le dicen.

translation:
Clara is **really gullible**. She believes anything you tell her.

cola *m.* penis • (lit.): tail.

colarse *v.* to cut in line, to sneak in, to gatecrash.

example:
Manuel intentó **colarse** en la fiesta de Rosalía pero no pudo.

translation:
Manuel tried to **sneak into** Rosalia's party but he couldn't.

SYNONYM -1:
deslizarse *v.* • (lit.): to slide, to slip.

SYNONYM -2:
escurrirse *v.* • (lit.): to drain, to drip, to trickle, to slip.

SYNONYM -3:
meterse delante de *exp.* • (lit.): to put in front of.

colgados *m.pl. (Mexico)* sagging breasts of an old woman • (lit.): hanging things (from the verb *colgar* meaning "to hang").

colgajos *m.pl.* testicles • (lit.): bunch (of fruit).

colgantes *m.pl.* testicles, "balls" • (lit.): "danglers" – from the verb *colgar* meaning "to hang" or "to dangle."

colmo (ser el) *exp.* to take the cake, to be the last straw • (lit.): to be the culmination.

example:
David no ha pagado el alquiler en tres meses. ¡Esto **es el colmo**!

translation:
David hasn't paid the rent for three months. That **takes the cake**!

VARIATION:
colmo de los colmos (ser el) *exp.* • (lit.): to be the culmination of culminations.

comadrera *f.* blabbermouth.

example:
¿Cómo sabías que me iba a casar? ¿Te lo dijo la **comadrera** de Cristina?

translation:
How did you know I was getting married? Did that **blabbermouth** Christina tell you?

NOTE:
This is from the feminine noun *comadre* meaning "gossip."

SYNONYMS:
SEE – **blabbermouth**, *p. 208*.

comebasura *n. & adj.* idiot; stupid • (lit.): garbage-eater.

example:
Alfredo es un verdadero **comebasura**. Le dice a todo el mundo que pertenece a la realeza.

translation:
Alfredo is a real **idiot**. He tells everyone that he is royalty.

SYNONYM:
comemierda *n. & adj.* • (lit.): shit-eater.

comecocos *m.* a person who tries to push his/her opinion on others.

example:
Javier es un **comecocos**. Piensa que lo que le gusta a él, le debe gustar a todos.

translation:
Javier always **tries to push his opinion on others**. He thinks that whatever he likes, everyone else should like, too.

SYNONYM -1:
comebolas *m. (Cuba).*

SYNONYM -2:
rollo *m. (Spain)* • (lit.): roll.

comilón/ona *n. & adj.* one who eats a lot, pig; piggy.

example:
¿Has visto todo lo que se ha comido Alfonso para almorzar? ¡Qué **comilón**!

translation:
Did you see how much food Alfonso ate during lunch? What a **pig**!

NOTE:
This is from the verb *comer* meaning "to eat."

comemierda *n. & adj.* jerk; jerky • (lit.): shit-eater.

example:
José es un **comemierda**. No creo que nadie quiera casarse con él.

translation:
Juan is such an **idiot**. I don't think anyone's ever going to want to marry him.

comer *v. (Chile, Colombia, Ecuador, Peru, Venezuela)* to perform oral sex • (lit.): to eat.

comer como un desfondado *exp.* to eat like a pig, to pig out • (lit.): to eat like someone without a bottom (to eat like a bottomless pit).

example:
Fernando está tan gordo porque siempre **come como un desfondado**.

translation:
Fernando is so fat because he always **eats like a pig**.

SYNONYM -1:
comer como si fuera la última cena *exp.* • (lit.): to eat as if it were the last supper.

SYNONYM -2:
comer como si no hubiera comido nunca *exp.* • (lit.): to eat as if one never ate before.

NOTE:
The noun *desfondado* comes from the verb *desfondar* meaning "to go through" or "to break the bottom of."

comerse el coco *exp.* • **1.** to worry, to get all worked up about something • **2.** to convince someone to do something • (lit.): to eat someone's head (since the masculine noun *coco,* literally meaning "coconut," is used in Spanish slang to mean "head" or "noggin").

example (1):
No **te comas el coco**. Mañana será otro día.

translation:
Don't **get all worked up about it**. Tomorrow will be a new beginning.

example (2):
Voy a **comerle el coco** a Javier para que me dé dinero.

translation:
I'm going to **convince** Javier to give me some money.

SYNONYM -1:
darle manija *exp.* *(Argentina)* • (lit.): to give oneself a handle.

SYNONYM -2:
perder la cabeza *exp.* *(Cuba)* • (lit.): to lose one's head.

SYNONYM -3:
rascar el coco *exp. (Mexico)* • (lit.): to scratch one's head or "coconut."

ALSO:
romperse el coco *exp.* to rack one's brain · (lit.): to break one's brain.

cometer la equivocación *exp.* to get married • (lit.): to make the mistake.

example:
Antonio finalmente ha decidido **cometer la equivocación**.
translation:
Antonio has finally decided **to get married**.

como (ser) *exp.* (referring to time) approximately, about • (lit.): to be like.
example:
Tengo mucho sueño. ¡Ya **son como** las dos de la madrugada!
translation:
I'm very sleepy. It's **about** two o'clock in the morning!

como anillo al dedo (quedar) exp. to fit to a T • (lit.): to fit like a ring to a finger.
example:
Ese vestido te queda **como anillo al dedo**.
translation:
That dress **fits you to a T**.
SYNONYM:
sentar de maravilla *exp.* • (lit.): to sit marvelously.

como bocina de avión (estar/ser) *exp. (Argentina)* to be as useless as a screen door on a submarine • (lit.): to be like a horn in a plane.
example:
No te va a poder ayudar. **Es como una bocina de avión**.
translation:
He's not going to be able to help you. **He's as useless as a screen door on a submarine**.
VARIATION:
inútil como bocina de avión (estar/ser) *exp.* • (lit.): useless as a horn in a plane.

como llovido del cielo *exp.* like manna from heaven, heaven sent • (lit.): like rained from the sky.
example:
Ese dinero me vino **como llovido del cielo**.
translation:
That money came **like manna from heaven**.

como Pedro por su casa *exp.* to feel right at home, to act like one owns the place • (lit.): like Pedro in his house.
example:
Juan siempre anda en la oficina **como Pedro por su casa**.
translation:
Juan always walks around the office **as if he owned the place**.

como pez en el agua (sentirse) *exp.* to feel right at home • (lit.): to feel like a fish in water.

example:
Estoy muy contento. **Me siento como pez en el agua**.

translation:
I'm so happy. **I feel right at home**.

SYNONYM:
como Pedro por su casa (andar) *exp.* • (lit.): like Pedro in his house.

ANTONYM -1:
como gallina en corral ajeno (estar) *exp.* • (lit.): to be like a chicken in a strange pen.

ANTONYM -2:
como [un] pez fuera del agua (estar) *exp.* to feel out of place, to feel like a fish out of water • (lit.): to be like a fish out of water.

ANTONYM -3:
como perro en barrio ajeno (estar) *exp.* • (lit.): to be like a dog in a strange neighborhood.

como un cenicero de moto (estar/ser) *exp.* *(Argentina)* to be totally useless • (lit.): to be like an ashtray on a motorcycle.

example:
No te voy a poder ayudar con la tarea. Cuando se trata de matemáticas soy **como un cenicero de moto**.

translation:
I'm not going to be able to help you with your homework. When it comes to math, I'm as **useless as a screen door on a submarine**.

VARIATION:
inútil como un cenicero de moto (estar/ser) *exp.* • (lit.): to be as useless as an ashtray on a motorcycle.

comprometido/a (estar) *adj.* • to be engaged, to get married • (lit.): to be compromised.

example:
Acabo de enterarme de que estás **comprometido**. ¡Enhorabuena!

translation:
I just found out that you're **engaged**. Congratulations!

con el corazón en la mano *exp.* in all frankness, in all honesty • (lit.): with the heart in the hand.

example:
Te lo digo **con el corazón en la mano**. Creo que no debes casarte con él.

translation:
I'm telling you **in all honesty**. I think you shouldn't marry him.

con los brazos abiertos *exp.* with open arms.

example:
Cuando Juan volvió de la guerra, lo recibimos **con los brazos abiertos**.

translation:
When Juan came back from the war, we welcomed him **with open arms**.

coña *f.* • **1.** vagina • **2.** joking.

NOTE:
This is a variation of the masculine noun *coño* which is an extremely vulgar term for "vagina."

ALSO -1:
¡No me des la coña! *interj.* Go away! • (lit.): Don't give me the cunt!

ALSO -2:
de coña *exp. (Spain)* by pure luck • *Conseguí este trabajo de coña;* I got this job by pure luck.

coñazo (ser un) *n.* • **1.** to be a pain in the neck • **2.** to be a horrible bore • **3.** to be a complete idiot.

example -1:
Mi hermanito me sigue por todos lados. ¡Qué **coñazo**!

translation:
My little brother follows me around everywhere. What a **pain in the neck**!

example -2:
Esa fue la peor película que he visto. ¡Qué **coñazo**!

translation:
That was the worst movie I've ever seen. What a **bore**!

example -3:
¡Carlos puso sal en su café en lugar de azúcar! ¡Qué **coñazo**!

translation:
Carlos put salt in his coffee instead of sugar! What a **complete idiot**!

NOTE:
This is a variation of the masculine noun *coño* meaning "vagina."

concha *f. (Argentina, Central America, Cuba, Uruguay)* a vulgar term for "vagina" • (lit.): seashell.

ALSO:
¡La concha de tu madre! *interj.* an extremely vulgar insult literally meaning "Your mother's vagina!"

VARIATION:
concho *m.*

NOTE:
The term *concha* literally means "seashell" but is used in slang to mean "vagina," so be careful how you use it! For example:

> ***Voy a la playa a buscar conchas.***

Common Translation:
I'm going to the beach to look for **seashells**.
Translation in Mexico:
I'm going to the beach to look for **vaginas**.

SYNONYMS:
SEE – **vagina**, *p. 263*.

conchudo/a *n. & adj.* lazy bum; lazy.
example:
Mi hermano Raudo es un **conchudo**. No hace nada todo el día.
translation:
My brother Raudo is a **lazy bum**. He doesn't do a thing all day.

conejo *m.* a vulgar term for "vagina" • (lit.): rabbit.

NOTE:
The term *conejo* literally means "rabbit" but is used in slang to mean "vagina," so be careful how you use it! For example:

> ***Mi madre me va a comprar un conejo para mi cumpleaños.***

Common Translation:
My mother's going to buy me a **rabbit** for my birthday.
Translation in Mexico:
My mother's going to buy me a **vagina** for my birthday.

SYNONYMS:
SEE – **vagina**, *p. 263*.

congalera *f.* prostitute, "whore" • (lit.): someone who works at a bordello.

coño *m.* a vulgar term for "vagina."

NOTE:
This term is commonly used in many Spanish-speaking countries (with the exception of Mexico and Argentina) as an interjection denoting surprise, anger, or annoyance. For example: *¡Coño! ¡No sabía que iba a llover!;* Damn! I didn't know it was supposed to rain!

SYNONYMS:
SEE – **vagina**, *p. 263*.

conocer a alguien *exp.* • **1.** *(when used in the past tense)* to meet someone • **2.** *(when used in the present tense)* to be acquainted with someone.

example:
Ayer **conocí** a mis nuevos vecinos. Parecen muy buena gente.
translation:
Yesterday I **met** my new neighbors. They seem to be good people.

ALSO -1:
conocer a alguien de nombre *exp.* to know someone by name.

ALSO -2:
conocer a alguien de vista *exp.* to know someone by sight.

consolador *m.* dildo • (lit.): comforter, consoler.

consultarlo con la almohada *exp.* to sleep on it • (lit.): to consult it with the pillow.

example:
Esa decisión tan importante, tendré que **consultarla con la almohada**.
translation:
It's such a big decision, I will have **to sleep on it**.

contra viento y marea *exp.* against all odds • (lit.): against wind and tide.
example:
Ese corredor ganó la carrera **contra viento y marea**.
translation:
That runner won the race **against all odds**.

corbejo *m. (Puerto Rico)* old whore.

corchito *m. (Argentina)* • (lit.): little cork.
example:
El **corchito** de Joseph me pidió salir el sábado por la noche.
translation:
That **little runt** Joseph asked me out on Saturday night.

corcho *m. (El Salvador)* annoying person or idiot • (lit.): cork.
example:
Guillermo me sigue a todas partes. ¡Es un **corcho**!
translation:
Guillermo follows me everywhere. He's such a **pain in the neck**!

correr *v.* to go fast or faster • (lit.): to run.

example:
Quiero **correr** más pero no puedo porque hay mucho tráfico.

translation:
I want to **go faster** but I can't because there is a lot of traffic.

SYNONYM -1:
acelerar el paso *exp.* to speed up • (lit.): to accelerate the step.

SYNONYM -2:
apretar el acelerador *exp.* to accelerate quickly • (lit.): to squeeze the accelerator.

ALSO:
carretera y manta *exp.* *(very popular)* to hit the road • (lit.): road and blanket.

correr el rumor *exp.* to be rumored • (lit.): to run the rumor.

example:
Corre el rumor que mañana van a despedir a Carlos.

translation:
It's been rumored that Carlos is going to get fired tomorrow.

correrse *v.* to ejaculate, to have an orgasm.

NOTE:
The intransitive form of this verb *correr* literally means "to run." However, in the reflexive form, it carries a sexual connotation.

cortar por lo sano *exp.* to take drastic measures • (lit.): to cut (something off) and leave only the healthy parts.

example:
Voy a **cortar por lo sano** y empezar de nuevo.

translation:
I'm going **to take drastic measures** and start over.

corte (dar un) *exp.* to cut someone off, to answer someone back in an aggressive way • (lit.): to cut.

example:
Quise ayudar a Ismael pero me **dio un corte** y me dijo no, gracias.

translation:
I wanted to help Ismael but he **cut me off** and said no thank you.

ALSO -1:
darse corte *exp.* to brag about something.

ALSO -2:
¡Qué corte! *exp.* • **1.** What a disappointment! • **2.** How embarrassing!

NOTE:
Interestingly enough, simply by removing the indefinite article *un* from the expression *dar un corte,* another popular expression is created: **dar corte** *exp.* to be ashamed or embarrassed.

SYNONYM -1:
cortarón (dar un) *exp.* *(Argentina).*

SYNONYM -2:
corte pastelillo (dar un) *exp. (Puerto Rico).*

NOTE:
pastelillo *m.* • (lit.): a fried pastry that has been folded in half and cut.

cortejo *m. (Puerto Rico)* pimp • (lit.): escort.

corto/a de mate *adj. (Argentina)* crazy, touched in the head • (lit.): short in the gourd.

example:
Creo que nuestra profesora está un poco **corta del mate**. En sus clases se empieza a reír sin motivo.

translation:
I think our new teacher is a little **touched in the head**. During her lectures, she starts laughing for no reason.

SYNONYM:
corto/a entendedera *exp. (Argentina)* (from the verb *entender* meaning "to understand").

cosa de *exp.* approximately, about • (lit.): thing of.

example:
Vuelvo en **cosa de** dos horas.

translation:
I'll be back **in approximately** two hours.

NOTE:
ser cosas de_____ *exp.* to be the way_____ is • (lit.): to be things of • *Esas son cosas de Javier;* That's just the way Javier is.

cosita *f.* penis • (lit.): little thing.

example:
Cada vez que mi hermanito tiene que orinar, se toca la **cosita**.

translation:
Every time my little brother has to urinate, he holds his **peepee**.

SYNONYMS:
SEE – **penis**, *p. 243*.

costar trabajo hacer algo *exp.* to have trouble believing/swallowing something • (lit.): to cost work.

example:
Me cuesta trabajo creer que Pedro ganó la apuesta.

translation:
I have trouble believing that Pedro won the bet.

costar un ojo de la cara *exp.* to cost an arm and a leg • (lit.): to cost an eye from the face.

example:
Ese abrigo **me costó un ojo de la cara**.

translation:
That coat **cost me an arm and a leg**.

SYNONYM -1:
costar un huevo [y medio] *exp. (Bolivia, Colombia, Ecuador, Peru, Spain, Venezuela)* • (lit.): to cost an egg.

NOTE:
This common expression is somewhat rude since the masculine noun *huevo* is commonly used to mean "testicle" in many Spanish-speaking countries.

cotorra *f.* blabbermouth • (lit.): parrot.
example:
¡Le conté un secreto a Ana y se lo contó a todo el mundo! Se me había olvidado lo **cotorra** que es.
translation:
I told a secret to Ana and she told everyone! I forgot what a **blabbermouth** she is.

SYNONYMS:
SEE – **blabbermouth**, *p. 208*.

coyón/na *n. & adj.* scaredy-cat; scared.
example:
¡Soy demasiado **coyón** para tirarme en paracaídas!
translation:
I'm too much of a **scaredy-cat** to try parachuting!

creído/a *adj.* snob, conceited person • (lit.): thought or believed.
example:
Manuel es un **creído**. Se cree que es mejor que nadie.
translation:
Manuel is a **snob**. He thinks he's better than anybody else.

SYNONYM -1:
esnob *m.*

SYNONYM -2:
snob *m.*

SYNONYM -3:
zarpado/a *n. (Argentina)*.

crema *f.* semen • (lit.): cream.

cretinita *f. & adj. (Argentina)* idiotic little girl; jerky • (lit.): little cretin.
example:
¡Esa **cretinita** me ha robado el bolígrafo!
translation:
That **little cretin** stole my pen!

cretino *m. & adj.* jerk, idiot; jerky • (lit.): cretin.
example:
El hermano de Steve es un pequeño **cretino**. No para de desatarme los cordones de mis zapatos.
translation:
Steve's brother is a little **cretin**. He keeps untying my shoes.

crica *f. (Puerto Rico)* vagina • (lit.): vagina.

SYNONYMS:
SEE – **vagina**, *p. 263*.

curda *f.* hangover • (lit.): raw.

example:
Si bebes mucho hoy, mañana tendrás una **cruda**.

translation:
If you drink a lot today, you'll have a **hangover** tomorrow.

SYNONYM -1:
goma (estar de) *exp.* to be like rubber.

SYNONYM -2:
resaca *f.* • (lit.): undertow.

cua-cua *m. (Puerto Rico)* derogatory for "homosexual."

NOTE:
This is the sound a duck makes and is applied to homosexuals who walk with fast little steps much like a duck.

cuadrado/a (estar) *adj.* (pronounced *cuadrao* in Cuba and Puerto Rico) to be strong, muscular • (lit.): to be squared.

example:
Ricardo está **cuadrado**, se nota que hace ejercicio.

translation:
Ricardo is so **strong**, you can tell he exercises.

SYNONYM:
mula (estar como una) *exp.* • (lit.): to be like a mule.

cualquiera *f.* prostitute • (lit.): anyone.

cuando más *exp.* at most • (lit.): when more.

example:
Javier debe tener diez y ocho años **cuando más**.

translation:
Javier must be eighteen years old **at most**.

NOTE:
This common expression is used primarily in Latin-American countries. • (lit.): when more.

ANTONYM:
cuando menos *exp.* at least • (lit.): when less.

cuarenta y uno *m. (Mexico)* derogatory for "homosexual" • (lit.): forty-one.

NOTE:
This expression may have originated since some people think that if a person is over forty and not married, it may be a sign of homosexuality.

cuartito *m.* bathroom, the "john" • (lit.): small room

example:
Necesito ir al **cuartito**.

translation:
I need to visit the **bathroom**.

cuate *m. (Mexico)* buddy, friend • (lit.): twin.

example:
Alfredo es mi **cuate**. Siempre puedo contar con él.

translation:
Alfredo is my **buddy**. I can always count on him.

SYNONYM -1:
amigote *m.* • (lit.); big friend (from the noun *amigo*).

SYNONYM -2:
camarada *m.* • (lit.): comrade.

SYNONYM -3:
carnal *m.* • (lit.): related by blood.

SYNONYM -4:
compadre *m.* • (lit.): godfather.

SYNONYM -5:
hermano *m.* • (lit.): brother.

SYNONYM -6:
jefe *m.* • (lit.): boss.

SYNONYM -7:
mano *m.*

NOTE:
This is a shortened version of *hermano* meaning "brother."

SYNONYM -8:
tío *m. (Cuba/Spain)* • (lit.): uncle.

cuatro ojos *m.* a person who wears glasses, "four-eyes" • (lit.): four eyes.

example:
Mi maestro de literatura es un **cuatroojos**.

translation:
My literature teacher is **four-eyed**.

NOTE:
Also spelled: *cuatrojos*.

SYNONYM -1:
bisco/a *n. (Argentina)* cross-eyed.

SYNONYM -2:
cegato/a *adj.* • (lit.): from the masculine noun *ciego* meaning "blind person."

SYNONYM -3:
chicato/a *adj. (Argentina)*.

SYNONYM -4:
corto de vista *exp.* near-sighted • (lit.): shortsighted.

SYNONYM -5:
gafitas *adj.* • (lit.): from the masculine noun *gafas* meaning "glasses."

SYNONYM -6:
gafudo/a *adj.* • (lit.): from the masculine noun *gafas* meaning "glasses."

cuca *f. (El Salvador, Venezuela)* vagina • (lit.): clever, smart.

SYNONYMS:
SEE – **vagina**, *p. 263*.

cuchi *m.* fatso • (lit.): variation of *cochino* meaning "filthy."

example:
Como te comas todo eso, te vas a poner **cuchi**.
translation:
If you eat all that, you're going to turn into a **fat pig**.

cuello duro *m. & adj.* snob; stuck up • (lit.): hard or stiff neck (from keeping one's nose in the air).

example:
Miguel es un **cuello duro**. Sólo viaja en primera clase.
translation:
Miguel is a **snob**. He'll only travel first class.

cuentero/a *n. & adj.* *(Argentina)* a gossip; gossipy• (lit.): one who tells tales.

example:
¿Le contaste un secreto a Antonio? No fue buena idea. Es todo un **cuentero**.
translation:
You told Antonio a secret? That wasn't a good idea. He's such a **blabbermouth**.

SYNONYMS:
SEE – **blabbermouth**, *p. 208*.

cuentista *m. & f.* gossip • (lit.): story teller.

example:
Juan siempre está hablando de otras personas. ¡Es un **cuentista**!
translation:
Juan is always talking about other people. He's such a **gossip**!

SYNONYM -1:
cantamañanas *m.*

SYNONYM -2:
chismoso *m. (Argentina).*

SYNONYM -3:
mitotero/a *n. (Mexico).*

cuentón *m.* • **1.** big bill, check • **2.** long story.

example (1):
¡Casi me da un ataque cardíaco cuando me llegó el **cuentón** y me di cuenta cuánto costaba comer en ese restaurante!
translation:
I almost had a heart attack when I got the **check** and found out how much our meal cost at the restaurant!

example (2):
Si quieres, te cuento lo que me pasó hoy en la escuela pero es un **cuentón**.
translation:
If you want, I'll tell you what happened to me at school today but it's a **long story**.

SYNONYM -1:
dolorosa *f. (Argentina, Puerto Rico)* • (lit.): that which causes pain (from the masculine noun *dolor* meaning "pain").

SYNONYM -2:
importe *m.*

SYNONYM -3:
monto *m.*

NOTE:
The synonyms above apply to definition **1** only.

ANTONYM:
cuentecilla *f.* small bill or check.

cuero *m. & adj.* • **1.** hunk; hunky • **2.** *(Puerto Rico)* prostitute who is into leather • (lit.): leather.

example:
Tu hermano es tan **cuero**. ¿Tiene novia?

translation:
Your brother is so **hunky**. Does he have a girlfriend?

ALSO:
en cueros (estar) *exp.* to be butt-naked • (lit.): to be in leathers.

cuesco *m.* fart • (lit.): stone, punch.

example:
¡Acabo de oír al vecino tirarse un **cuesco**!

translation:
I just heard the next door neighbor **fart**!

cuete (ponerse) *adj.* to get drunk • (lit.): slice of rump (of beef).

example:
Benito nunca parece demasiado sano. Yo creo que **se pone cuete** todo el tiempo.

translation:
Benito never looks very healthy. I think he **gets drunk** all the time.

cuevita *f.* vagina • (lit.): little cave.

SYNONYMS:
SEE – **vagina**, *p. 263*.

culastrón *m. (Argentina)* derogatory for "homosexual."

NOTE:
This is a variation of the masculine noun *culo* meaning "ass."

culero *m.* **1.** a drug thief who smuggles drugs by hiding them in the rectum (from the masculine noun *culo* meaning "ass") • **2.** derogatory for "homosexual" • **3.** brown-noser.

culicagado *m.* little brat • (lit.): shit-covered ass.

example:
Dormí apenas cuatro horas anoche. ¡Los **culicagados** de mi vecinidad estaban gritando en las primeras horas de la mañana!

translation:
I only got four hours of sleep last night. The **little brats** in my neighborhood were screaming first thing in the morning!

culo *m.* ass.

ALSO -1:
culo mal asiento (estar hecho un) *exp.* to be fidgety • (lit.): to be made an ass that won't sit right.

ALSO -2:
culón *m.* one with a big ass.

ALSO -3:
ir con el culo a rastras *exp.* • **1.** to be in a jam • **2.** to be broke • (lit.): to go with the ass dragging.

ALSO -4:
ir de culo *exp.* to go downhill, to deteriorate • (lit.): to go on its ass.

ALSO -5:
lamer el culo a alguien *exp.* to kiss up to someone • (lit.): to lick someone's ass.

culo (estar de) *exp.* to feel out of sorts • (lit.): to be like an asshole.

example:
Normalmente, me gustaría ir contigo al cine pero hoy **estoy de culo**. Creo que voy a quedarme en casa para leer un buen libro.

translation:
Ordinarily, I'd love to go with you to the movies but I feel **out of it** today. I think I'm just going to stay home and read a good book.

culo mal hecho (estar un) *exp.* to be fidgety • (lit.): to have an ass that won't sit right.

example:
¿Estás preocupado de algo? Estás un **culo mal hecho** hoy.

translation:
Are you worried about something? You're **fidgety** today.

ALSO:
culo (estar hecho un) *exp.* to look awful • (lit.): to be made [to look like] an ass or buttock.

culón *m.* one with a big ass, lard-ass.

example:
Trabajo en un escritorio todo el día. Si no empiezo a hacer ejercicios, voy a convertirme en un **culón**.

translation:
I work behind a desk all day long. If I don't start getting some exercise, I'm going to turn into a **lard-ass**!

cundango *m.* derogatory for "homosexual."

curo *m. (Cuba)* penis • (lit.): leather strap.

SYNONYMS:
SEE – **penis**, *p. 243*.

currar *v.* to work.

example:
Me encanta **currar** en este restaurante porque así nunca tengo hambre.
translation:
I love **working** at this restaurant because that way I never go hungry.

SYNONYM:
chambear *v.*

NOTE:
chamba *m.* job.

cusca *f.* prostitute, slut • (lit.): prostitute.

chacón *f. (Argentina)* vagina • (lit.): an inversion of the feminine term *concha* meaning "seashell."

SYNONYMS:
SEE – **vagina**, *p. 263.*

chaira *f.* penis • (lit.): cobbler's knife.

SYNONYMS:
SEE – **penis**, *p. 243.*

chamaco/a *n. (Mexico)* little kid, small child.
example:
Esos **chamacos** pasan todo el día jugando en el parque.
translation:
Those **kids** spend all day playing at the park.

SYNONYM -1:
chiquillo/a *n.*

NOTE:
This noun comes from the adjective *chico/a* meaning "small."

SYNONYM -2:
chiquitín/a *n.*

NOTE:
This noun comes from the adjective *chico/a* meaning "small."

SYNONYM -3:
crío/a *m.* • (lit.): a nursing-baby.

SYNONYM -4:
enano/a *n. (Spain)* short person • (lit.): dwarf.

SYNONYM -5:
gurrumino/a *n.* • (lit.): weak or sickly person, "whimp."

SYNONYM -6:
mocoso/a *n.* • (lit.): snot-nosed person.

SYNONYM -7:
párvulo *m.* • (lit.): tot.

SYNONYM -8:
pequeñajo/a *n.*

NOTE:
This noun comes from the adjective *pequeño/a* meaning "small."

SYNONYM -9:
pendejo/a *n. (Argentina).*

ANTONYM -1:
grandote *m.*

NOTE:
This noun comes from the adjective *grande* meaning "big."

ANTONYM -2:
grandulón/a *n.* big kid.

NOTE:
This noun comes from the adjective *grande* meaning "big."

chambear *v.* to work.

example:
Hoy no tengo ganas de **chambear**. Estoy muy cansado.

translation:
Today I don't feel like **working**. I'm really tired.

NOTE:
chamba *f.* job.

SYNONYM -1:
currar *v. (Spain).*

SYNONYM -2:
doblar el lomo *exp. (Puerto Rico)* to work hard • (lit.): to fold one's back in two.

champe *m. (Cuba)* derogatory for "homosexual."

NOTE:
This is a variation of the masculine noun *champí* meaning "a tiny insect."

chancho *m.* • (lit.): fat pig.

example:
Ese **chancho** se acaba de comer siete hamburguesas. No me sorprende que esté así.

translation:
That **fat slob** just ate seven hamburgers. It doesn't surprise me he looks like that.

chango *m.* vagina • (lit.): monkey.

SYNONYMS:
SEE – **vagina**, *p. 263*.

chao *good-bye.*

example:
¡**Chao**! ¡Hasta la vista!

translation:
Good-bye! See ya!

NOTE:
This slang term comes from the Italian word "*ciao*" meaning "good-bye" and is extremely popular among Spanish-speakers as well as French.

NOTE:
In Argentina, this is spelled *chau*.

chaparro/a *n. & adj.* runt; runty.

example:
¡Hey **chaparro**! ¡Muévete!
translation:
Hey, **shorty**! Move it!

chapero *m. (Spain)* male prostitute.

chapete *f.* an easy lay.
example:
Me gustaría salir con Elvia. He oído que es una **chapete**.
translation:
I'd like to go out with Elvia. I hear she's a **real easy lay**.

chaquetear *v.* to masturbate.

VARIATION:
hacer una chaqueta *exp.* to make a jacket.

charlar *v.* to chat.
example:
A Pepa le gusta **charlar** mucho con las amigas.
translation:
Pepa loves to **chat** with her friends.

SYNONYM -1:
charlatear *v.*

SYNONYM -2:
charlotear *v.*

SYNONYM -3:
cuchichear *v.*

SYNONYM -4:
parlotear *v.*

NOTE:
This term comes from the verb *parlar* meaning "to talk" or "to chat."

SYNONYM -5:
platicar *v. (extremely common in Mexico).*

ALSO:
tener una charla *exp.* to have a conversation.

chava bien [buena] *f.* beautiful girl, hot chick • (lit.): young girl well good.
example:
Mira a esa **chava bien [buena]**. Me pregunto si ella es un modelo.
translation:
Look at that **hot girl**. I wonder if she's a model.

chavo bien [bueno] *m.* handsome guy, hunk • (lit.): young guy well good.
example:
¡Tu hermano es un **chavo bien [bueno]**!
translation:
Your brother is a **hunk**!

¡Che dejá de dormir, fiaca de mierda, movete un poco! *exp. (Argentina)* used in response to seeing a lazy person • (lit.): Hey, stop sleeping, you lazy piece of shit, and move around a little!

example:
¡Che dejá de dormir, fiaca de mierda, movete un poco! ¡Tenemos mucho trabajo que hacer!

translation:
Hey, stop sleeping, you lazy piece of shit, and move around a little! We have a lot of work to do!

¡Che estás tan gordo que vas a reventar! *exp.* *(Argentina)* in response to seeing someone very fat • (lit.): Hey fatso, you're going to explode!

example:
¡**Che estás tan gordo que vas a reventar**! ¡Deja de comer tanto!

translation:
Hey fatso, you're going to explode! Stop eating so much!

chela *f.* beer • (lit.): blond.

example:
En ese restaurante sirven **chelas** de México.

translation:
They serve Mexican **beer** in that restaurant.

SYNONYM -1:
birra *f. (Argentina).*

SYNONYM -2:
palo *m. (Puerto Rico)* beer or any strong drink • (lit.): stick (since when one gets drunk, it could be compared to being hit on the head with a stick, causing dizziness and fogginess).

chica de alterne *f.* prostitute • (lit.): alternating girl.

chichis *m.pl.* breasts, "tits."

NOTE:
Interestingly, there is a well-known female impersonator in Los Angeles named Miss Chichi, yet most Americans are probably unaware that her name comes from Spanish and is in reference to her large breasts.

chichona *f.* a woman with big breasts (from the masculine plural noun *chichis* meaning "breasts."

example:
Carolina tiene solamente catorce años y ya está bien dotada. En pocos años, ella va a ser una **chichona**.

translation:
Carolina is only fourteen years old and she's already very endowed. In another few years, she's going to be a real **breasty woman**.

chicloso *m.* anus • (lit.): made of chewing-gum.

chico *m.* boy, guy, "dude."

example:
Ese **chico** siempre se viste bien.
translation:
That **guy** always dresses well.

NOTE:
chica *f.* girl, "chick."

SYNONYM -1:
chamaco/a *n. (Mexico, Puerto Rico).*

SYNONYM -2:
guambito *m. (Columbia).*

SYNONYM -3:
patojo/a *n. (Guatemala).*

SYNONYM -4:
pibe *n. (Argentina, Spain, Uruguay).*

SYNONYM -5:
tío *m. (Cuba, Spain)* • (lit.): uncle.

chiflado/a *n. & adj.* crackpot; crazy, nuts • (lit.): whistled (from the verb *chiflar* meaning "to whistle").
example:
Si crees que puedes conducir de San Francisco a Los Angeles en sólo tres horas, ¡estás **chiflado**!
translation:
If you think you can drive to Los Angeles from San Francisco in only three hours, you're **nuts**!

chiflo *m.* penis • (lit.): whistle.

SYNONYMS:
SEE – **penis**, *p. 243.*

chile *m. (Mexico)* penis • (lit.): chile, hot pepper.

SYNONYMS:
SEE – **penis**, *p. 243.*

chilito *m. (Mexico, Spain)* an insulting term for a little penis • (lit.): small chile, small hot pepper.

SYNONYMS:
SEE – **penis**, *p. 243.*

chimba *f. (Colombia)* vagina.

NOTE:
This is a variation of the masculine noun *chimbo* which is a type of dessert.

SYNONYMS:
SEE – **vagina**, *p. 263.*

chinaloa *f. (Mexico)* opium, heroin.

¡Chinga tu madre! *interj.* a common insult meaning "Go to hell!" • (lit.): Fuck your mother!

chingado/a [noun] *adj.* fucking [noun] (i.e. *chingado idiota;* fucking idiot).
example:
¡David es tan **chingado idiota**! ¡Pusó agua en su carro en lugar de gasolina!
translation:
David is such a **fucking idiot**! He put water in his car instead of gasoline!

¡Chingao! *interj.* Fuck! • (lit.): Fucked!

VARIATION:
concho *m.*

chingar *v.* **1.** to fuck • **2.** to cheat • **3.** to tire someone • **4.** to annoy.

chingar a alguien *v.* to annoy someone greatly • to fuck someone.

example:
Rosa **me chinga** con todas sus preguntas estúpidas.

translation:
Rosa **bugs the shit out of me** with all of her stupid questions.

¡Chíngate!
interj. (Mexico) Fuck you! (from the verb *chingar* meaning "to fuck").

chingón *m.* fucker (from the verb *chingar* meaning "to fuck").

example:
¡Nunca confiaré en un **chingón** como Oliver!

translation:
I would never trust a **fucker** like Oliver!

NOTE:
This term is also used in reference to a person who is very good at something. For example: *Fernando es un chingón en matemáticas;* Fernando is fucking good at math.

chiquito *m.* a tiny anus • (lit.): very small, tiny.

chirusa *f. (Argentina)* idiotic little girl • (lit.): ignorant young woman.

example:
¿Conociste a la hija de Marcela? ¡Qué **chirusa**!

translation:
Did you meet Marcela's daughter? What a little **geek**!

chis *m. (Mexico – children's language)* urine, piss.

example:
Huele a **chis** en este baño.

translation:
It smells of **urine** in this bathroom.

NOTE:
As an interjection, *chis* may be used to mean "shhh!" or "pst!"

chismear *v.* to gossip.

example:
A Pablo le encanta **chismear** con sus compañeros de trabajo.

translation:
Pablo loves to **gossip** with his coworkers.

VARIATION:
chismorrear *v.*

ALSO:
chisme *m.* a juicy piece of gossip.

example:
¡Cuéntame los **chismes**!

translation:
Give me the **dirt**!

SYNONYM:
cotillear *v. (Spain).*

chismolero/a *n. & adj.* one who spreads gossip or *chismes;* gossipy.
example:
No le cuentes nunca nada a Ana. ¡Es una **chismolera**!
translation:
Don't ever tell anything to Ana. She's a **gossip**!

chismoso/a *n.* one who spreads gossip or *chismes*.
example:
No le cuentes a Jorge nada personal. Es un **chismoso**.
translation:
Don't tell anything personal to Jorge. He's a **gossip**.

chivo *m.* pimp • (lit.): goat.

chocante *adj.* annoying, unpleasant.
example:
Ese tío habla demasiado y además tiene una voz muy **chocante**.
translation:
That guy talks too much and besides he has an **annoying** voice.

NOTE:
chocar *v.* to annoy, to get annoyed, to hate something or someone • (lit.): to crash, to collide.
example:
Me **choca** ir de compras cuando hay mucha gente en las tiendas.
translation:
I **hate** to go shopping when there are a lot of people in the stores.

chocha *f. (Cuba)* vagina • (lit.): woodcock (a type of game bird).

SYNONYMS:
SEE – **vagina**, *p. 263.*

chocho *m. (Mexico, Spain)* vagina • (lit.): floppy.

SYNONYMS:
SEE – **vagina**, *p. 263.*

chocolate de fu man chu *m. (Mexico)* opium, heroin • (lit.): chocolate of fu manchu.

chollo *m.* good deal.
example:
Solo pagué trescientos dólares por este automóvil. ¡Qué **chollo**!
translation:
I only paid three hundred dollars for this car. What a **deal**!

SYNONYM -1:
buena ganga (una) *f. (Argentina, Puerto Rico).*

SYNONYM -2:
curro *m. (Argentina).*

cholo *m. (Mexico, Puerto Rico)* • **1.** pimp • **2.** half-breed, the product of a mixed marriage.

choncha *f.* penis.

SYNONYMS:
SEE – **penis**, *p. 243*.

chora *f.* **1.** penis • **2.** *(Mexico)* marijuana • (lit.): female thief.

SYNONYMS:
SEE – **penis**, *p. 243*.

chorizo *m.* penis • (lit.): pork sausage.

NOTE:
The term *chorizo* literally means "pork sausage" but is used in slang to mean "penis," so be careful how you use it! For example:

Me comí un chorizo entero a la hora del desayuno.

Common Translation #1:
I ate a whole **pork sausage** for breakfast.

Common Translation #2:
I ate a whole **penis** for breakfast.

SYNONYMS:
SEE – **penis**, *p. 243*.

chorra *f.* good luck.

example:
¡No te puedes imaginar la **chorra** que he tenido! ¡Me tocó la lotería!

translation:
You won't believe my **luck**! I won the lottery!

ALSO:
tener chorra *exp.* to be lucky.

chorrada *f.* stupid or despicable act.

example:
No puedo creer que Pablo haya hecho una **chorrada** como ésa.

translation:
I can't believe Pablo would do a **stupid thing** like that.

NOTE:
The noun *chorrada* may also be used when referring to something very easy to do.

SYNONYM -1:
burrada *f. (Mexico)* a stupid act or remark • (lit.): a drove of donkeys • *decir burradas;* to talk nonsense.

SYNONYM -2:
trastada *f. (Puerto Rico)* despicable act or dirty trick.

chorrico *m.* penis • (lit.): constant flow or stream.

SYNONYMS:
SEE – **penis**, *p. 243*.

chucha *f.* vagina • (lit.): bitch dog *(Chile)*.

NOTE:
The term *chucha* literally means "bitch dog" but is used

in slang to mean "vagina," so be careful how you use it! For example:

Mi chucha acaba de parir.

Common Translation:
My **female** dog just had babies.

Translation in Chile:
My **vagina** just had babies.

SYNONYMS:
SEE – **vagina**, *p. 263*.

chufle *f.* penis.

SYNONYMS:
SEE – **penis**, *p. 243*.

chulada *f.* said of something "cool," neat.

example:
¡Este automóvil es una verdadera **chulada**!

translation:
This car is so **cool**!

SYNONYM -1:
copado/a *adj. (Argentina).*

SYNONYM -2:
rebueno/a *adj. (Argentina).*

NOTE:
In Argentina, it's very common to add re before an adjective to add greater emphasis.

SYNONYM -3:
tumba (estar que) *exp. (Puerto Rico)* • (lit.): to fall (for).

ANTONYM:
chungo/a *adj.* "uncool," ugly, lousy.

chulear *v.* to act cool, to be vain or conceited, to show off.

example:
Le encanta **chulear** de coche porque tiene un coche muy caro.

translation:
He loves to **show off** his car because he drives an expensive car.

NOTE:
chulo/a *adj.* cool, neat, good looking.

example:
¡Qué **chulo** que estás con ese traje!

translation:
You look really cool with that **suit**!

SYNONYM:
echándosear *v. (Cuba, Puerto Rico).*

chulo *m. (Spain)* hunk • (lit.): • **1.** bull-fighter's assistant • **2.** pimp.

example:
¿Has visto al nuevo estudiante? ¡Es un verdadero **chulo**!

translation:
Did you see the new student? He's such a **hunk**!

chumino *m.* vagina.

SYNONYMS:
SEE – **vagina**, *p. 263*.

chungo/a *adj.* "uncool," lousy, ugly.

example:
Esa película es muy **chunga**. Cuando fui a verla me quedé dormido.

translation:
That's a really **lousy** movie. When I went to see it I fell asleep.

SYNONYM -1:
chango/a *adj. (Puerto Rico)*.

SYNONYM -2:
flojo/a *adj. (Mexico, Puerto Rico)*.

ANTONYM:
chulo/a *adj.* cool, neat, great, good-looking.

¡Chupame la pinga/pija! *interj. (an insult of contempt)* • (lit.): Suck my penis!

¡Chupame la polla! *interj.* Suck my penis! • (lit.): Suck my young chicken!

¡Chupame la verga! *interj.* Suck my penis! • (lit.): Suck my penis (of an animal).

¡Chúpame, puto! *interj.* Go to hell, you jerk! • (lit.): Suck me, you faggot!

¡Chúpamela! *interj.* Go to hell! • (lit.): Suck it!

chupandín *m. (Argentina)* drunkard, lush • (lit.): big sucker (from the verb *chupar* meaning "to suck").

example:
¿Viste cuánto alcohol bebió Jack ayer por la noche? ¡No tenía idea de que fuera tan **chupandín**!

translation:
Did you see how much alcohol Jack drank last night? I had no idea he was such a **lush**!

chupar *v.* to drink • (lit.): to suck.

example:
A Manolo le gusta **chupar** demasiado.

translation:
Manolo likes to **drink** too much.

SYNONYM -1:
darle al chupe *exp.* to drink • (lit.): to take the pacifier (baby's comforter).

SYNONYM -2:
dar palos *exp. (Puerto Rico)* • (lit.): to give (oneself) sticks (a slang expression meaning "drinks" perhaps since the state of drunkenness could be compared to being hit on the head with a stick, causing dizziness and fogginess).

chupar/mamar la pinga *exp.* to perform oral sex • (lit.): to suck the "penis."

example:
¡Angela le **chupó la pinga** a Tomás en su carro!

translation:
Angela **performed oral sex** on Thomas last night in his car!

NOTE -1:
Any slang synonym for "penis" can be used in the expression. SEE – **penis**, *p. 243*.

NOTE -2:
In Argentina, the slang term for penis in this expression would be *pija* (literally, "fool").

chuparosa *f.* derogatory for "homosexual."

NOTE:
This is a variation of the masculine noun *chupaflor* meaning "humming bird."

chuperson *m. (Mexico)* penis.

SYNONYMS:
SEE – **penis**, *p. 243*.

chupón *m.* a player who tends to hog the ball.

example:
Ernesto es un **chupón**. Nunca les pasa la pelota a los demás jugadores.

translation:
Ernesto **hogs the ball**. He never passes the ball to the rest of the players.

NOTE:
This term is used mostly in soccer games.

SYNONYM:
peleón *m. (Puerto Rico)* one who plays like the famous soccer player, Pelé.

churro *m.* • **1.** turd • **2.** penis • (lit.): long fritter (*churro;* a long, straight fried pastry).

example:
¡Ese perro acaba de largar un enorme **churro**!

translation:
That dog just laid the biggest **turd**!

NOTE -1:
The noun *churro* is also used to refer to a failure. For example: *La película fue un churro;* The movie was a bomb.

NOTE -2:
In Argentina and Colombia, a *churro* means "a sexy guy."

NOTE -3:
The term *churro* literally means "fritter" but is used in slang to mean "turd" or "penis," so be careful how you use it! For example:

> ***¡Mira! Ese hombre está vendiendo churros.***

Common Translation:
Look! That man is selling **fritters**!

Common Translation in Mexico:
Look! That man is selling **penises**!

SYNONYMS:
SEE – **penis**, *p. 243*.

chusma *f.* despicable people, "scumbags."

example:
Yo no voy a invitar ni a Jorge ni a Pedro a mi fiesta porque son muy **chusma**.

translation:
I'm not inviting Jorge or Pedro to my party because they're **scum**.

daga *f. (Puerto Rico)* penis • (lit.): dagger.

SYNONYMS:
SEE – **penis**, *p. 243*.

dar [tanta] rabia *exp.* to make one [so] mad • (lit.): to give rage.

example:
Me da tanta rabia cuando la gente llega tarde a una cita.

translation:
It gets me so ticked off when people arrive late to an appointment.

dar a luz a *exp.* to give birth to • (lit.): to give light to.

example:
Marta **dio a luz a** una preciosa niña.

translation:
Marta **gave birth to** a beautiful girl.

dar calabazas a alguien *exp.* to dump someone • (lit.): to give pumpkins to someone.

example:
Yo pensé que Carlos y yo nos íbamos a casar, y de repente sin ninguna razón, **¡me dio calabazas**!

translation:
I thought Carlos and I were going to get married. Then for no reason, **he dumped me**!

dar candela por el culo *exp. (Cuba)* to participate in anal sex • (lit.): to give fire up the ass.

dar en el clavo *exp.* to hit the nail on the head, to put one's finger on it • (lit.): to hit on the nail.

example:
¡Tienes razón! ¡Has **dado en el clavo**!

translation:
You're right! You just **hit the nail on the head**!

SYNONYM -1:
dar el hito *exp.* • (lit.): to hit on the stone.

SYNONYM -2:
dar la tecla *exp.* • (lit.): to give in the key (of a muscial instrument – in other words, to hit the right note).

ALSO -1:
dar con (algo) *exp.* to find (something) • (lit.): to give with.

ALSO -2:
dar en *exp.* to hit on • (lit.): to give on.

dar un esquinazo a [alguien] *exp.* to avoid [someone], to ditch someone • (lit.): to give [someone] a corner.

example:
¡Tengo ganas de **darle esquinazo** a Julio! Es un pesado.

translation:
Let's **ditch** Julio! He's so annoying.

SYNONYM:
dejar plantado a *exp.* • (lit.): to leave someone planted.

dar gato por liebre *exp.* to pull the wool over someone's eyes • (lit.): to give a cat instead of a hare.

example:
Le dieron gato por liebre cuando Jorge compró esa casa. Tenía muchos problemas de plomería.

translation:
They **pulled the wool over his eyes** when Jorge bought that house. It was full of plumbing problems.

dar mala espina *exp.* to arouse one's suspicions • (lit.): to give a bad thorn.

example:
A Mario **le dio mala espina** cuando vio a una persona salir del banco corriendo.

translation:
It **aroused** Mario's **suspicions** when he saw a person running out of the bank.

dar por [el] culo *exp.* to have anal intercourse • (lit.): to give through the ass.

dar por donde amarga el pepino *exp.* to fornicate doggie-style • (lit.): to give where the cucumber is bitter.

dar un portazo *exp.* to slam the door • (lit.): to give a slam (of a door).

example:
¡No **des portazos** por favor!

translation:
Please don't **slam the door**!

SYNONYM:
tirar la puerta *exp.* • (lit.): to throw the door.

dar una mamada *exp.* to give a blow job • (lit.): to give a sucking.

example:
¡Esta puta le está **dando una mamada** a este tipo en plena calle!

translation:
That prostitute is **giving a blow job** to that guy right on the street!

dar una vuelta *exp.* to take a stroll, a walk • (lit.): to give a turn.

example:
Hace un día muy bonito. Vamos a **dar una vuelta**.

translation:
It's a beautiful day. Let's **go for a stroll**.

SYNONYM -1:
dar un paseo *exp.* • (lit.): to give a passage.

SYNONYM -2:
pasear a pie *exp.* • (lit.): to walk by foot.

SYNONYM -3:
tomar aire *exp.* • (lit.): to take the air.

darse el lote *exp. (Spain)* to kiss, to make out • (lit.): to give each other the portion or allotment (of kisses).

example:
¿Sabías que Marco y Alicia salían? Los he visto hoy **dándose el lote** en el parque.

translation:
Did you know that Marco and Alicia were going out? I saw them **making out** in the park today.

darse lija *exp.* to put on airs, to act pretentious, to have an attitude problem • (lit.): to give oneself sandpaper.

example:
A Ricardo le gusta **darse lija**. Cree que es mejor que nadie.

translation:
Ricardo likes to **put on airs**. He thinks he's better than anybody else.

SYNONYM:
ser un broncas *adj. (Spain)* to have a bad attitude, said of someone who is always in fights.

darse una buena calentada *exp. (Mexico)* to kiss • (lit.): to give each other a good heating up.

example:
¡Ven rápido! ¡Carol y Juan se están **dando una buena calentada** en público!

translation:
Come quickly! Carol and Juan are **making out** in public!

de antemano *exp.* ahead of time • (lit.): of beforehand.

example:
Te aviso **de antemano** que voy a ir contigo a la fiesta pero no me voy a quedar hasta tarde.

translation:
I'm warning you **beforehand** that I'm going with you to the party but I'm not staying late.

de buenas a primeras *exp.* suddenly (and unexpectedly), right off the bat, from the very start • (lit.): from the good ones to the first ones.

example:
De buenas a primeras Ana me dijo que no quería salir más conmigo.

translation:
Right off the bat Ana told me she didn't want to go out with me anymore.

SYNONYM -1:
de repente *exp.* • (lit.): suddenly (of sudden movement).

SYNONYM -2:
luego, luego *adv. (Mexico)* right away • (lit.): later, later.

NOTE:
Although its literal translation is indeed "later, later," when *luego* is repeated twice, it means, oddly enough, "right away" or "immediately."

de cabo a rabo *exp.* from beginning to end • (lit.): from end to tail.

example:
Me leí "El Quijote" **de cabo a rabo**.

translation:
I read "Don Quixote" **from beginning to end**.

SYNONYM -1:
de cabo a cabo *exp.* • (lit.): from end to end.

SYNONYM -2:
de punta a punta *exp.* • (lit.): from point to point.

de gala (estar) *exp.* to be all dressed up, to be in formal attire, to be dressed to kill • (lit.): to be in full regalia.

example:
Siempre que voy a una fiesta me visto **de gala**.
translation:
I always get **all dressed up** when I go to a party.

VARIATION:
vestirse de gala *exp.* • (lit.): to dress oneself in full regalia.

de la acera de enfrente *exp.* derogatory for "homosexual" • (lit.): (someone) from the other side of the street.
example:
¿Tu hermana quiere salir con Enrique? Creo que va a estar frustrada cuando sepa que él **es de la acera de enfrente**.
translation:
Your sister wants to go out with Enrique? I think she's going to be disappointed when she finds out he's **gay**.

de la cáscara amarga *exp.* derogatory for "homosexual" • (lit.): (someone) from the bitter peel (of fruit)

de la otra acera *exp.* derogatory for "homosexual" • (lit.): (someone) from the other side of the street.
example:
Por fin mi hermana conoció a un tipo que le gusta mucho. ¡Qué pena que él sea **de la otra acera**!
translation:
My sister finally met a guy that she really likes. It's too bad he's **gay**!

de los otros *m.* derogatory for "homosexual" • (lit.): one of them.

de mal en peor (ir) *exp.* to go from bad to worse • (lit.): [same].
example:
Las cosas van **de mal en peor** entre Fernando y Verónica.
translation:
Things are going **from bad to worse** between Fernando and Veronica.

de moda (estar) *exp.* to be fashionable, to be chic, to be in style • (lit.): to be of fashion.
example:
Verónica siempre **se viste de moda**.
translation:
Verónica always **dresses in style**.

VARIATION:
a la moda (estar) *exp.* • (lit.): of good tone.

SYNONYM:
de buen tono *exp.* • (lit.): of good tone.

de pedo *adv.* by luck • (lit.): by fart (something that happens as easily as a fart).

example:
Gané el concurso **de pedo**.
translation:
I won the contest **by luck**.

de tal palo tal astilla *exp.* like father like son, a chip off the old block • (lit.): from such stick comes such splinter.

example:
Alvaro quiere ser policía como su papá. **De tal palo tal astilla**.
translation:
Alvaro wants to become a policeman like his dad. **Like father like son**.

de todas maneras *exp.* at any rate, in any case • (lit.): in all manners.

example:
No puedo creer cuánto trabajo tengo. **De todas maneras**, me voy a Inglaterra por la mañana.
translation:
I can't believe how much work I have to do. **At any rate**, I'm leaving for England in the morning.

SYNONYM:
de todos modos *exp.* • (lit.): in all modes.

de un humor de perros (estar) *exp.* to be in a lousy mood • (lit.): to be in a mood of dogs.

example:
Estoy de un humor de perros porque alguien me robó mi bicicleta.
translation:
I'm in a lousy mood because someone stole my bicycle today.

SYNONYM:
tener malas pulgas *exp.* • (lit.): to have bad fleas.

NOTE:
The expression *de perros* meaning "lousy" can be used to modify other nouns as well. A variation of *de perros* is *perro/a*. For example: *Pasé una noche perra;* I had a hell of a night.

de un modo u otro *exp.* one way or another • (lit.): of a way or another.

example:
De un modo u otro, iré a visitarte este verano.
translation:
One way or another, I'll visit you next summer.

de una vez por todas *exp.* once and for all • (lit.): for one time and for all.

example:
Voy a terminar este proyecto **de una vez por todas**.
translation:
I'm going to finish this project **once and for all**.

SYNONYM -1:
de una vez *exp.* • (lit.): for one time.

SYNONYM -2:
de una vez y para siempre *exp.* • (lit.): for one time and for always.

de vida fácil *exp.* said of someone who has an active sex life • (lit.): of an easy (or loose) life.

example:
Emilio tiene muchas novias. Verdaderamente, es un hombre **de vida fácil**.

translation:
Emilio has a lot of girlfriends. He certainly does have **an active sex life**.

dejar a alguien *exp.* to dump someone • (lit.): to leave someone.

example:
Sandra **me dejó** por otro tipo.

translation:
Sandra **dumped me** for another guy.

dejar a alguien a su suerte *exp.* to dump someone • (lit.): to leave someone to his/her luck.

example:
El día de nuestra boda, ¡Manuel **me dejó a mi suerte**!

translation:
On our wedding day, Manuel **dumped me**!

dejar clavado/a *exp.* to stand someone up [on a date] • (lit.): to leave nailed (in one place).

example:
Llevo una hora esperando aquí. ¡No me puedo creer que Guillermo me haya **dejado clavada**!

translation:
I've been waiting here for an hour. I can't believe that Guillermo **stood me up**!

dejar plantado/a *exp.* to stand someone up [on a date] • (lit.): to leave planted.

example:
¿Llevas dos horas esperando a Marco? Creo que deberías marcharte. Me temo que **te ha dejado plantada**.

translation:
You've been waiting for Marco for two hours? I think you should just leave. I'm afraid he's **stood you up**.

del dicho al hecho hay mucho trecho *exp.* easier said than done • (lit.): from what someone says to the facts, there's a long way to go.

example:
Mi jefe me prometió un aumento de sueldo pero **del dicho al hecho hay mucho trecho**.

translation:
My boss promised me a raise but **it's easier said than done**.

ALSO -1:
dicho de otro modo *exp.* in other words • (lit.): said in another way.

ALSO -2:
dicho sea de paso *exp.* let it be said in passing.

del rejue *exp. (Guatemala, Mexico)* prostitute.

del rejuego *exp. (Guatemala, Mexico)* prostitute.

NOTE:
This is a variation of: *del rejue.*

delantera *f.* breasts • (lit.): front part.

denso/a *n. & adj. (Argentina)* pain in the neck; annoying • (lit.): dense.

example:
Ahí está Dennis. Espero que no venga y me empiece a hablar. ¡Es tan **denso**!

translation:
There's Dennis. I hope he doesn't come over here and start talking to me. He's so **annoying**!

dentro de poco *exp.* any moment, soon • (lit.): in a little bit.

example:
Carlos llegará **dentro de poco**.

translation:
Carlos will arrive **any moment**.

desbeber *v.* to urinate, to take a leak • (lit.): to "un-drink."

example:
Después de beber toda esa agua, de verdad necesito **desbeber**.

translation:
After drinking all that water, I really need **to take a leak**.

deshacerse de alguien *exp.* to get rid of someone, to ditch someone • (lit.): to undo oneself of someone.

example:
Juan es muy aburrido. Quería **deshacerme de** él pero no sabía cómo.

translation:
Juan is very boring. I wanted to get **rid of** him, but I didn't know how.

SYNONYM:
darle un esquinazo a alguien *exp.* • (lit.): to give a corner to someone.

desmadre *m.* chaotic mess, chaos.

example:
¡Esta boda es un **desmadre**! Nadie sabe donde sentarse.

translation:
This wedding is a **chaotic mess**! Nobody knows where to sit.

ALSO -1:
armar un desmadre *exp.* to kick up a rumpus.

ALSO -2:
¡Qué desmadre! *interj.* What a mess!

SYNONYMS:
SEE – **gazpacho**, *p. 99*.

desocupar *v.* to defecate • (lit.): to empty.

example:
¡Huele como si alguien hubiera **desocupado** dentro del tren!

translation:
It smells like people **crapped** in this train!

diablito *m.* penis • (lit.): little devil or mischievous one.

SYNONYMS:
SEE – **penis**, *p. 243*.

diligencia (hacer una) *exp.* to go to the bathroom (urinate or defecate) • (lit.): to do an errand.

example:
Antes de salir a trabajar, siempre hago una **diligencia** primero.

translation:
Before I leave for work, I always go to the **bathroom** first.

dinero contante y sonante *exp.* cold hard cash • (lit.): cash money and sounding.

example:
Alfonso pagó su casa con **dinero contante y sonante**.

translation:
Alfonso paid for his house with **cold hard cash**.

SYNONYM -1:
dinero al contado *exp.* • (lit.): counting money.

SYNONYM -2:
dinero en efectivo *exp.* • (lit.): effective money.

discreto/a como pedo de monja *exp.* to be very discrete • (lit.): as discrete as a nun's fart.

example:
Puedes confiar en él y contarle todos tus problemas porque él es tan **discreto como pedo de monja**.

translation:
You can confide in him and tell him all your problems because he's **very discrete**.

dolorosa *f.* humorous for "check" at a restaurant since it causes *dolor* or "pain."

dominguero *m.* • **1.** a bad driver, Sunday driver • **2.** a person who likes to go out, a party animal.

example -1:
Parece que todos los **domingueros** decidieron salir al mismo tiempo.

translation:
It looks like all the **Sunday drivers** decided to go out at the same time.

example -2:
El es un **dominguero**. Anda de fiesta en fiesta.

translation:
He's a **party animal**. He goes from party to party.

NOTE:
This comes from the masculine noun *domingo* meaning "Sunday."

SYNONYM:
bago *m. (Mexico).*

Don Juan (ser un) *m.* to be a womanizer • (lit.): to be a Don Juan (a fictitious character known for being a womanizer).

example:
¿Estás saliendo con Ricardo? Ten cuidado. Ese hombre es un **Don Juan**. ¡Tiene un montón de novias!

translation:
You're going out with Ricardo? Be careful. That guy's such a **playboy**. He has tons of girlfriends!

Don mierda (ser un) *exp.* to be a real nobody • (lit.): to be a Mr. Shit.

dona *f.* vagina • (lit.): doughnut.

SYNONYMS:
SEE – **vagina**, *p. 263*.

donnadie *m.* loser • (lit.): Mr. Nobody.

example:
Es tipo es un **donnadie**, no tiene dinero ni para pagar el alquiler.

translation:
That guy is such a **loser**. He doesn't even have enough money to pay rent.

SYNONYM:
matada/o *n. (Spain).*

ANTONYM:
casinadie *m.* a very important person • (lit.): almost nobody.

dormilón/ona *n. & adj.* lazy bum; lazy • (lit.): one who sleeps a lot (from the verb *dormir* meaning "to sleep").

example:
El tío de Enrique es un **dormilón**. Está todo el día durmiendo.

translation:
Enrique's uncle is such a **lazy bum**. All he does is sleep all day.

dormir [a fondo] boca abajo *exp.* to sleep on one's stomach • (lit.): to sleep [deeply] with the mouth under.

example:
Desde que Laura se dañó la espalda, sólo puede **dormir [a fondo] boca abajo**.

translation:
Ever since Laura hurt her back, she can only **sleep on her stomach**.

SYNONYM -1:
dormir como un tronco *exp.* • (lit.): to sleep like a trunk.

SYNONYM -2:
dormir como un lirón *exp.* (lit.): to sleep like a dormouse.

dulzura *f.* a term of endearment such as "sweetheart."

NOTE:
This comes from the adjective *dulce* meaning "sweet."

example:
Lynda es una **dulzura**. Siempre está sonriendo.

translation:
Lynda is a **sweetheart**. She is always smiling.

SYNONYM -1:
amor *m.* • (lit.): love.

SYNONYM -2:
bombón *m.* • (lit.): a type of chocolate candy.

SYNONYM -3:
caramelo *m.* • (lit.): candy.

SYNONYM -4:
ternura *f.* • (lit.): tenderness.

echar a alguien a la calle *exp.* to fire someone, to can someone • (lit.): to throw someone to the street.

example:
Parece que a Tomás lo **echaron a la calle** porque siempre llegaba tarde al trabajo.

translation:
It looks like they **fired** Tomas because he was always late to work.

SYNONYM -1:
arrojar a la calle *exp.* • (lit.): to throw [someone/something] to the street.

SYNONYM -2:
correr *v. (Mexico).* • (lit.): to run.

SYNONYM -3:
despedir *v.* • (lit.): to say good-bye to.

echar chispas *exp.* to be furious, to be mad or angry • (lit.): to throw sparks.

example:
El jefe estaba **echando chispas** cuando se enteró que Andrés llamó diciendo que estaba enfermo tres veces esta semana.

translation:
The boss **was furious** when he found out Andres called in sick for the third time this week.

SYNONYM -1:
echar fuego por las orejas *exp.* • (lit.): to throw fire through the ears.

echar espumarajos [por la boca] *exp.* to be furious, to foam at the mouth with rage • (lit.): to throw foam [from the mouth].

example:
Rafael está **echando espumarajos [por la boca]** porque le robaron su coche.

translation:
Rafael is **furious** because somebody stole his car.

SYNONYM -1:
echar humo *exp.* • (lit.): to throw smoke (in the air).

SYNONYM -2:
enchilarse *v. (Mexico)* • (lit.): to get red in the face from eating chilies.

echarle flores [a alguien] *exp.* to flatter [someone], to butter [someone] up • (lit.): to throw flowers at someone.

example:
Por más que le **eches flores** a Ramón, no va a cambiar de opinión.

translation:
Even if you **flatter** Ramón, he's not going to change his mind.

SYNONYM -1:
darle la suave a uno *exp. (Mexico)* • (lit.): to give the soft to someone.

SYNONYM -2:
pasarle la mano a alguien *exp.* • (lit.): to pass one's hand to someone.

SYNONYM -3:
pasarle la mano por el lomo *exp.* • (lit.): to pass the hand by the back (of an animal).

echarse/tirarse un pedo *exp.* to fart • (lit.): to throw a fart.

example:
Aquí huele muy mal. Parece que Carlos se ha **tirado un pedo** otra vez.

translation:
It smells really bad in here. I think Carlos **let one go** again.

VARIATION -1:
tirarse un peillo *exp.*

VARIATION -2:
tirarse un peo *exp.*

echar los perros *exp.* to flirt • (lit.): to throw dogs.

example:
Siempre que Alfonso ve a una mujer guapa, empieza a **echarle los perros**.

translation:
Every time Alfonso sees a pretty girl, he starts **to flirt**.

echarse/largarse un erupto *exp.* to burp • (lit.): to throw an eruption.

example:
¡Luis **se echó un erupto** en medio de la clase!

translation:
Luis **burped** in the middle of class!

echarle una mano a alguien *exp.* to lend someone a hand • (lit.): to throw someone a hand.

example:
Voy a **echarle una mano** a Juan con esas cajas.

translation:
I'm going **to lend** Juan **a hand** Juan with those boxes.

SYNONYM -1:
darle una mano a alguien *exp.* • (lit.): to give someone a hand.

SYNONYM -2:
echarse la mano a alguien *exp.* • (lit.): to throw the hand to someone.

echar/tirar la casa por la ventana *exp.* to go overboard • (lit.): to throw the house out the window.

example:
¿Viste cómo Cristina decoró su nueva casa? La verdad es que esta vez **echó la casa por la ventana**.

translation:
Did you see how Cristina decorated her new house? She really **went overboard**.

echarse un trago *exp.* to have a drink • (lit.): to throw a swallow.

example:
A mi papá le gusta **echarse un trago** después del trabajo.

translation:
My father likes **to have a drink** after work.

NOTE:
The verb *tragar*, literally meaning "to swallow," is commonly used to mean "to eat voraciously." It is interesting to note that as a noun, *trago* means "a drink." However, when used as a verb, *tragar* takes on the meaning of "to eat" • *¿Quieres echar un trago?*; Would you care for a drink? • *¿Qué quieres tragar?*; What would you like to eat?

SYNONYM -1:
echarse un fogonazo *exp.* *(Mexico)* • (lit.): to throw oneself a flash.

SYNONYM -2:
empinar el cacho *exp.* *(Chile)* • (lit.): to raise the piece.

SYNONYM -3:
empinar el codo *exp.* • (lit.): to raise the elbow.

SYNONYM -4:
pegarse un palo *exp. (Colombia, Cuba, Dominican Republic, Puerto Rico)* • (lit.): to stick oneself a gulp.

el brazo derecho *exp.* right-hand man • (lit.): the right arm.

example:
Alfonso es **el brazo derecho** de Carlos.

translation:
Alfonso is Carlos's **right-hand man**.

el coño de la Bernarda *exp.* a real mess • (lit.): Bernarda's vagina.

NOTE:
The masculine noun *coño* is an extremely vulgar slang term for "vagina."

MEXICO:
el buey de la Bernarda *exp.*

¡El coño de tu madre! *interj. (Cuba – an insult of contempt)* • (lit.): The vagina of your mother!

NOTE: The masculine noun *coño* is an extremely vulgar slang term for "vagina."

MEXICO:
¡El carajo de tu madre! *interj.*

el de atrás *exp. (Mexico)* asshole • (lit.): the thing from the bottom.

el hábito no hace al monje *exp.* you can't judge a book by its cover • (lit.): the habit (attire) doesn't make the monk.

example:
Ramón siempre va muy bien vestido pero en realidad, no tiene dinero. **El hábito no hace al monje**.

translation:
Ramón is always dressed in expensive clothes but he actually has no money. **You can't judge a book by its cover**.

el sin mangas *exp. (Mexico)* condom • (lit.): the one without sleeves.

elbi *m. (Puerto Rico)* penis.

SYNONYMS:
SEE – **penis**, *p. 243*.

elefante *m. & adj.* fatso; fat • (lit.): elephant.

example:
Después de comer tanto dulce, me siento como un **elefante**.

translation:
After eating so much dessert, I feel like a **fat pig**.

NOTE:
Although this is a masculine noun, it can be applied to a woman as well.

elote *m.* penis • (lit.): corn on the cob.

SYNONYMS:
SEE – **penis**, *p. 243*.

embarazada *f.* • (lit.): pregnant.

NOTE:
The term *embarazada* literally means "pregnant" but looks a lot like the English word "embarrassed," so be careful how you use it... adespecially if you're a man! For example:

Estoy muy embarazada.

Mistaken Translation:
I'm very embarrassed.
Actual Translation:
I'm very pregnant.

empalmado (estar) *adj.* to get an erection • (lit.): to be connected.

empalmarse *v.* to get an erection • (lit.): to connect.
example:
El pobre Adolfo. ¡Estuvo muy avergonzado porque **se empalmó** enfrente de la clase!
translation:
Poor Adolfo. He got so embarrassed because he **got an erection** in front of the entire class!

empezar con buen pie *exp.* to get off to a good start • (lit.): to begin with a good foot.
example:
Esta mañana gané la lotería. **Empecé con buen pie**.
translation:
I won the lottery this morning. **I got off to a good start**.

SYNONYM:
levantarse con el pie derecho *exp.* • (lit.): to get up on the right foot.

empollón/na *n.* • **1.** nerd, geek, pain in the neck • **2.** lazy bum; lazy.
example -1:
Francisco siempre está estudiando. Es un verdadero **empollón**.
translation:
Francisco is always studying. He's a real **nerd**.
example -2:
Mi jefe es tan **empollón**, que al final termino haciendo yo todo el trabajo.
translation:
My boss is so **lazy** that I end up doing all of his work!

NOTE:
empollar *v.* to study hard • (lit.): to hatch, brood.

SYNONYMS:
SEE – **adoquín**, *p. 6.*

en brasas (estar) *exp.* to be on pins and needles, to be on tenterhooks, be uneasy • (lit.): to be in live coal.

example:
Susan está esperando ver si le dieron su ascenso. ¡Está **en brasas**!

translation:
Susan is waiting to see if she got a promotion. She's **on pins and needles**!

SYNONYM:
estar como en brasas *exp.* • (lit.): to be like in live coal.

en cueros (estar) *exp.* naked, in one's birthday suit • (lit.): in one's own hide.

example:
Carlos siempre anda **en cueros** por la casa.

translation:
Carlos always goes around the house **completely naked**.

SYNONYM -1:
en cueros vivos *exp.* • (lit.): in one's own living hide.

SYNONYM -2:
en el traje de Adán *exp.* • (lit.): in the suit of Adam.

SYNONYM -3:
en pelotas *exp. (Spain)* • (lit.): in balls.

SYNONYM -4:
en pila *f. (Bolivia, Ecuador, Peru)* • (lit.): heap, pile.

SYNONYM -5:
encuerado/a *adj.* • (lit.): skinned.

en el acto *exp.* • **1.** right away, immediately • **2.** in the act [of doing something] • (lit.): in the act.

example:
Voy a hacer la tarea **en el acto**.

translation:
I'm going to do my homework **right away**.

SYNONYM -1:
acto continuo/seguido *exp.* same as definition **1** above • (lit.): continuous /consecutive act.

SYNONYM -2:
ahora mismo *exp.* same as **1** and **2** above • (lit.): now the same.

SYNONYM -3:
de inmediato *exp.* same as definition **1** above • (lit.): of immediate.

en el fondo *exp.* deep down, at heart • (lit.): at the bottom.

example:
En el fondo, Felipe es una buena persona.

translation:
Deep down, Felipe is a good person.

en el pellejo de alguien (estar) *exp.* to be in someone's shoes • (lit.): to be in someone's skin (hide).

example:
No me gustaría **estar en su pellejo** cuando le pida un aumento al jefe.

translation:
I wouldn't like **to be in his shoes** when he asks the boss for a raise.

SYNONYM:
en la piel de (estar) *exp.* • (lit.): to be in one's skin.

en menos de lo que canta un gallo *exp.* in a flash, as quick as a wink, in the winking of an eye • (lit.): in less time than a rooster can sing.

example:
David siempre termina su almuerzo **en menos de lo que canta un gallo**.

translation:
David always finishes his lunch **in a flash**.

enamoradísimo/a (estar) *adj.* to be very much in love • (lit.): to be super enamored.

example:
Creo que David está **enamoradísimo** de su profesora de piano.

translation:
I think David is **big-time in love** with his piano teacher.

enano/a *n. & adj.* runt; runty. • (lit.): dwarf.

example:
John se cree que es un tipo duro, pero no es más que un **enano**.

translation:
John thinks he's so tough but he's nothing but a **runt**.

SYNONYM:
hombrecito *m. (Cuba).*

encalomar *v.* to fornicate • (lit.): to become overheated.

encular *v.* to perform anal sex • (lit.): to enter the *culo* meaning "ass."

enfermo mental (ser un) *exp.* to be crazy • (lit.): to be a mentally corrupt person.

example:
No puedo creer que Cynthia vaya a ser madre. ¡Es una **enferma mental**!

translation:
I can't believe Cynthia is going to be a mother. She's such a **mental case**!

enfermo sexual (ser un) *m.* to be a sex pervert • (lit.): to be a sexually corrupt person.

example:
Juan siempre está pensando en el sexo. Yo creo que es un **enfermo sexual**.

translation:
All Juan ever thinks about is sex. I think he's a **sex maniac**.

engazado/a *adj.* to be drunk • (lit.): gassed up.
example:
Ricardo se puso **engazado** en mi fiesta.
translation:
Ricardo got **plastered** at my party.

enjaretarse a *v.* to fornicate • (lit.): to do (something) in a rush.

enredador/a *n. (Spain)* a gossip • (lit.): meddler.
example:
Le conté a Armando todos mis problemas personales y se los contó a todos sus amigos. ¡Nunca volveré a confiar en ese **enredador**!
translation:
I told Armando all about my personal problems and he told all of his friends. I'll never trust that **blabbermouth** again!

SYNONYMS:
SEE – **blabbermouth**, *p. 208*.

enredoso/a *n. & adj. (Chile, Mexico)* a gossip; gossipy • (lit.): fraught with difficulties.
example:
A Mateo le encanta expandir rumores. Es un **enredoso**.
translation:
Mateo likes to spread rumors. He's a **gossip**.

enrollarse *v.* **1.** to talk up a storm • **2.** to get involved romantically with someone • (lit.): to roll up, to wind.
example (1):
A mi madre le gusta mucho **enrollarse** cuando viene visita a la casa.
translation:
My mother loves to **talk up a storm** when she has company at her house.
example (2):
Me encantaría **enrollarme** con esa tía porque es muy simpática y guapa.
translation:
I'd love to **get involved** with that girl because she's very nice and beautiful.

SYNONYM:
cotorrear *v. (Cuba, Puerto Rico)* • (lit.): to squawk.

NOTE:
charlatán/ana *n.* blabbermouth.

enrucado (estar) *adj.* to get an erection.

entabicar *v.* to fornicate • (lit.): to board up, to wall up.

enterarse *v.* to find out • (lit.): to inform oneself.

example:
¿Te enteraste de cómo se llega a la casa de Alfredo?
translation:
Did you **find out** how get to Alfredo's house?

entrar por detrás *exp.* to fornicate doggie-style • (lit.): to enter from the rear.

entrar por un oído y salir por el otro *exp.* to go in one ear and out the other • (lit.): to go in one ear and out the other.
example:
Todo lo que le digo a Isabel **le entra por un oído y le sale por el otro**.
translation:
Anything that I tell Isabel **goes in one ear and out the other**.

SYNONYM:
hacer caso omiso de *exp.* • (lit.): to take no notice of.

escaso/a de fondos (andar/estar) *exp.* to be short of money • (lit.): to lack funds.
example:
No puedo ir contigo al cine porque **ando escaso de fondos**.
translation:
I can't go with you to the movies because I'm **short of money**.

SYNONYM -1:
no tener ni un duro *exp.* *(Spain)* • (lit.): not to have even a *duro*.

NOTE:
duro *m.* a coin equal to five *pesetas* which is the national currency of Spain.

SYNONYM -2:
no tener plata *exp.* *(South America)* • (lit.): not to have any silver.

ANTONYM -1:
estar nadando en dinero *exp.* to be rolling in money• (lit.): to be swimming in money.

ANTONYM -2:
estar podrido/a en dinero *exp.* to be fithy-rich • (lit.): to be rotten in money.

ANTONYM -3:
tener más lana que un borrego *exp.* to have more wool than a lamb (since *lana*, or "wool" is a slang term for "money").

escuincle *m.* little kid, small child.

example:
¡No me lo puedo creer! Luisa ya tiene siete **escuincles** y ¡está embarazada otra vez!

translation:
I can't believe it! Luisa already has seven **kids** and she's pregnant again!

SYNONYM -1:
chiquillo/a *n.*

NOTE:
This noun comes from the adjective *chico/a* meaning "small."

SYNONYM -2:
chiquitín/a *n.*

NOTE:
This noun comes from the adjective *chico/a* meaning "small."

SYNONYM -3:
crío/a *m. (Spain)* • (lit.): a nursing-baby.

SYNONYM -4:
gurrumino/a *n.* • (lit.): weak or sickly person, "whimp."

VARIATION:
gurrumín *m.*

SYNONYM -5:
mocoso/a *n.* • (lit.): snot-nosed person.

SYNONYM -6:
nené *m. (Cuba, Puerto Rico).*

NOTE:
By putting an accent over the second "e" in *nene,* this standard term for "baby" acquires a slang connotation.

SYNONYM -7:
párvulo *m.* • (lit.): tot.

SYNONYM -8:
pequeñajo/a *n.*

VARIATION:
pequeñuelo n.

NOTE:
These nouns come from the adjective *pequeño/a* meaning "small."

ANTONYM -1:
grandote *m.*

NOTE:
This noun comes from the adjective *grande* meaning "big."

ANTONYM -2:
grandulón/a *n.* big kid.

NOTE:
This noun comes from the adjective *grande* meaning "big."

escupir *v.* to spit • (lit.): to spit.

example:
Es ilegal **escupir** en el tren.

translation:
It's illegal **to spit** in the train.

estafiate *m. (El Savador)* asshole.

estar de buenas *exp.* to be in a good mood • (lit.): to be in good.

example:
Lynda es una mujer muy feliz. Siempre **está de buenas**.
translation:
Lynda is a very happy woman. She is always **in a good mood**.

ANTONYM -1:
estar de malas *exp*. to be in a bad mood • (lit.): to be in bad.

ANTONYM -2:
estar de un humor de perros *exp*. • (lit.): to be in the mood of dogs.

ANTONYM -3:
tener malas pulgas *exp*. • (lit.): to have bad fleas.

estar hecho una sopa *exp*. to be soaking wet, drenched • (lit.): to be made into a soup.
example:
Susana llegó al trabajo **hecha una sopa**.
translation:
Susana was **soaking wet** by the time she got to work.

SYNONYM:
estar empapado/a *adj*. • (lit.): to be soaking wet.

¡Esto es cagarse! *exp*. This is a fine mess! • (lit.): This is to shit oneself!

¡Esto es una cagada! *exp*. This is a fine mess! • (lit.): This is a shit!

estorbo *m*. pain in the neck • (lit.): obstacle.
example:
Cada vez que doy mi opinión sobre algo, Oscar discute conmigo. Es un **estorbo**.
translation:
Every time I give an opinion about something, Oscar argues with me. He's such a **pain in the neck**!

evaporarse *v*. to disappear, to vanish • (lit.): to evaporate.
example:
Me **evaporé** cuando me di cuenta que Juan estaba en la fiesta.
translation:
I **disappeared** when I realized Juan was at the party.

SYNONYM -1:
colarse *v*. *(Mexico)* • (lit.): to slip away.

SYNONYM -2:
escaquearse *v*. *(Spain)* • (lit.): to check or checker oneself.

SYNONYM -3:
escurrirse *v*. • (lit.): to slip, to slide, to sneak out.

SYNONYM -4:
esfumarse *v*. • (lit.): to vanish.

explorador *m*. penis • (lit.): the explorer.

SYNONYMS:
SEE – **penis**, *p. 243*.

expulsar *v.* to ejaculate • (lit.): to expel, eject.

fachar *v. (Venezuela)* to have sex with a woman.

fácil *adj.* to be sexually easy • (lit.): easy.

example:
Vilma parecerá inocente, pero en realidad es **fácil**.

translation:
Vilma may look innocent, but she's really **easy**.

facilito/a *n. & adj.* easy lay; easy • (lit.): a little easy one.

example:
Clarissa es una **facilita**. Se acuesta con un tipo diferente cada noche.

translation:
Clarissa is an **easy lay**. She has sex with a different guy every night.

falo *m.* penis • (lit.): phallus, penis.

SYNONYMS:
SEE – **penis**, *p. 243*.

faltar un tornillo *exp.* to have a screw loose • (lit.): to miss a screw.

example:
Yo creo que a Paco le **falta un tornillo**.

translation:
I think Paco **has a screw loose**.

SYNONYM -1:
estar chiflado/a *exp.* • (lit.): to be crazy.

SYNONYM -2:
estar loco/a como una cabra *exp.* • (lit.): to be like a goat.

SYNONYM -3:
estar tocado/a de la cabeza *exp. (Spain)* • (lit.): to be touched in the head.

SYNONYM -4:
estar un poco loco/a *exp.* • (lit.): to be a little bit crazy.

SYNONYM -5:
estar un poco sacado/a de onda *exp. (Mexico)* • (lit.): to be a little taken from a wave.

SYNONYM -6:
tener flojos los tornillos *exp.* • (lit.): to have loose screws.

SYNONYM -7:
tener los alambres pelados *exp. (Chile)* • (lit.): to have peeled cables.

SYNONYM -8:
tener los cables cruzados *exp. (Mexico)* • (lit.): to have crossed cables.

farandulero/a *n. & adj.* a gossip; gossipy • (lit.): actor, strolling player.

example:
Benito y yo éramos buenos amigos hasta que descubrí que era un **farandulero**. No puedo volver a confiar en él.

translation:
Benito and I used to be good friends until I discovered that he was a **gossip**. I can never trust him again.

farolero/a (ser un/a) *n. & adj.* show-off; showy • (lit.): lantern maker.

example:
Nancy es una **farolera**. Yo creo que le gusta llamar la atención.

translation:
Nancy is such a **show-off**. I think she likes a lot of attention.

fichado/a (tener) *adj.* to be on someone's bad side, to be on someone's bad list • (lit.): to be posted or affixed.

example:
Creo que el maestro **tiene fichado** a Pepe porque siempre le está gritando.

translation:
I think Pepe's on the teacher's **bad side** because he's always yelling at him.

VARIATION:
fichado/a (tener) *exp.* • (lit.): to have posted or affixed.

SYNONYM -1:
cazar a alguien *v. (Cuba)* • (lit.): to hunt someone down.

SYNONYM -2:
tener en la mirilla *exp.* • (lit.): to have someone on target.

fierro *m. (Mexico)* penis • (lit.): iron.

SYNONYMS:
SEE – **penis**, *p. 243*.

finquita *f. (Puerto Rico)* vagina • (lit.): small piece of property.

SYNONYMS:
SEE – **vagina**, *p. 263*.

flaco/a de mierda *n. (Argentina)* an insult meaning "a skinny person" • (lit.): thin one of shit.

NOTE:
The noun *flaco/a* may certainly be used without *mierda*, in which case it is not considered insulting.

flojo/a *n. & adj.* lazy bum; lazy • (lit.): loose, weak.

<u>example:</u>
Eres demasiado **flojo**. Tienes que intentar motivarte.
<u>translation:</u>
You're so **lazy**. You need to try and get motivated.

flote (estar a) *exp.* to be well off (monetarily).
<u>example:</u>
Parece que Pedro está **a flote**. ¿Viste qué cochazo tiene?
<u>translation:</u>
It seems like Pedro is **well off**. Did you see what a great car he drives?

foca *f.* a very fat woman • (lit.): seal.
<u>example:</u>
Adriana es una **foca**. Parece que siempre está comiendo.
<u>translation:</u>
Adriana is really **fat**. It seems like she's always eating.

SYNONYM -1:
elefante *m.* • (lit.): elephant.

SYNONYM -2:
gordita *f. (Cuba).*

SYNONYM -3:
vaca *f. (Puerto Rico* • (lit.): cow.

follar *v.* • **1.** to fart silently • **2.** to have sex.
<u>example -1:</u>
Algo huele mal. Creo que el niño se ha **follado**.
<u>translation:</u>
Something smells funny. I think the baby **farted**.

<u>example -2:</u>
Verónica es una mujer muy bella. Me encantaría **follármela**.
<u>translation:</u>
Veronica is a beautiful woman. I would love **to have sex with her**.

NOTE:
follón *m.* a silent fart, an SBD ("silent but deadly").

VARIATION -1:
follarse *v.*

VARIATION -2:
follonarse *v.*

follón *m.* • **1.** mess, jam • **2.** trouble, uproar • **3.** silent fart, an SBD ("silent but deadly") • **4. follón/na** *n.* lazy bum; lazy.
<u>example (1):</u>
El tráfico de Chicago es un **follón**.
<u>translation:</u>
The traffic in Chicago is a **mess**.
<u>example (2):</u>
Si nuestro equipo pierde el partido se va a armar un gran **follón**.
<u>translation:</u>
If our team loses the games, there is going to be an **uproar** here.

example -3:
¡Creo que el niño se ha tirado un **follón**!
translation:
I think the baby let lose an **SBD**!
example -4:
Tienes que dejar de ser un **follón** o nunca encontrarás trabajo.
translation:
You've got to stop being such a **lazy bum** or you'll never find a job.

SYNONYMS:
SEE – **gazpacho**, *p. 99*.

ALSO -1:
armar un follón *exp.* to kick up a rumpus.

ALSO -2:
¡**Menudo follón**! *exp.* What a mess!

ALSO -3:
¡**Qué follón**! *exp.* What a mess!

NOTE:
The term *follón* has different meanings depending on the context and the country, so be careful how you use it!
For example:

¡Qué follón tan horrible!

Common Translation:
What a horrible **mess**!
Translation in Mexico:
What a horrible **fart**!

follonarse *v.* to fart silently.
example:
Después de comerme toda esa comida picante, creo que voy a **follonarme**.
translation:
After eating all that spicy food, I think I'm going **to fart**.

NOTE:
This is a variation of the term **follar**.

fondo de la espalda *m.* buttocks • (lit.): lower back.

foquin *adj. (Puerto Rico)* fucking.

NOTE:
This is a Puerto Rican adaptation of the English adjective "fucking."

forro *m.* condom • (lit.): lining, covering.

fregado/a *n. & adj.* annoying person, pain in the neck; annoying • (lit.): scrubbing.
example:
Jaime es un **fregado**. ¡Me llama por teléfono cinco veces al día!
translation:
Jaime is such a **pain in the neck**. He calls me on the telephone five times a day!

fregón/ona *n. & adj.* pain in the neck; annoying • (lit.): one who scrubs.

example:
Victor es un **fregón**. Cada vez que hablamos no hace más que contarme sus problemas.

translation:
Victor is a **pain in the neck**. Every time we talk, he does nothing but tell me about his problems.

NOTE:
This term is also commonly used to describe someone who is extremely impressive and "cool."

fresco *m.* derogatory for "homosexual" • (lit.): fresh.

fufú *m. & adj.* snob; stuck up • (lit.): Cuban dish made of plantain & pork rind.

example:
Desde que Arnaldo se hizo rico, se ha convertido en un **fufú**.

translation:
Ever since Arnaldo became rich, he's become a **snob**.

fufurufu *n. & adj.* snob; stuck up.

example:
Mi tio es millonario pero no es un **fufurufu** para nada. Tiene los pies en la tierra.

translation:
My uncle is a millionaire but he's not a **snob** at all. He's very down-to-earth.

fulana *f.* prostitute • (lit.): so-and-so (anyone).

funda *f.* condom • (lit.): lining, covering.

fundillero *m.* pimp.

fundillo *m.* anus, asshole.

NOTE:
This is a variation of the masculine noun *fondillos* meaning "seat of trousers."

furcia *f.* prostitute • (lit.):doll, chick.

gafitas *m. (Spain)* lazy bum • (lit.): small eyeglasses.

example:
He decidido echar a Adolfo. Es buen chico pero es un **gafitas**.

translation:
I've decided to fire Adolfo. He's a very good guy but he's a **lazy bum**.

gafudo/a • **1.** *adj.* said of one who wears glasses, "four-eyed" • **2.** *n.* one who wears glasses, "four-eyes."

example (1):
Ese policía **gafudo** me dio una multa.

translation:
That **four-eyed** policeman gave me a ticket.

example (2):
Ese **gafudo** es mi nuevo profesor de biología.

translation:
That **four-eyed man** is my new biology teacher.

SYNONYM -1:
anteojudo *m. (Argentina)*.

SYNONYM -2:
cuatro ojos *m.* • (lit.): four-eyes.

SYNONYM -3:
gafas *f.pl. (Cuba)* • (lit.): glasses.

SYNONYM -4:
gafitas *adj. & n.* • (lit.): small pair of glasses.

galán *adj.* hunk, good-looking guy.

example:
Claudio es un **galán**. Se nota que se cuida.

translation:
Claudio is a **hunk**. You can tell he takes care of himself.

SYNONYM -1:
apuesto/a *adj.* • (lit.): neat, elegant.

SYNONYM -2:
bien parecido/a *adj.* • (lit.): well appearing.

SYNONYM -3:
chorbo/a *adj. (Spain)*.

SYNONYM -4:
gallardo *adj.* • (lit.): elegant, graceful.

NOTE:
There is no feminine form of this adjective since it can only refer to a man.

SYNONYM -5:
majo/a *adj.* • (lit.): showy, flashy, dressed up.

SYNONYM -6:
tío bueno *m.* / **tía buena** *f. (Spain)*.

galleta *f. (Costa Rica)* penis • (lit.): cracker, cookie.

SYNONYMS:
SEE – **penis**, *p. 243*.

gancho *m.* pimp • (lit.): hook.

gandul/a *n. & adj.* lazy bum; lazy.

example:
La razón por la que se está hundiendo esta compañía es porque hay demasiados **gandules** en ella.

translation:
The reason this company isn't surviving is because there are too many **lazy people** in it.

garraleta *f.* cheap whore.

garrote *m.* penis • (lit.): club or stick.

SYNONYMS:
SEE – **penis**, *p. 243*.

gastar saliva en balde *exp.* to waste one's breath [while explaining something to someone] • (lit.): to waste one's saliva in vain.

example:
No me gusta **gastar saliva en balde**. Yo sé que de todas maneras no me entenderías.

translation:
I don't like to **waste my breath**. I know you wouldn't understand me anyway.

gata *f.* vagina • (lit.): female cat.

SYNONYMS:
SEE – **vagina**, *p. 263*.

gay *adj.* homosexual, gay • (lit.): [same].

gazpacho *m. (Spain)* mess, predicament, jam • (lit.): a type of Spanish tomato soup.

example:
El tráfico de Los Angeles es un verdadero **gazpacho**.

translation:
Los Angeles traffic is a real **mess**.

SYNONYM -1:
broncón *m. (Mexico)*.

SYNONYM -2:
caos *m.* • (lit.): chaos.

SYNONYM -3:
desbarajuste *m.* • (lit.): disorder, confusion.

SYNONYM -4:
despelote *m.*

SYNONYM -5:
embole *m. (Argentina)*.

SYNONYM -6:
embrollo *m.* • (lit.): muddle, tangle, confusion.

SYNONYM -7:
enredo *m.* • (lit.): tangle, snarl (in wool).

SYNONYM -8:
follón *m.* • (lit.): lazy, idle.

SYNONYM -9:
garrón *m. (Argentina)*.

SYNONYM -10:
golpaso *m. (Mexico)* • (lit.): heavy or violent blow.

SYNONYM -11:
jaleo *m.* • (lit.): noisy party.

SYNONYM -12:
kilombo *m. (Argentina)*.

SYNONYM -13:
lío *m.* • (lit.): bundle, package.

SYNONYM -14:
marrón *m. (Spain).*

SYNONYM -15:
mogollón *m.*

SYNONYM -16:
paquete *m. (Cuba)* • (lit.): package.

SYNONYM -17:
revoltijo *m.* • (lit.): jumble, mix-up.

SYNONYM -18:
revoltillo *m.* • (lit.) mix-up, jumble.

SYNONYM -19:
revuelo *m. (Cuba)* • (lit.): second flight.

ALSO:
revoltillo de huevos *m.* scrambled eggs • (lit.): a jumble of eggs.

SYNONYM -18:
sángano *m. (Puerto Rico).*

gentío *m.* crowd, people.

example:
No me gusta ir a los partidos de béisbol porque siempre hay mucho **gentío**.

translation:
I don't like going to baseball games because there are always big **crowds** there.

SYNONYM:
gente *f.* people, folks, relatives.

ALSO:
gente gorda *f.* bigwigs • (lit.): fat people.

gilipollas *m. (Spain)* idiot, jerk • (lit.): stupid dick.

example:
No te creas nada de lo que te diga ese **gilipollas**. Es un mentiroso.

translation:
Don't believe anything that **jerk** tells you. He's a big liar.

globo *m.* condom • (lit.): balloon.

golfa *f.* prostitute • (lit.): prostitute.

goma *f.* condom • (lit.): rubber.

gomita *f.* condom • (lit.): small rubber.

gordinflón/na *adj.* fat pig, obese person.

example:
Darío es un **gordinflón**. Parece que nunca para de comer.

translation:
Darío is a **fat pig**. It seems like he never stops eating.

SYNONYM -1:
mofletudo/a *adj.* • (lit.): chubby-cheeked.

SYNONYM -2:
rechoncho/a *adj.* • (lit.): chubby, tubby.

SYNONYM -3:
regordete *adj.*

NOTE:
This comes from the adjective *gordo/a* meaning "fat."

SYNONYM -4:
tripón *adj.*

NOTE:
This comes from the feminine noun *tripa* meaning "tripe," "guts" or "stomach."

ANTONYM:
canijo *adj.* skinny person.

gordo/a chancho *n. & adj.* *(Argentina)* fatso; fat • (lit.): fat hog-like person.

example:
Nuestro jefe es un **gordo chancho**. No sé por qué no se pone a dieta.

translation:
Our new boss is a **fat pig**. I don't know why he doesn't go on a diet.

gordo/a como una ballena *exp.* to be very fat • (lit.): as fat as a whale an elephant.

example:
Si te comes la tarta entera, te vas a poner **gordo como una ballena**.

translation:
If you eat the entire cake, you are going to be as **fat as a pig**.

VARIATION:
gordo/a como un elefante *adj.* • (lit.): fat as an elephant.

gordo/a de mierda *n.* *(Argentina)* an insult for "fatso" • (lit.): fat one of shit.

example:
¡Ese **gordo de mierda** me estafó!

translation:
That **fat pig** ripped me off!

gorro *m.* condom • (lit.): cap, bonnet.

gorrona *f.* prostitute • (lit.): libertine.

gozador/a *adj.* big spender, person who likes to have fun all the time.

example:
Francisco es un gran **gozador**. Le encanta pasarlo bien.

translation:
Francisco is such a **big spender**. He loves to have fun.

NOTE:
This comes from the verb *gozar* meaning "to enjoy."

SYNONYM -1:
gastador *m. (Argentina, Cuba).*

SYNONYM -2:
manirroto *m. (Spain).*

gozar *v.* to ejaculate • (lit.): to enjoy.

grandote boludo *m.* *(Argentina)* idiot, jerk • (lit.): big-balled (testicles) one.

example:
¿Has visto el sombrero que lleva Miguel? ¡Parece un **grandote boludo**!

translation:
Have you seen the hat Miguel is wearing? He looks like an **idiot**!

grieta *f.* vagina • (lit.): crack.

SYNONYMS:
SEE – **vagina**, *p. 263*.

grifear *v.* *(Mexico)* to smoke marijuana.

grifo *m.* *(Mexico)* drug addict • (lit.): faucet, tap.

grilla *f.* *(Mexico, Central and South America)* marijuana • (lit.): female cricket.

gritar como unos descosidos *exp.* to scream one's lungs out • (lit.): to scream like something unstiched.

example:
Cuando fuimos al restaurante, mis niños estaban **gritando como unos descosidos**.

translation:
When we went to the restaurant, my kids were **screaming out of control**.

NOTE:
This expression comes from the verb *descoser* meaning "to unstitch." Therefore, this expression could be loosely translated as "to come apart at the seams."

ALSO:
reír como descosidos *exp.* to laugh out of control • *¡Nos reímos como descosidos!;* We laughed our heads off!

gritón/ona *n. & adj.* loudmouth; gossipy.

example:
Habla bajo. Esto es una biblioteca. ¡Eres un **gritón**!

translation:
Keep your voice down. This is a library. You're such a **loudmouth**!

NOTE:
This is from the verb *gritar* meaning "to shout."

guabina *f.* *(Cuba)* idiot.

example:
¡Qué **guabina**! Paula está todo el día tirada viendo la televisión.

translation:
What an **idiot**! Paula just sits around and watches television all day.

guaje *m. & adj.* *(El Salvador, Mexico)* idiot; stupid.

example:
Con ese sombrero Pancho parece un **guaje**.
translation:
With that hat Pancho is wearing he looks like a **jerk**.

guante *m.* condom • (lit.): glove.

guay *adj.* cool, neat.
example:
¡Qué **guay**! ¡Esa motocicleta tiene tres ruedas!
translation:
Cool! That motorcycle has three wheels!

SYNONYM -1:
chulo *adj.*

SYNONYM -2:
padre *adj.* • (lit.): father.

ALSO:
¡Guay de mí! *interj.* Woe is me!

guerrillera *f. (Puerto Rico)* prostitute, whore • (lit.): guerrilla, partisan.

güey *m. & adj.* jerk, idiot; jerky • (lit.): variation of *buey* meaning "ox" or "bullock."
example:
Ño me puedo creer que salgas con Antonio; ¡es un **güey**!
translation:
I can't believe you're going out with Antonio. He's such a **jerk**!

gumersinda *f.* heroin or opium.

gustar los bebes *exp.* to rob the cradle • (lit.): to like babies.
example:
Roberto siempre sale con mujeres mucho más jóvenes que él. Yo creo que le **gustan los bebes**.
translation:
Roberto always dates women much younger than he is. I think he likes **to rob the cradle**.

haber gato encerrado *exp.* there's more than meets the eye, there's something fishy • (lit.): there's a locked cat (here).
example:
Aquí **hay gato encerrado**. Esto no puede ser tan fácil.
translation:
There's more here than meets the eye. This can't be so easy.

hablador/a *n. & adj.* blabbermouth; gossipy.
example:
¿Le contaste a Jesús mi secreto? ¡Qué **hablador**!

translation:
You told Jesús my secret? What a **blabbermouth**!

NOTE:
This is from the verb *hablar* meaning "to speak."

SYNONYMS:
SEE – **blabbermouth**, *p. 208*.

hablar [hasta] por los codos *exp.* to speak nonstop • (lit.): to talk even with the elbows.

example:
Pablo siempre **habla hasta por los codos** cuando viene a mi casa.

translation:
Pablo always **talks nonstop** when he comes to my house.

SYNONYM -1:
hablar como loco/a *exp.* • (lit.): to speak like a crazy person.

SYNONYM -2:
hablar como una cotorra *exp.* • (lit.): to talk like a parrot.

SYNONYM -3:
no parar la boca *exp.* *(Mexico)*. • (lit.): not to let the mouth stop.

SYNONYM -4:
ser de lengua larga *exp.* to be gossipy • (lit.): to be of long tongue.

hablar a mil por hora *exp.* to talk very fast, to talk a mile a minute • (lit.): to talk at one thousand kilometers per hour.

example:
Lynda **habla a mil por hora**.

translation:
Lynda **talks too fast**.

SYNONYM:
hablar a borbotones *exp.* • (lit.): to talk like a torrent.

hablar como loco/a *exp.* to talk too much, to go on and on • (lit.): to talk like a crazy person.

example:
Gabriela **habla como loca**. Nunca se calla.

translation:
Gabriela **goes on and on**. She never shuts up.

SYNONYM -1:
hablar como un loro *exp.* *(Spain)* • (lit.): to talk like a parrot.

SYNONYM -2:
hablar como una cotorra *exp.* • (lit.): to talk like a parrot.

SYNONYM -3:
hablar hasta por las narices *exp.* *(Spain)* • (lit.): to talk even through the nose.

SYNONYM -4:
hablar más que siete *exp.* • (lit.): to talk more than seven (people).

SYNONYM -5:
hablar por los codos *exp.* • (lit.): to talk through the elbows.

SYNONYM -6:
no parar la boca *exp.* *(Mexico)* • (lit.): not to let the mouth stop.

hacer acto de presencia *exp.* to put in an appearance, to show up • (lit.): to make an act of presence.

example:
Voy a la fiesta de la escuela para **hacer acto de presencia**.

translation:
I'm going to the school party **to put in an appearance**.

hacer añicos *exp.* • **1.** (of objects) to smash to smithereens • **2.** (of paper) to rip to shreds • (lit.): to make (into) fragments or bits.

example:
Elena **hizo añicos** mi plato favorito.

translation:
Elena **smashed** my favorite plate **to smithereens**.

SYNONYM:
hacer pedazitos *exp.* • (lit.): to make little pieces.

hacer el equipaje *exp.* to pack one's bags • (lit.): to make one's luggage.

example:
Estoy **haciendo el equipaje** para ir a España.

translation:
I'm **packing my bags** to go to Spain.

SYNONYM -1:
empacar los belices *exp.* *(Mexico)* • (lit.): to pack the bags.

SYNONYM -2:
hacer las maletas *exp.* • (lit.): to make one's trunks.

SYNONYM -3:
hacer las valijas *exp.* *(Argentina)* • to make one's suitcases or valises.

hacer frente a *exp.* to face up • (lit.): to make the front to.

example:
Tenemos que **hacer frente** al enemigo.

translation:
We have **to face up to** the enemy.

hacer frente al hecho *exp.* to face up to the fact that • (lit.): to face up to the fact.

example:
Tenemos que **hacer frente** al hecho de que nuestra empresa está perdiendo dinero.

translation:
We have **to face up to the fact** that our company is losing money.

SYNONYM:
dar la cara a *exp.* • (lit.): to give the face to.

hacer la barba *exp.* to brown-nose • (lit.): to do the beard.

example:
La razón por la que Ricardo ha conseguido un ascenso es porque siempre está **haciendo la barba**.

translation:
The reason Ricardo got a promotion is because he always **brown-noses**.

hacer la pelotilla *exp.* to brown-nose • (lit.): to do the testicle or "lick someone's balls" (since *pelotilla* , literally meaning "small balls," is used in Spanish slang to mean "small testicles").

example:
David ha debido **hacer la pelotilla** para conseguir que le subieran el sueldo.

translation:
David must have **brown-nosed** to get a raise.

hacer la sopa *exp.* to perform oral sex to a woman • (lit.): to make a soup.

hacer las paces *exp.* to make up after a quarrel • (lit.): to make peace.

example:
Josefina y Gerardo se pelearon pero luego **hicieron las paces**.

translation:
Joesphina and Geraldo had a big fight but they finally **made up**.

SYNONYM:
echar pelillos a la mar *exp. (Southern Spain)* to throw little hairs to the sea.

ANTONYM:
romper con *exp.* to have a falling out • (lit.): to break with.

hacer mal/buen papel *exp.* to make a bad/good impression • (lit.): to do a bad/good (theatrical) role.

example:
Hiciste un buen papel anoche.

translation:
You made a good impression last night.

SYNONYM:
caer mal/bien *exp.* • (lit.): to fall badly/well.

hacer pipí *exp.* to urinate • (lit.): to make peepee.

example:
No te olvides de **hacer pipí** antes de irte a la cama.

translation:
Don't forget **to go peepee** before you go to bed.

hacer puente *exp.* to take a long weekend, to take a three-day weekend • (lit.): to make a bridge.

example:
La próxima semana voy a **hacer puente** y voy a ir a esquiar.

translation:
Next week I'm going to take **a long weekend** and go skiing.

hacer su agosto *exp.* to make a killing • (lit.): to make one's August.

example:
Alfredo y Eva **hicieron su agosto** en el casino.

translation:
Alfredo and Eva **made a killing** at the casino.

hacer un cuadro *exp.* *(Cuba)* to make a daisy chain • (lit.): to make a picture.

hacer un favor *exp.* to fornicate • (lit.): to do a favor.

NOTE:
The difference between the slang meaning and the literal meaning depends on the connotation.

hacer un gran furor *exp.* to be a big event, to make a big splash • (lit.): to make fury.

example:
¡Oí que **hiciste un gran furor** con el jefe!

translation:
I heard you **made a big splash** with the boss!

SYNONYM:
tener un éxito padre *exp.* *(Mexico)* to have a father success.

hacer una cubana *exp.* *(Spain)* (said of a man) to reach orgasm by rubbing the penis between a woman's breasts • (lit.): to do it Cuban-style.

hacer una paja *exp.* to masturbate (someone else), to give someone a hand-job.

SYNONYMS:
SEE – **masturbate**, *p. 239*.

VARIATION:
hacerse la paja *exp.* to masturbate oneself • (lit.): to make a straw.

hacerse agua la boca *exp.* to make one's mouth water • (lit.): to make one's mouth water.

example:
Se me está **hacecerse agua la boca** con el olor de ese pan.

translation:
The smell of that bread is **making my mouth water**.

VARIATION:
hacerse la boca agua *exp.*

hacer amigos *exp.* to make friends• (lit.): [same].

example:
Fernando siempre **hace amigos** cuando viaja porque le gusta hablar con la gente.

translation:
Fernando always **makes friends** because he likes to talk to people.

hacer[se] amigo de *exp.* to make friends with • (lit.): to make friends of.

example:
Me hice amigo de Pedro porque es muy simpático.

translation:
I made friends with Pedro because he's very nice.

SYNONYM:
hacer buenas migas con *exp.* • (lit.): to make good bread crumbs with.

hacerse las puñetas *exp.* to masturbate • (lit.): to make oneself cuffs.

SYNONYMS:
SEE – **masturbate**, *p. 239*.

hacerse un pajote *exp.* to masturbate • (lit.): to make a large straw.

SYNONYMS:
SEE – **masturbate**, *p. 239*.

hacerse un solitario *exp.* to masturbate • (lit.): to do a solitary.

SYNONYMS:
SEE – **masturbate**, *p. 239*.

hacerse una bartola *exp.* to masturbate • (lit.): to do a careless act.

SYNONYMS:
SEE – **masturbate**, *p. 239*.

hacerse una canuta *exp.* to masturbate • (lit.): to make a tubular container.

SYNONYMS:
SEE – **masturbate**, *p. 239*.

hacerse una carlota *exp.* to masturbate • (lit.): to do a Carlota *(a woman's name)*.

SYNONYMS:
SEE – **masturbate**, *p. 239*.

hacerse una chaqueta *exp. (Mexico)* to masturbate • (lit.): to make a jacket.

SYNONYMS:
SEE – **masturbate**, *p. 239*.

hacerse una gallarda *exp.* to masturbate • (lit.): to make a galliard (a type of French dance).

SYNONYMS:
SEE – **masturbate**, *p. 239.*

hacerse una magnolia *exp.* to masturbate • (lit.): to make a magnolia.

SYNONYMS:
SEE – **masturbate**, *p. 239.*

hacerse una paja *exp.* to masturbate • (lit.): to make a straw.

SYNONYMS:
SEE – **masturbate**, *p. 239.*

hacerse una pera *exp.* to masturbate • (lit.): to make a pear.

SYNONYMS:
SEE – **masturbate**, *p. 239.*

hacerse una sombrillita *exp.* to masturbate • (lit.): to make a little umbrella.

SYNONYMS:
SEE – **masturbate**, *p. 239.*

haragán/ana *n. & adj.* lazy bum; lazy.

example:
Nunca he conocido a nadie tan **haragán** como Pedro. Está durmiendo todo el día.

translation:
I've never met anyone as **lazy** as Pedro. All he does is sleep all day.

harina de otro costal (ser) *exp.* to be another story, to be a horse of a different color • (lit.): to be flour of a different sack.

example:
¡Eso es **harina de otro costal**!

translation:
That's **a different story**!

SYNONYM -1:
no tener que ver con nada *exp.* • (lit.): not to have anything to do with anything.

SYNONYM -2:
no venir al cuento *exp.* • (lit.): not to come to the story.

SYNONYM -3:
ser otro cantar *exp.* • (lit.): to be another song.

hasta la coronilla de (estar) *exp.* to be fed up with, to be sick of [something or someone] • (lit.): to be up to the crown with.

example:
Estoy **hasta la coronilla de** Marcos.

translation:
I'm **fed up with** Marcos.

SYNONYM -1:
estar harto de [alguien] *exp.* • (lit.): to be fed up with [someone].

SYNONYM -2:
estar hasta las cejas de *exp.* • (lit.): to be up to the eyebrows • *Estoy hasta las cejas de trabajo;* I'm up to my eyebrows in work.

hasta la fecha *exp.* to date, up till now • (lit.): until that date.

example:
Hasta la fecha nunca había comido un pescado tan delicioso.

translation:
Up till now, I have never had such delicious fish.

SYNONYM -1:
hasta el día de hoy *exp.* • (lit.): until today.

SYNONYM -2:
hasta hoy *exp.* • (lit.): until today.

SYNONYM -3:
hasta la actualidad *exp.* • (lit.): until today.

¡Hay que joderse! *exp.* To hell with everything! • (lit.): One should fuck oneself!

hecho polvo *exp.* *(Spain)* said of a jerk • (lit.): made of dust.

example:
Arnaldo parece un **hecho polvo** con sus gafas nuevas.

translation:
Arnaldo looks like a **jerk** in his new glasses.

NOTE -1:
In Argentina and Mexico, this expression is used to mean "to ache." For example: *Mis pies están hechos polvo;* My feet are aching.

NOTE -2:
In Argentina, *hecho/a polvo* is also used to mean "exhausted" • *Estoy hecho polvo hoy;* I'm exhausted today.

hediondito *m.* vagina • (lit.): the little smelly one.

SYNONYMS:
SEE – **vagina**, *p. 263*.

hermano pequeño *m.* small penis • (lit.): little brother.

SYNONYMS:
SEE – **penis**, *p. 243*.

hierba *f.* *(Mexico)* marijuana • (lit.): grass or herb.

example:
Marco lo echaron de la escuela por fumar **hierba**.

translation:
Marco got thrown out of school for smoking **pot**.

NOTE:
Also spelled: *yerba.*

hierro *m. (Puerto Rico)* penis • (lit.): iron.

SYNONYMS:
SEE – **penis**, *p. 243.*

higo *m.* vagina • (lit.): fig (fruit).

SYNONYMS:
SEE – **vagina**, *p. 263.*

¡Hijo de tu chingada madre! *interj. (an insult of contempt)* • (lit.): Son of your fucking mother!
example:
¡Me has estropeado mi bicicleta nueva! ¡**Hijo de tu chingada madre**!
translation:
You ruined my new bicycle! **You son of a bitch**!

ALSO:
hijo de la chingada *exp.* son of a bitch • (lit.): son of a fucker.

hinchapelotas *m.* pain in the neck • (lit.): one who makes someone's testicles swell.
example:
No puedo aguantar a Marco. Es un **hinchapelotas**. ¡Siempre me anda molestando con preguntas estupidas!
translation:
I can't stand Marco. He's a **pain in the neck**. He always bugs me with stupid questions!

NOTE:
pelotas *f.pl.* testicles • (lit.): balls (in a game).

hocicar *v.* to fornicate • (lit.): to root, nuzzle, grub around in.

hocicón/ona *n. & adj.* loudmouth; gossipy • (lit.): mouthy (since this term comes from the masculine noun *hocico* meaning "snout").
example:
No quiero invitar a Anita a mi fiesta porque no la soporto. ¡Es tan **hocicona**!
translation:
I don't want to invite Anita to my party because I can't stand her. She's such a **loudmouth**!

hombre • **1.** *m.* husband • **2.** *interj.* Wow! • (lit.): man.
example (1):
No me puedo quejar. Mi **hombre** me trata muy bien.
translation:
I can't complain. My **husband** treats me very well.
example (2):
¡**Hombre**! ¡Esta mujer es guapísima!
translation:
Man! That girl is beautiful!

SYNONYM -1:
¡Ay Caray! *interj. (Cuba).*

SYNONYM -2:
¡Caballero! *interj.* • (lit.): Sir!

SYNONYM -3:
¡Che! *interj. (Argentina)* Hey!

SYNONYM -4:
¡Guau! *interj. (Puerto Rico, Spain – pronounced Wow!).*

VARIATION:
¡Guao!

SYNONYM -5:
¡Manitas! *interj. (Puerto Rico).*

SYNONYM -6:
¡Mujer! *interj. (Cuba)* • (lit.): woman.

SYNONYM -7:
¡Tío! *interj.* • (lit.): Uncle!

SYNONYM -8:
¡Ufa! *interj. (Argentina).*

NOTE:
This interjection is used in response to an annoying person.

horripilante *adj.* horrifying, terrifying.

example:
Esa película es **horripilante**. Me tuve que salir del cine.

translation:
That's a **horrifying** movie. I had to get out of the theater.

SYNONYM -1:
espeluznante *adj.* • (lit.): horrifying.

SYNONYM -2:
horroroso *adj.* • (lit.): horrible, dreadful, hideous.

SYNONYM -3:
pavorosa *adj.* • (lit.): frightful, terrifying.

¡Hostia puta! *interj.* Holy shit! • (lit.): Fucking sacred wafer!

example:
¡Hostia puta! ¡Mira cómo llueve!

translation:
Holy Shit! Look at all that rain!

hoy por hoy *exp.* nowadays • (lit.): today by today.

example:
Hoy por hoy, los hijos no respetan a sus padres como antes.

translation:
Nowadays, children don't respect their parents like they used to.

hoyo *m. (Puerto Rico)* vagina • (lit.): hole.

SYNONYMS:
SEE – **vagina**, *p. 263*.

hueso *m.* penis • (lit.): bone.

SYNONYMS:
SEE – **penis**, *p. 243*.

huevón/na *n. & adj.* lazy bum; lazy.

example:
Mario es un **huevón**. Nunca hace nada.

translation:
Mario is a **lazy bum**. He never does anything.

SYNONYM -1:
dejado/a *adj.* • (lit.): left (from the verb *dejar* meaning "to leave [something]").

SYNONYM -2:
flojo/a *adj. & n.* • (lit.): lazy, idle.

SYNONYM -3:
parado/a *adj. (Spain).*

NOTE:
This is pronounced: *parao* in Spain.

SYNONYM -4:
vago/a *adj. (Spain)* • (lit.): vague.

ALSO:
hacer la hueva *exp.* not to lift a finger, to do nothing • (lit.): to make a female egg.

huevos *m.pl.* testicles • (lit.): eggs.

NOTE -1:
The term *huevo* literally means "egg" but is used in slang to mean "testicle," so be careful how you use it! For example:

> ***¿Quieres que te fría un huevo?***

Common Translation #1:
Would you like me to fry you an **egg**?

Common Translation #2:
Would you like me to fry one of your **testicles**?

NOTE -2:
In Bolivia, when this term is used in the singular, it is a derogatory term for "homosexual."

ALSO -1:
costar un huevo *exp.* to be terribly expensive, "to cost one's left nut" • (lit.): to cost one testicle.

ALSO -2:
huevada *f.* stupidity.

ALSO -3:
huevón *adj.* a description of a lazy or stupid person • (lit.): one with big *huevos* or "balls."

ALSO -4:
tener huevos *exp.* to be courageous • (lit.): to have balls.

impermeable *m. (Mexico)* condom • (lit.): raincoat.

inga *f. (Cuba)* penis • (lit.): inga plant.

SYNONYMS:
SEE – **penis**, *p. 243*.

insinuarse a alguien *exp.* to lead someone on • (lit.): to hint oneself to someone.

example:
Tienes que dejar de **insinuártele a Eduardo** porque es un hombre casado.

translation:
You need to **stop leading Eduardo on** because he's a married man.

inspector de zócalo *m.* *(Argentina)* runt • (lit.): baseboard inspector.

example:
¿Le pediste a Enrique que te ayudara a mover el piano? ¡Pero si es un **inspector de zócalo**!

translation:
You asked Enrique to help you move your piano? But he's such a **little runt**!

instrumento *m.* penis • (lit.): instrument.

SYNONYMS:
SEE – **penis**, *p. 243*.

invertido *adj.* derogatory for "homosexual" • (lit.): inverted.

ir a botar el agua al canario *exp.* *(Cuba)* to go take a leak • (lit.): to go to throw away the canary's water.

example:
Creo que he bebido demasiado café; necesito **ir a botar el agua al canario** otra vez.

translation:
I think I drank too much coffee. I need **to take a leak** again.

ir a desgastar el petate *exp.* *(Mexico)* to have sex • (lit.): to go wear down the bedding.

example:
No pude dormir anoche porque ¡mis vecinos de la casa de al lado estaban **yendo a desgastar el petate** toda la noche!

translation:
I couldn't sleep last night because my next door neighbors were **having sex** all night!

SYNONYM -1:
ir a desvencigar la cama *exp.* *(Mexico)* to have sex • (lit.): to go break the bed.

SYNONYM -2:
ir a hacer de las aguas *exp.* *(Mexico)* to have sex • (lit.): to go make some water.

SYNONYM -3:
ir a la junta de conciliación *exp.* *(Mexico)* to have sex • (lit.): to go to a meeting.

SYNONYM -4:
ir a la lucha super libre a calzón *exp.* *(Mexico)* to

have sex • (lit.): to go see wrestling wearing nothing but underwear.

SYNONYM -5:
ir a percudir el colchón *exp. (Mexico)* to have sex • (lit.): to tarnish the mattress.

SYNONYM -6:
ir a rechinar la cama *exp. (Mexico)* to have sex • (lit.): to make the bed squeak.

SYNONYM -7:
ir a un entierro *exp. (Mexico)* to have sex • (lit.): to go to a funeral.

ir a medias *exp.* to go halfsies, fifty-fifty • (lit.): to go halves.

example:
Cuando salimos a cenar siempre **vamos a medias**.

translation:
When we go out for dinner we always split everything **fifty-fifty** on the bill.

SYNONYM -1:
a la holandesa *exp.* to go Dutch • (lit.): to go Holland style.

SYNONYM -2:
ir a la mitad *exp.* • (lit.): to go to the half.

SYNONYM -3:
ir mitad mitad *exp.* • (lit.): to go half-half.

ir al asunto *exp.* to get down to the facts • (lit.): to go to the subject.

example:
¡**Vamos al asunto**!

translation:
Let's get down to the facts!

ir con el culo a rastras *exp.* • **1.** to be in a jam • **2.** to be broke • (lit.): to go with the ass dragging.

ir de culo *exp.* to go downhill, to deteriorate • (lit.): to go on its ass.

example:
La fiesta fue muy divertida durante las primeras horas. Después **fue de culo** cuando la gente empezó a irse.

translation:
The party was a lot of fun for the first few hours. Then it **went downhill** when people started to leave.

ir sin decir *exp.* to go without saying • (lit.): [same].

example:
Eso **va sin decir**.

translation:
That **goes without saying**.

irse *v.* to ejaculate • (lit.): to leave, go away.

irse a la gloria *exp.* to ejaculate • (lit.): to go to the glory.

SYNONYM:
irse de la varilla *exp.* to ejaculate • (lit.): to go from the stick.

jaina *f.* prostitute.

jamón/ona *n. & adj.* fatso; fat • (lit.): ham.

example:
¡Vaya **jamona**! ¡Debe pesar una tonelada!

translation:
What a **fatso**! She must weigh a ton!

jardinera *f.* derogatory for "homosexual" • (lit.): female gardener.

jeba *f. (Puerto Rico)* prostitute, whore.

NOTE:
This is a humorous variation of the masculine noun *jebe* meaning "rubber" (since prostitutes are known for being able to get into many different sexual positions as if they were made of rubber).

jebo *m. (Puerto Rico)* pimp.

jeta *f.* face or "block."

example:
¡Le voy a romper la **jeta**!

translation:
I'm going to knock his **block** off!

jiñar *v.* • **1.** to urinate • **2.** to defecate.

example:
¡Tengo que encontrar un sitio donde **jiñar**!

translation:
I need to find somewhere **to relieve myself**!

joda *f.* • **1.** nuisance, pain in the neck • **2.** joke.

example -1:
¡Esta tarea es una **joda**!

translation:
This homework is such a **pain in the neck**!

example -2:
Raudo me contó una buena **joda**.

translation:
Raudo told me a funny **joke**.

joder *v.* • **1.** to have sex • **2.** to annoy • **3.** to steal • **4.** to botch up • **5.** (*joderse*) to fail, to flop • **6.** *interj.* Damn! (used to denote anger, surprise, disappointment) • (lit.): to fuck.

example -1:
¡Mis vecinos **joden** cada noche!

translation:
My neighbors **have sex** every night!

example -2:
¡No me **jodas**!

translation:
Leave me the **hell** alone!

example -3:
Alguien **jodió** mi carro esta mañana!

translation:
Someone **stole** my car this morning!

example -4:
¿Has visto el nuevo corte de peinado de Alicia? Es tan **jodido**!

translation:
Did you see Alicia's new haircut? It's so **screwed up**!

example -5:
Toda el mundo creía que la nueva película sería un gran éxito. Desgraciadamente, **se jodió**!

translation:
Everyone thought that the new movie was going to be a huge success. Unfortunately, it **flopped**!

example -6:
¡**Qué joder**! ¡Dejé mis llaves en el carro!

translation:
Damn! I locked my keys in the car!

joder como desesperados *exp.* to fornicate • (lit.): to fuck like desperate people.

joder como locos *exp.* to fornicate • (lit.): to fuck like crazy people.

joderse vivos *exp.* to fornicate • (lit.): to fuck alive.

¡Jódete y aprieta el culo! *exp. (Cuba – an insult of contempt)* • (lit.): Fuck you and hold your ass tight!

example:
¡Me has engañado! ¡Jódete y aprieta el culo!

translation:
You cheated me! **Go to hell**!

jodida/pinche puta *f. (an insult of contempt)* • (lit.): fucking whore.

example:
¡Ésa **jodida/pinche puta** me ha zancadilleado!

translation:
That **damned bitch** tripped me!

NOTE:
In Spain, the adjective *jodida* would be used in this expression, whereas in Mexico, the commonly used adjective would be *pinche*.

jodido/a *adj.* • **1.** exhausted, wiped out • **2.** difficult • **3.** fucking • **4.** ruined • **5.** destitute, broke • (lit.): fucked.

example -1:
Después de trabajar todo el fin de semana, estoy **jodido**.

translation:
After working all weekend, I'm **wiped out**.

example -2:
Yo creo que el examen era muy **jodido**.

translation:
I think the test was very **difficult**.

example -3:
¡Guillermo es un **jodido** idiota! He locked himself out of his house for the fourth time this week!

translation:
Guillermo is a **fucking** idiot!

example -4:
¡Derramé jugo de tomate en mi chaleco nuevo y lo **jodí**!

translation:
I spilled tomato juice on my new vest and **wrecked** it!

example -5:
Clarissa perdió un montón de dinero en las apuestas. Ahora está **jodida**.

translation:
Clarissa lost a pile of money gambling. Now she's **broke**.

jodido/a pero contento/a *exp*. a common response to someone asking how you're doing • (lit.): fucked but content.

example:
– ¡Hola Alfonso! ¿Cómo estás hoy?
– **Jodido pero contento**.

translation:
– Hi Alfonso! How are you today?
– **Same shit, different day but still happy**!

jodienda *f.* annoying person or thing, pain in the ass • (lit.): act of fucking.

example:
Mi jefe quiere que yo trabaje el proximo fín de semana. ¡Qué **jodienda**!

translation:
My boss wants me to work next weekend again. What a **pain in the ass**!

jodón/ona *n. & adj.* pain in the ass (from the verb *joder* meaning "to fuck").

jodontón/ona *n. & adj.* "horndog"; sexual, horny (from the verb *joder* meaning "to fuck").

example:
Mi hermano piensa en el sexo todo el tiempo. ¡Es tan **jodontón**!

translation:
My brother thinks about sex all the time. He's such a **horndog**!

josiadora *f. (Puerto Rico)* prostitute, whore.

joto *m. (Mexico)* derogatory for "homosexual" • (lit.): effeminate.

jugar el todo por el todo *exp.* to risk everything, to go for it • (lit.): to play (risk) everything for everything.
example:
Cuando invertí en la bolsa, me **jugué el todo por el todo**.
translation:
When I invested in the stock market, I **risked everything**.

jugo *m.* semen • (lit.): juice.

¡La concha de tu madre! *interj. (Uruguay)* an extremely vulgar insult literally meaning "Your mother's vagina!"

VARIATION:
El concho de tu madre! *interj.*

la gota que derrama el vaso (ser) *exp.* to be the last straw, the straw that broke the camel's back • (lit.): to be the drop that makes the glass spill over.
example:
Elle me mintió anoche. ¡Eso ya **fue la gota que derramó el vaso**!
translation:
She lied to me last night. That's **the last straw**!

SYNONYM -1:
es el colmo *exp.* • (lit.): it is the height (or: that's the limit).

SYNONYM -2:
es el colmo de los colmos *exp.* • (lit.): it is the limit of the limits.

SYNONYM -3:
la gota que colmó el vaso (ser) *exp.* • (lit.): to be the drop that makes the glass spill over.

SYNONYM -4:
la última gota que hace rebosar la copa *exp.* • (lit.): the last drop that makes the glass overflow.

¡La puta que te parió! *interj.* You son of a bitch! • (lit.): The whore that gave you birth!
example:
¿Cómo has podido hacer algo tan horrible? ¡**La puta que te parió**!
translation:
How could you do such a horrible thing? **You son of a bitch**!

lacho *m. (Puerto Rico)* vagina.

SYNONYMS:
SEE – **vagina**, *p. 263*.

lagarta *f.* • **1.** prostitute, whore • **2.** bitch • (lit.): lizard.

lagartona *f.* • **1.** prostitute, whore • **2.** bitch • (lit.): big lizard.

example:
Karen se acuesta con todos. ¡Estoy empezando a pensar que es una **lagarta**!

translation:
Karen has sex with everybody. I am starting to think she's a **whore**!

lambiscón/ona *n. & adj.* brown-noser.

example:
Eduardo Haskell es muy cumplido con mi madre; es un **lambiscón**.

translation:
Eduardo Haskell always gives my mother compliments. He's such a **brown-noser**.

lameculo[s] *m. & adj.* kiss-ass, brown-noser • (lit.): butt-licker.

example:
¿Has oido cómo le hablaba Ana al jefe? Nunca supe que fuera tan **lameculo[s]**.

translation:
Did you hear how Ana was talking to the boss? I never knew she was such a **kiss-ass**.

lamehuevos *m.* brown-noser • (lit.): egg (testicles) sucker.

example:
¡Ese **lamehuevos** acaba de ser ascendido!

translation:
That **brown-noser** just got a promotion!

lamepollas *m.* cocksucker • (lit.): [same].

example:
El primo de Pablo es un **lamepollas**. ¡No lo soporto!

translation:
Pablo's cousin is a **cocksucker**. I can't stand him!

lamer el culo de alguien *exp.* to kiss up to someone • (lit.): to lick someone's ass.

example:
La única razón por la que Erica recibió una promoción, es porque ¡ella siempre le **lame el culo al** jefe!

translation:
The only reason Erica got a promotion is because she always **kisses up to the** boss!

lamesuelas *m. & adj.* kiss-ass • (lit.): leather-licker.

example:
La razón por la que al jefe le gusta tanto Víctor es porque éste es un **lamesuelas**.

translation:
The reason the boss likes Victor so much is because he's such a **kiss-ass**.

lana *f. (Spain)* money • (lit.): wool.

example:
Se nota que Javier tiene **lana**. Siempre conduce un automóvil último modelo.

translation:
You can tell Javier has **money**. He always drives a late-model car.

SYNONYM -1:
guita *f. (Argentina)* • (lit.): twine.

SYNONYM -2:
pasta *f.* • (lit.): pasta, paste.

SYNONYM -3:
plata *f.* • (lit.): silver.

SYNONYM -4:
tela *f. (Argentina)* • (lit.): material, cloth, fabric.

lanzar *v.* to ejaculate • (lit.): to throw.

largarse *v.* to leave, to go away, to beat it.

example:
Como no me gustó el concierto, me **largué** en seguida.

translation:
Since I didn't like the concert, I **left** after only a little while.

SYNONYM -1:
escabullirse *v.* • (lit.): to slip (from, through, or out), to escape.

SYNONYM -2:
escurrirse *v.* • (lit.): to drain, to slide.

SYNONYM -3:
evaporarse *v.* • (lit.): to evaporate oneself.

SYNONYM -4:
marcharse *v.* • (lit.): to go away, to leave.

las malas lenguas *exp.* gossip • (lit.): the bad tongues.

example:
Dicen **las malas lenguas** que Darío va a dejar a Lucía por otra mujer.

translation:
According to **gossip**, Dario is going to leave Lucia for another woman.

lata *f.* • **1.** pain in the neck, annoyance, nuisance • **2.** boring person or thing • **3.** long boring speech or conversation • (lit.): tin can.

example:
Esta película es una verdadera **lata**.

translation:
This movie is so **boring**.

SYNONYM -1:
garrón *m. (Argentina)*.

SYNONYM -2:
moserga *f.* • (lit.): bore, nuisance.

SYNONYM -3:
rollo *m.* • (lit.): roll • SEE – *p. 178.*

SYNONYM -4:
tabarra *f.* • (lit.): bore, nuisance.

ALSO -1:
dar la lata *exp.* • **1.** to annoy • **2.** to bore • (lit.): to give the can.

ALSO -2:
¡Qué lata! *interj.* What a pain in the butt! • (lit.): What a tin can!

latón *n.* annoying person, pain in the neck.

example:
Por favor, no invites a Pedro a la fiesta mañana. ¡Es un **latón**!

translation:
Please don't invite Pedro to the party tonight. He's such a **pain in the neck**!

SYNONYM -1:
chinche *m.* *(Puerto Rico / Cuba)* • **1.** annoying person • **2.** in a bad mood • (lit.): an annoying little bug • *¿Qué te pasa? ¡Estás chinche hoy!;* What happened? Are you in a bad mood?

SYNONYM -2:
dolor de cabeza (ser un) *exp. (Cuba)* • (lit.): to be a pain in the head or headache.

SYNONYM -3:
lata *f.* a pain in the neck • (lit.): tin can.

NOTE:
Both *latón* and *lata* may be used when referring either to people or to things: *¡Qué lata!* or *¡Qué latón!* = What a pain in the neck!

SYNONYM -4:
latoso/a *n. (Mexico).*

SYNONYM -5:
marrón *m. (Spain).*

latoso/a *n. & adj.* pain in the neck; annoying person • (lit.): made of tin can.

example:
Diana es una **latosa**. No hace más que pedirme favores.

translation:
Diana is a **pain in the neck**. All she ever does is ask me for favors.

leche *f.* semen • (lit.): milk.

NOTE:
This term may also be used as an expletive.

ALSO -1:
de mala leche *adj.* said of someone who is mean • (lit.): of bad semen.

ALSO -2:
hay mucha mala leche entre ellos *exp.* there are a lot of bad feelings between them • (lit.): there's a lot of bad semen between them.

ALSO -3:
tener mala leche *exp.* to be in a bad mood • (lit.): to have bad semen.

lechero *m.* penis.

NOTE:
This is from the noun *leche* literally meaning "milk" but used in slang to mean "semen."

SYNONYMS:
SEE – **penis**, *p. 243*.

leña *f. (Cuba)* penis • (lit.): firewood.

SYNONYMS:
SEE – **penis**, *p. 243*.

leñazo *m.* blow, bump, accident • (lit.): large piece of firewood.

example:
Ayer Luis se dio un **leñazo** con el coche.

translation:
Yesterday Luis had a car **accident**.

SYNONYM -1:
batacazo *m.* • (lit.): thud.

SYNONYM -2:
golpetazo *m.* • (lit.): great blow or knock.

VARIATION:
golpazo *m.*

NOTE:
From the verb *golpear* meaning "to hit."

SYNONYM -3:
porrazo *m.* • (lit.): great blow or knock.

SYNONYM -4:
topetazo *m.* • (lit.): great blow or knock.

SYNONYM -5:
trancazo *m.* • (lit.): great blow or knock.

SYNONYM -6:
trompazo *m.* • (lit.): great blow or knock.

ALSO:
dar/pegar un leñazo *exp.* to hit something or someone, to have an accident.

lengua larga (tener) *exp. (Argentina)* to be a blabbermouth • (lit.): to have a long tongue.

example:
A Angel le encanta chismear. **Tiene la lengua larga**.

translation:
Angel loves to gossip. **He's a blabbermouth**.

SYNONYMS:
SEE – **blabbermouth**, *p. 208*.

lenguasuelta *n. & adj. (Mexico)* a gossip; gossipy • (lit.): loose tongue.

example:
¡Para de ser **lenguasuelta**! Ésas no son más que mentiras.

translation:
Stop being a **gossip**! Those are nothing but lies.

lenguatuda *f. (Argentina)* blabbermouth • (lit.): one with a long tongue (used for blabbing).

example:
Consuela no puede guardar un secreto. Es una **lenguatuda**.

translation:
Consuela can't keep a secret. She's such a **blabbermouth**.

SYNONYMS:
SEE–**blabbermouth**, *p. 208*.

liarse *v.* to get involved (with someone), to go out with • (lit.): to tie up, to wrap up.

example:
Parece que Alfonso se ha **liado** con Lynda.

translation:
It seems like Alfonso is **involved** with Lynda.

SYNONYM -1:
engancharse *v. (Argentina)* • (lit.): to get hooked up (with someone).

SYNONYM -2:
enrollarse *v.* • (lit.): to roll up.

SYNONYM -3:
juntarse *v.* • (lit.): to join, to unite.

SYNONYM -4:
ligarse *v. (Cuba, Mexico, Spain)* • (lit.): to tie oneself up (with someone).

ALSO:
liarse a golpes *exp.* to come to blows.

licor *m.* semen • (lit.): liquor.

limones *m.pl.* breasts • (lit.): lemons.

limpiar el sable *exp.* to fornicate • (lit.): to clean the saber.

lina *f. (Mexico)* line of cocaine • (lit.): line.

listillo/a *adj. (Spain)* smart, clever person.

example:
Fernando es un **listillo**. Siempre tiene la respuesta adecuada.

translation:
Fernando is so **smart**. He always has the right answer.

SYNONYM -1:
agosado/a *adj. (Cuban, Puerto Rico)*.

NOTE:
In Puerto Rico and Cuba, this is pronounced: *agosao/agosah*.

SYNONYM -2:
avispado/a *adj.* • (lit.): clever, sharp.

NOTE:
This comes from the term *avispa* meaning "wasp."

SYNONYM -3:
despabilado/a *adj.* • (lit.): awakened.

NOTE:
This comes from the verb *despavilar* meaning "to wake up."

SYNONYM -4:
pillo *adj.* • (lit.): roguish, mischievous.

SYNONYM -5:
vivo/a *adj.* • (lit.): alive.

ANTONYM -1:
adoquín *m.* jerk, fool, moron, simpleton • (lit.): paving block.

ANTONYM -2:
bruto/a *adj.* • (lit.): stupid, crude.

ANTONYM -3:
cabezota *adj.*

NOTE:
This comes from the feminine noun *cabeza* meaning "head." The suffix *-ota* is commonly used to modify the meaning of the noun changing it literally to "big head."

ANTONYM -4:
tosco/a *adj.* • (lit.): coarse, crude, unrefined.

ANTONYM -5:
zopenco/a *adj.* • (lit.): dull, stupid.

lo dicho, dicho *exp.* what I said, goes • (lit.): I said it, said.

example:
¡Ya no te quiero ver más! **Lo dicho, dicho**.

translation:
I don't want to see you again! **What I said, goes**.

VARIATION:
lo dicho, dicho está *exp.*

loca *m. (Venezuela)* derogatory for "homosexual," "drag queen" • (lit.): crazy woman.

example:
¡Marta se pone tanto maquillaje que aparece una **loca**!

translation:
Marta puts on so much make-up, she looks like a **drag queen**!

loco/a como una cabra (estar) *exp.* to be crazy • (lit.): to be as crazy as a nanny goat.

example:
Si yo fuera tú no confiaría en él. ¡Está **loco como una cabra**!

translation:
I wouldn't trust him if I were you. He's **out of his mind**!

loco/a de remate (estar) *exp.* to be totally crazy, nuts, hopelessly mad • (lit.): crazy of end.

example:
Eduardo está **loco de remate**. Siempre habla consigo mismo en público.

translation:
Eduardo is **totally crazy**. He always talks to himself in public.

SYNONYM -1:
como una cabra (estar) *exp.* • (lit.): to be like a goat.

SYNONYM -2:
loco/a de atar (estar) *exp.* • (lit.): to be crazy to restrict.

locote *n.* big idiot.

example:
Mi hermana es psiquiatra y trabaja con **locotes** todo el día.

translation:
My sister is a psychiatrist who works with **crazy people** all day long.

NOTE:
This term comes from the adjective *loco/a* meaning "crazy."

longaniza *f.* penis • (lit.): pork sausage.

SYNONYMS:
SEE – **penis**, *p. 243*.

lurio/a *adj. (Mexico)* crazy • (lit.): mad, crazy.

example:
Si te crees que te puedes comer esa tarta entera, ¡tú estás completamente **lurio**!

translation:
If you think you can eat that entire cake, you're totally **crazy**!

VARIATION:
lurias *adj.*

luz *f. (Argentina)* smart person • (lit.): light.

example:
Mi sobrina es una verdadera **luz**. ¡Tiene sólo siete años y ya puede resolver problemas de álgebra!

translation:
My niece is a real **smarty**. She's only seven years old but she can do algebra!

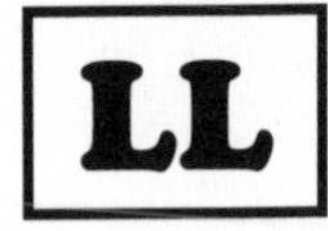

LL

llamar al pan pan y al vino vino *exp.* to call it like it is • (lit.): to call bread, bread and wine, wine.

example:
Yo siempre **llamo al pan pan y al vino vino**.

translation:
I always **call it like it is**.

SYNONYM:
llamar a las cosas por su nombre *exp.* • (lit.): to call things by their name.

llamar la atención *exp.* to attract attention • (lit.): to call for attention.

example:
Magda siempre **llama la atención** cuando se pone esa minifalda.

translation:
Magda always **attracts attention** when she wears that mini-skirt.

llello *m. (Mexico, Puerto Rico)* cocaine, crack.

lleno/a de humos *adj.* *(Argentina)* snobby • (lit.): full of smoke.

example:
La tía de David está **llena de humos**. Se niega a hablar con la gente que no es rica.

translation:
David's aunt is **very snobby**. She refuses to speak to people who aren't rich.

llevar/seguir la corriente *exp.* to humor someone, to go along with • (lit.): to carry/follow the current to someone.

example:
Siempre **le llevo la corriente** a mi esposa porque no me gusta discutir con ella.

translation:
I always **go along with** my wife because I don't like to argue with her.

NOTE:
This comes from the verb *correr* meaning "to run." Therefore, *una corriente* could be loosely translated as "a woman who runs around with more than one man."

llevar los pantalones *exp.* to wear the pants, to be in command • (lit.): to wear the pants.

example:
En mi casa yo **llevo los pantalones**.

translation:
In my house, **I wear the pants in the family**.

SYNONYM -1:
llevar la batuta *exp.* • (lit.): to carry the baton.

SYNONYM -2:
llevar los calzones *exp.* • (lit.): to wear underwear.

llevarse como perro y gato *exp.* not to get along, to fight like cats and dogs • (lit.): to carry each other like dog and cat.

example:
Teresa y Carlos **se llevan como perro y gato**.

translation:
Teresa and Carlos **fight like cats and dogs**.

NOTE:
Make sure to be aware of the difference between the Spanish expression and its English equivalent. In the Spanish expression, it's *perro y gato* ("dog and cat") both singular. However, in English the order is opposite and both are plural: "to fight like cats and dogs."

SYNONYM -1:
llevarse mal con *exp.* • (lit.): to carry oneself off badly with.

SYNONYM -2:
no hacer buenas migas con *exp.* • (lit.): not to make good bread crumbs with.

ANTONYM -1:
hacer buenas migas con *exp.* to get along well with • (lit.): to make good bread crumbs with.

ANTONYM -2:
llevarse bien con *exp.* to get along well with • (lit.): to carry oneself off well with.

llover a cántaros *exp.* to rain cats and dogs • (lit.): to rain pitcherfuls.

example:
No podemos ir al parque porque está **lloviendo a cántaros**.

translation:
We can't go to the park because **it's raining cats and dogs**.

SYNONYM -1:
caer burros aparejados *exp. (Cuba, Dominican Republic, Puerto Rico)* • (lit.): to fall prepared donkeys.

SYNONYM -2:
caer el diluvio *exp.* • (lit.): to fall the Flood (as in the Bible).

SYNONYM -3:
caer un chaparrón *exp.* • (lit.): to fall a downpour (but of short duration).

SYNONYM -4:
llover a chorros *exp.* • (lit.): to rain in spurts.

SYNONYM -5:
llover con rabia *exp. (Cuba, Dominican Republic, Puerto Rico, Southern Spain)* • (lit.): to rain with anger (or fury).

lluvia dorada *f.* golden shower • (lit.): golden rain.

NOTE:
This is a deviate sexual act where one partner urinates on the other.

macana *f.* penis • (lit.): heavy wooden club.

SYNONYMS:
SEE – **penis**, *p. 243*.

macha *f. & adj.* lesbian • (lit.): the feminine form of *macho* meaning "very masculine."

machaca *f.* penis • (lit.): crusher, pounder.

SYNONYMS:
SEE – **penis**, *p. 243*.

machacar *v.* to repeat, to go on and on about.

example:
Estás siempre **machacando** con lo mismo. Déjame en paz.

translation:
You always **go on and on** about the same thing. Leave me alone.

machete *m.* penis • (lit.): machete.

SYNONYMS:
SEE – **penis**, *p. 243*.

machorra *f.* lesbian.

NOTE:
This is a variation of the masculine noun *macho* meaning "manly."

madama *f. (Mexico)* madame of a brothel.

madre *f. (Mexico)* motherfucker • (lit.): mother.

ALSO:
me vale madre *exp.* I don't give a fuck • (lit.): it's worth a mother to me.

madre superiora *f. (Mexico)* may be used in slang to mean "a madame of a brothel" • (lit.): mother superior.

madrina *f. (Mexico)* a madame of a brothel • (lit.): godmother.

madrota *f. (Mexico)* a madame of a brothel.

NOTE:
This is a variation of the feminine noun *madrona* meaning "pampering mother."

magras *f.pl.* buttocks • (lit.): slice of ham, rasher.

maja *adj.* elegant.

example:
¿Has visto a Sandra? ¡Ella es muy **maja**!

translation:
Have you seen Sandra? She's really **elegant**!

maje *adj.* crazy.

example:
Tú estás **maje** si crees que el jefe te va a conceder un ascenso.

translation:
You're **out of your mind** if you think the boss is going to give you a raise.

NOTE:
This is from the verb *majar* meaning "to crush, pound, mash."

majo *m.* classy guy.

example:
¿Crees que David es un **majo**?

translation:
Do you believe that David is a **classy guy**?

mal aire *m.* fart • (lit.): bad air.

example:
¡Qué asco! ¡Creo que huelo un **mal aire**!

translation:
Yuck! I think I smell a **fart**!

mala semana *f.* menstruation • (lit.): bad week.

maldita puta *f.* damned bitch • (lit.): damned whore.

example:
¡Esa **maldita puta** ha derramado jugo de tomate en mi chaleco nuevo!

translation:
That **bitch** spilled tomato juice on my new sweater!

maleta *f.* prostitute, whore • (lit.): suitcase.

malísimamente *adv.* really badly, terribly (from the adverb *mal* meaning "poorly").

example:
Juan jugó **malísimamente**.

translation:
Juan played **really badly**.

SYNONYM -1:
de pena *exp.* • (lit.): of shame.

SYNONYM -2:
pésimamente *adv.* • (lit.): very badly, wretchedly.

ANTONYM:
buenísimamente *adv.* (from the adverb *bueno* meaning "good") really well, fantastically.

malva *f. (Mexico)* marijuana • (lit.): mallow.

mamada *f.* blow job • (lit.): sucking.

mamón/ona *n. & adj.* • **1.** brown-noser • **2.** obnoxious person • (lit.): unweaned.
example:
Rolando le ha comprado el almuerzo al jefe por tercera vez en esta semana. ¡Qué **mamón**!
translation:
Rolando bought the boss lunch for the third time this week. What a **brown-noser**!

NOTE:
This is from the verb *mamar* meaning "to suck."

mamplora *f. (El Salvador)* derogatory for "homosexual."

manchas *f.pl.* breasts, "tits" • (lit.): spots or stains.

mandar a alguien a bañarse *exp.* to tell someone to go take a flying leap, to tell someone to go fly a kite • (lit.): to send someone to take a bath.

example (1):
¡**Vete a bañar**!
translation:
Go fly a kite!
example (2):
Cuando Adolfo me pidió dinero por tercera vez, ¡**lo mandé a bañarse**!
translation:
When Adolfo asked me to lend him money for the third time, I told him **to go take a flying leap**!

SYNONYM -1:
¡Vete a echar pulgas a otra parte! *exp.* • (lit.): Go throw fleas somewhere else!

SYNONYM -2:
¡Vete a freír chongos! *exp. (Mexico)* • (lit.): Go fry buns!

SYNONYM -3:
¡Vete a freír espárragos! *exp.* • (lit.): Go fry asparagus!

SYNONYM -4:
¡Vete a freír mocos! *exp. (Ecuador, Peru, Bolivia)* • (lit.): Go fry mucus!

SYNONYM -5:
¡Vete a freir monos! *exp. (Colombia & Spain)* • (lit.): Go fry monkeys!

SYNONYM -6:
¡Vete a ver si ya puso la cochina/ puerca! *exp. (Latin America)* • (lit.): Go see if the sow has already laid an egg!

mandarria *f. (Cuba)* penis • (lit.): sledge hammer.

SYNONYMS:
SEE – **penis**, *p. 243*.

manga *f. (Mexico)* condom • (lit.): sleeve.

mangante *m.* thief.

example:
Anoche entró un **mangante** a mi casa y se llevó mis joyas.

translation:
Last night a **thief** broke into my house and stole my jewelry.

SYNONYM -1:
caco *m.* • (lit.): thief.

SYNONYM -2:
chorizo *m.* • (lit.): a type of Spanish sausage.

SYNONYM -3:
chorro *m. (Argentina)*.

SYNONYM -4:
pillo *m. (Puerto Rico)* • (lit.): mischievious.

SYNONYM -5:
ratero *m. (Mexico)* • (lit.): petty thief.

mangar *v.* to steal, to rob.

example:
Ese tipo quiso **mangar** el banco pero lo atrapó la policía.

translation:
That guy tried to **rob** the bank but he was caught by the police.

SYNONYM -1:
afanar *v. (Argentina)* • **1.** to steal, to swipe • **2.** to work hard (as seen earlier).

SYNONYM -2:
escamotear *v.*

SYNONYM -3:
hurtar *v.*

mango *m.* sexy person, hot number • (lit.): mango.

example:
¡Mi maestra de biología es un **mango**!

translation:
My biology teacher is a **hot number**!

manguera *f.* penis • (lit.): water hose.

SYNONYMS:
SEE – **penis**, *p. 243*.

manitas *m.* handyman • (lit.): little hands.

example:
Pepe arregla todo en su casa. ¡Es un verdadero **manitas**!

translation:
Pepe fixes everything in his house himself. He's a real **handyman**!

SYNONYM:
arreglatodo *m.* (said of a man or woman) • (lit.): a "fix-everything."

VARIATION:
arreglalotodo *m.*

ANTONYM -1:
chambón *adj.* • (lit.): awkward.

ANTONYM -2:
desmañado/a *adj.* • (lit.): clumsy or awkward person.

ANTONYM -3:
incapaz *adj.* • (lit.): incapable, unable.

ANTONYM -4:
patoso/a *adj.* • (lit.): boring, dull.

ANTONYM -5:
torpe *adj.* clumsy

ANTONYM -6:
zopenco/a *adj.*

manitas (hacer) *exp.* to play footsie.

example:
No pienso volver a salir con Alejandro. ¡Empezó a **hacer manitas** conmigo en el restaurante!

translation:
I'm never going out with Alejandro again. He started **playing footsie** with me at the restaurant!

NOTE:
This is from the feminine noun *mano* meaning "hand."

manolo *m.* penis.

NOTE:
This is a variation of the name *Manuel.*

SYNONYMS:
SEE – **penis**, *p. 243*.

manosear *v.* to finger [someone] • (lit.): to touch with one's hands.

manudo/a *n. (El Salvador)* drunkard.

example:
No pienso volver a invitar nunca más al **manudo** de Rafael a mi casa. ¡Fue tan vergonzoso!

translation:
I'm never inviting that **drunkard** Rafael to my house again. He was so embarrassing!

marchatrás *m. (Argentina)* derogatory for "homosexual" • (lit.): one who goes backward.

margaritas *f.pl.* breasts, "tits" • (lit.): pearls.

marica *m.* derogatory for "homosexual" • (lit.): magpie.

maricón *m.* **1.** anus • **2.** derogatory for "homosexual" • (lit.): sissy, homosexual, queer.

maricona *f.* derogatory for "homosexual" • (lit.): homosexual.

marimacha *f.* a derogatory term for "lesbian."

NOTE:
This is a variation of the feminine noun *marica* meaning "sissy" and the adjective *macho* meaning "manly."

mariposa *f. (Mexico)* derogatory for "homosexual" • (lit.): butterfly.

NOTE:
The term *mariposa* literally means "butterfly" but is used in slang to mean "homosexual," so be careful how you use it! For example:

Vamos a buscar mariposas.

Common Translation:
We're going to find **butterflies**.

Translation in Argentina, Chile, Mexico
We're going to find **homosexuals**.

mariquita *f.* a derogatory term for "homosexual male" • (lit.): ladybird.

mariscala *f. (Mexico)* a madame of a brothel.

mary *f. (Mexico)* marijuana.

NOTE:
This is much like the American-English slang term *Mary Jane*.

más vale prevenir que curar *exp.* better to be safe than sorry • (lit.): it's worth more to prevent than to cure.

example:
Más vale prevenir que curar. Voy a traer el paraguas por si llueve.

translation:
Better safe than sorry. I'm going to bring my umbrella just in case it rains.

más vale tarde que nunca *exp.* better late than never • (lit.): it is worth more late than never.

example:
Menos mal que llegaste. **Más vale tarde que nunca**.

translation:
Good thing you showed up. **Better late than never**.

mastuerzo *m. (Mexico)* marijuana.

matasanos *m.* doctor • (lit.): killer of healthy people (from the verb *matar* meaning "to kill" and *sano* meaning "heath").

example:
El marido de Gloria es un **matasanos**.

translation:
Gloria's husband is a **doctor**.

NOTE:
Although this term literally has a negative meaning, it is commonly used in jest to refer to a doctor in general.

SYNONYM:
doc *m. (Argentina)*.

mazo *m.* penis • (lit.): mallet.

SYNONYMS:
SEE – **penis**, *p. 243*.

¡Me cago en el recontra-coño de tu reputísima madre! *exp. (Cuba – an insult of contempt)* • (lit.): I shit on the big vagina of your big whore mother!

NOTE:
The masculine term *coño* is an extremely vulgar slang term for "vagina."

¡Me cago en la madre que te parió! *exp. (an insult of contempt)* • (lit.): I shit in the mother who gave you birth!

¡Me cago en la mar! *exp. (Spain – an insult of contempt)* • (lit.): I shit in the ocean!

¡Me cago en la purimísima hostia! *exp. (an insult of contempt)* • (lit.): I shit on the holiest communion wafer!

¡Me cago en tú! *exp. (an insult of contempt)* • (lit.): I shit on you!

¡Me cago en tu leche! *interj. (an insult of contempt)* • (lit.): I shit in your milk!

example:
¡Como te atreves a decirme eso! ¡**Me cago en tu leche**!

translation: How dare you say that to me! **Go to hell**!

¡Me cago en tu madre! *exp. (an insult of contempt)* • (lit.): I shit on your mother!

example:
¡Cómo eres capaz de hacerme eso! ¡**Me cago en tu madre**!

translation:
How dare you do such a mean thing to me! **Go to hell**!

VARIATION:
¡Me cago en el recontra-coño de tu reputísima madre! *exp. (Cuba)* • (lit.): I shit on the big vagina of your big whore mother!

¡Me cago en tus huesos! *exp. (an insult of contempt)* • (lit.): I shit in your bones!

¡Me cago en tus mulas! *exp. (an insult of contempt)* • (lit.): I shit in your mules!

meadero *m.* urinal (from the verb *mear* meaning "to piss").

example:
El **meadero** en este baño está muy limpio.

translation:
The **urinal** in this bathroom is very clean.

meado[s] *m.pl.* urine, piss (from the verb *mear* meaning "to piss").

example:
El olor a **meado** me pone enfermo.

translation:
The smell of **urine** makes me sick.

mear *v.* to urinate, to piss.

example:
Creo que tengo que llevar a mi hija al baño. Parece que necesita **mear**.

translation:
I think I need to take my daughter to the bathroom. She looks like she need **to take a leak**.

NOTE:
mearse de risa *exp.* to laugh so hard as to urinate in one's pants • (lit.): [same].

mecasala *f. (El Salvador)* penis.

SYNONYMS:
SEE – **penis**, *p. 243*.

media naranja *exp.* better half, spouse • (lit.): **1.** half an orange • **2.** dome, cupola.

example:
A mi **media naranja** y a mí nos encanta ir a México de vacaciones.

translation:
My **wife** and I love going to Mexico on vacation.

NOTE -1:
In Spanish, a dome is called a *media naranja* (literally, "half an orange") due to its shape.

NOTE -2:
Media naranja is commonly used as a humorous and affectionate term for one's spouse, since one half completes the other as would two halves of an orange.

SYNONYM:
jermu *f. (Argentina)* a reverse transformation of the word *mujer* ("jer-mu") meaning woman or wife.

melocotones *m.pl.* breasts, "tits" • (lit.): peaches.

NOTE:
The term *melocotones* literally means "peaches" but is used in slang to mean "breasts," so be careful how you use it! For example:

¡Esos melocotones son enormes!

Common Translation:
Those **peaches** are enormous!

Translation in Mexico:
Those **boobs** are enormous!

melones *m.pl.* breasts, "tits" • (lit.): melons.

mendigo/a *n. & adj.* tightwad; stingy • (lit.): beggar, mendicant.

example:
¿Viste el regalo tan barato que me hizo Geraldo para mi cumpleaños? ¡Qué **mendigo**!

translation:
Did you see the cheap gift Geraldo gave me for my birthday? What a **cheapskate**!

menearse *v.* to move, dance • (lit.): to wag (as in *menear la cola;* to wag the tail).

example:
Me encanta cómo **se menea** Alberto. Baila muy bien.

translation:
I love how Alberto **moves**. He really dances well.

SYNONYM -1:
bailotear *v.*

NOTE:
This term comes from the verb *bailar* meaning "to dance."

SYNONYM -2:
moverse *v.* • (lit.): to move.

ALSO:
mover la colita *exp.* • (lit.): to move or shake one's tail.

NOTE:
This expression comes from a popular Spanish song meaning "to shake one's booty."

meneársela *v.* to masturbate, to beat off • (lit.): to shake it for oneself.

SYNONYMS:
SEE – **masturbate**, *p. 239*.

menso/a *(Mexico) n. & adj.* idiot; jerky • (lit.): foolish, stupid.

example:
Acabo de enterarme de que Carla está en un hospital psiquiátrico. No sabía que estaba **mensa**.

translation:
I just heard that Carla is in a mental hospital. I didn't know she was **nuts**.

meón *n.* baby, "little pisher" (from the verb *mear* meaning "to piss").

example:
¡Roberto es un **meón**!

translation:
Robert is a **baby**!

merengue *m.* beautiful woman, "knockout" • (lit.): meringue, a type of pie.

example:
Ana es la chica más guapa de la escuela. ¡Es un verdadero **merengue**!

translation:
Ana is the most beautiful girl at school. She's a real **babe**!

SYNONYM -1:
bollito *m. (Spain)* • (lit.): a small sweet cake.

SYNONYM -2:
bombón *m.* bonbon • (lit.): (a type of chocolate candy).

SYNONYM -3:
buena moza *f.* • (lit.): good maid.

SYNONYM -4:
buenona *f.*

NOTE:
This noun comes from the adjective *bueno/a* meaning "good."

SYNONYM -5:
diosa *f. (Argentina)* goddess.

SYNONYM -6:
maja *f.* • (lit.): flashy or showy.

SYNONYM -7:
mamasita *f.* • (lit.): little mother.

SYNONYM -8:
pimpollo *m.* • (lit.): flower bud or bloom.

SYNONYM -9:
tía buena *f. (Cuba, Spain)* • (lit.): good aunt.

SYNONYM -10:
venus *f.* • (lit.): Venus (the goddess of beauty).

mermelada de membrillo *f. (Mexico)* semen • (lit.): marmalade of the smaller limb (quince jam).

NOTE:
dulce de membrillo *f. (Argentina)*.

mesero sin charola *m.* derogatory for "homosexual" • (lit.): waiter without a tray (since the hand is in an effeminate position with the palm facing upward).

meter el dedo *exp.* to finger [someone] • (lit.): to put the finger.

meter las narices en lo que a uno no le importa *exp.* to butt into other people's business, to stick one's nose into everything • (lit.): to put the nose into that which doesn't concern one.

example:
Francisco siempre **mete las narices en dónde no le importa**.

translation:
Francisco always **sticks his nose into everything**.

meter un gol *exp.* to score a goal • (lit.): to put in a goal.

example:
No me puedo creer que Luis **metió seis goles** en el partido de ayer.

translation:
I can't believe Luis **scored six goals** in yesterday's game.

NOTE:
This expression is used primarily in soccer games although it may also be used in similar sports such as hockey, waterpolo, etc.

meterla de mira quien viene *exp. (Cuba)* to fornicate doggie-style, to fornicate through the anus • (lit.): to put it in looking to see who is coming.

VARIATION:
singar de mira quien viene *exp.*

meterla hasta la empuñadura *exp.* to fornicate • (lit.): to put in up to the sword hilt.

meterla hasta las cachas *exp.* to fornicate • (lit.): to put it up to the buttocks.

meterla hasta los huevos *exp.* to fornicate • (lit.): to put it up to the balls (testicles).

meterla hasta los puños *exp.* to fornicate • (lit.): to put it up to the fists.

meterse en un [buen] berenjenal *exp.* to get oneself into a [real] jam, to get oneself into a fine mess • (lit.): to get into a good eggplant patch.

example:
No mientas sobre lo que pasó o te vas a **meter en un buen berenjenal**.

translation:
Every time I go to that bar **I get myself into a mess**.

SYNONYM -1:
meterse en un buen lío *exp.* • (lit.): to put oneself in a good bundle.

SYNONYM -2:
meterse en un callejón sin salida *exp.* • (lit.): to get oneself in a dead-end alley.

metérsela a alguien *exp.* to fornicate • (lit.): to put it in someone.

¡Métetelo por el culo! *exp.* Shove it up your ass! • (lit.): Put it in your ass!

mico/a *n. (Central America)* vagina • (lit.): car jack.

SYNONYMS:
SEE – **vagina**, *p. 263*.

miembrillo *m. (Mexico)* penis • (lit.): small member.

SYNONYMS:
SEE – **penis**, *p. 243*.

mierda • **1.** *interj.* shit (used to express surprise, anger, disappointment) • **2.** filth • (lit.): shit.

example -1:
Mierda! ¡Perdí mi cartera!

translation:
Shit! I lost my wallet!

example -2:
¿De dónde viene toda esa **mierda** en mi chaqueta nueva?

translation:
Where did all of this **shit** on my new jacket come from?

mierda (ser una) *exp.* • **1.**said of a despicable person, asshole • **2.** said of something lousy or "shitty" • (lit.): to be a shit.

example -1:
¿Invitaste a Marco a la fiesta? ¿No puedo soportarlo! ¡Es una **mierda**!

translation:
You invited Marco to your party? I can't stand him! He's such an **asshole**!

example -2:
Ese regalo que Pedro me dio el día de mi cumpleaños es **una mierda**.

translation:
That gift that Pedro gave me for my birthday was **for shit**.

mierdecilla *f.* runt • (lit.) little shit.

example:
Ese **mierdecilla** es un presuntuoso y no le gusta a na nadie.

translation:
That **little runt** acts so conceited but no one even likes him.

mierdero *m. (Nicaragua)* scum • (lit.): a place where there is a lot of shit.

mierdita *f.* a worthless piece of shit • (lit.): little shit.

example:
Mi carro se rompió por tercera vez esta semana. ¡No puedo creer que pagó tanto dinero por esta **mierdita**!

translation:
My car broke down for the third time this week. I can't believe I paid so much money for this **piece of shit**!

minga *f.* penis • (lit.): communal work.

SYNONYMS:
SEE – **penis**, *p. 243*.

minina *f. (child's language)* penis, "peepee" • (lit.): kitty cat.

minino *m. (child's language)* vagina • (lit.): kitty cat.

SYNONYMS:
SEE – **vagina**, *p. 263*.

mirar por sus [proprios] intereses *exp.* to look out for oneself, to look out for number one • (lit.): to look out for one's [own] interests.

example:
A Simón no le importa la gente. Solo **mira por sus [propios] intereses**.

translation:
Simon doesn't care about other people. He only **looks out for number one**.

SYNONYM -1:
mirar por sí mismo *exp.* • (lit.): to look by oneself.

SYNONYM -2:
preocuparse sólo de uno mismo *exp.* to worry only about oneself • (lit.): [same].

mirasol *m.* penis • (lit.): sunflower.

SYNONYMS:
SEE – **penis**, *p. 243*.

misma imagen (ser la) *exp.* to be the spitting image of • (lit.): to be the same image.

example:
David es **la misma imagen** de su padre.

translation:
David is the **spitting image** of his father.

SYNONYM -1:
ser escupido/a de *exp.* • (lit.): to be the spit of.

SYNONYM -2:
ser viva imagen de *exp.* • (lit.): to be the live image of.

mitotero/a *n. & adj.* a gossip; gossipy • (lit.): rowdy, noisy person.

example:
Te lo advierto, Margarita es una verdadera **mitotera**. No le cuentes nada personal.

translation:
I'm warning you. Margarita is a real **gossip**. Don't tell her anything personal.

mitra *f. (Puerto Rico)* penis • (lit.): mitre.

SYNONYMS:
SEE – **penis**, *p. 243*.

mocongó *m. (Puerto Rico)* penis.

SYNONYMS:
SEE – **penis**, *p. 243*.

mocoso/a de mierda *n. (Argentina)* snot-nosed little brat • (lit.): snotty one of shit.

example:
¿Conociste a los nuevos vecinos? Tienen dos **mocosos de mierda** que nunca paran de gritar.

translation:
Did you meet the new neighbors? They have two **brats** who never stop screaming.

mojar [el churro] *exp.* to fornicate • (lit.): to wet [the long fritter].

NOTE:
churro *m.* a long, straight fried pastry.

molesto/a como mosca de letrina *exp.* annoying • (lit.): annoying as an outhouse fly.

example:
¡Vete! ¡Eres **molesto como una mosca de letrina**!

translation:
Go away! You're **so annoying**!

mona *f. (El Salvador)* penis • (lit.): female monkey.

SYNONYMS:
SEE – **penis**, *p. 243*.

montar *v.* to fornicate • (lit.): to climb up (on someone).

montón m. a bunch of, a lot of • (lit.): crowd.

example:
Alfonso tiene un **montón** de amigos en todas partes porque es muy simpático.

translation:
Alfonso has **a lot of** friends everywhere because he's very nice.

SYNONYM:
pila *f.* • (lit.): a pile.

ALSO -1:
a montones *exp.* in large quantities, abundantly • *libros a montones* (literally, "a mountain of books").

ALSO -2:
ser del montón *exp.* to be mediocre • (lit.): to be of the crowd.

moravia *f. (Mexico)* marijuana.

morcilla *f.* penis • (lit.): blood sausage.

SYNONYMS:
SEE – **penis**, *p. 243*.

morder *v.* to give a French kiss • (lit.): to bite.

morderse la lengua *exp.* to hold or control one's tongue • (lit.): to bite one's tongue.

example:
¡**Muérdete la lengua**!

translation:
Bite your tongue!

ANTONYM -1:
cantar claro *exp.* to speak clearly • (lit.): to sing clearly.

ANTONYM -2:
no morderse la lengua *exp.* not to mince words, to speak straight from the shoulder • (lit.): not to bite one's tongue.

ANTONYM -3:
no tener pelos en la lengua *exp.* • (lit.): not to have hairs on the tongue.

ANTONYM -4:
ser claridoso/a *exp. (Central America, Venezuela)* • (lit.): to be very clear.

morir de ganas *exp.* to be dying to do something, to feel like • (lit.): to die of wish.

example:
Me muero de ganas de ver a María.

translation:
I'm dying to see Maria.

SYNONYM:
tener muchas ganas de *exp.* • (lit.): to have many desires to.

morisqueta *f. (Mexico)* marijuana • (lit.): speck.

morreo *m.* French kiss.

NOTE:
This is a variation of the masculine noun *morro* meaning "snout."

morrocotudo/a *adj.* • **1.** neat, cool, terrific, fabulous • **2.** very important • **3.** difficult • **4.** wealthy • **5.** big, enormous.

example (1):
El nuevo automóvil de Carlos es muy **morrocotudo**.

translation:
Carlos' new car is really **cool**.

example (2):
Mi entrevista con el presidente fue **morrocotuda**.

translation:
My interview with the President was **very important**.

example (3):
Este problema de matemáticas es **morrocotudo**.

translation:
This math problem is very **difficult**.

example (4):
Pablo es un **morrocotudo**. ¡Debes de ver la casa nueva que se ha comprado!

translation:
Pablo is very **wealthy**. You should see the new house he bought!

example (5):
¡Ese barco es **morrocotudo**!

translation:
That ship is **enormous**!

NOTE:
The following are synonyms for example (1) only:

SYNONYM -1:
alucinante *adj. (Argentina).*

SYNONYM -2:
chulo/a *adj. (Spain)* neat, cool, terrific.

SYNONYM -3:
del carah *adj. (Puerto Rico).*

SYNONYM -4:
molón *adj. (Spain).*

ANTONYM:
chungo/a *adj.* ugly, "uncool."

NOTE:
This is an antonym for the previous example (1) only.

morronga *f. (Central America)* penis • (lit.): a female cat.

SYNONYMS:
SEE – **penis**, *p. 243*.

morrongo *m. (Mexico)* penis • (lit.): male cat.

SYNONYMS:
SEE – **penis**, *p. 243*.

mota *f. (Mexico) marijuana.*

motivosa *f. (Mexico)* marijuana.

NOTE:
This is a variation of the masculine noun *motivo* meaning "motive" or "reason."

motocicleta *f. (Mexico)* marijuana • (lit.): motorcycle.

motor de chorro *m. (Mexico)* marijuana • (lit.): jet engine.

motorizar *v. (Mexico, Central and South America)* to smoke marijuana • (lit.): to motorize.

muchachas putierrez *f.pl. (Guatemala, Mexico)* prostitutes • (lit.): Putierrez girls.

NOTE:
The feminine noun *putierrez* is a variation of the term *puta* meaning prostitute and is used here in jest as the girls' last name.

mucho ruido y pocas nueces *exp.* much ado about nothing, a big fuss about nothing • (lit.): a lot of noise and very few walnuts.

example:
Antonio tuvo una emergencia y me pidió que viniera enseguida. Pero en realidad era **mucho ruido y pocas nueces**.

translation:
Antonio had an emergency and asked me to come over immediately. But it was really **a big fuss about nothing**.

muerdo *m.* a French kiss, a kiss with the tongue.

NOTE:
This comes from the verb *morder* meaning "to bite."

mugre *f.* filth, grime, dirt.

example:
¡Oye Paco! Tu automóvil está lleno de **mugre**. ¡Parece que nunca lo lavas!

translation:
Hey Paco! Your car is so full of **dirt**. It looks like you never wash it!

SYNONYM -1:
cochambre *f.* • (lit.): greasy.

SYNONYM -2:
porquería *f.* • (lit.): junk.

mujer de la calle *f.* prostitute • (lit.): a woman of the street.

mujer de la vida galante *f.* prostitute • (lit.): woman of luxurious lifestyle.

mujer fatal *f.* prostitute • (lit.): wicked woman.

mujeriego *m. & adj.* skirt-chaser; obsessed with women • (lit.): one who is obsessed with women (from the feminine noun *mujer* meaning "woman").

example:
Nunca saldría con alguien tan **mujeriego** como Simón. No creo que él pueda serle fiel a nadie.

translation:
I would never go out with such a **skirt-chaser** as Simón. I don't think he could ever be faithful.

muñeco *m. (Mexico)* vagina • (lit.): doll, puppet.

SYNONYMS:
SEE – **vagina**, *p. 263.*

muy ligero/a de palabra (ser) *exp.* to be a blabbermouth • (lit.): to be very light in words.

example:
Rafael es **muy ligero de palabra**. Le gusta hablar demasiado.

translation:
Rafael is a **blabbermouth**. He likes to talk too much.

SYNONYM -1:
charlatán (ser un) *adj.* • (lit.): to be a charlatan.

SYNONYM -2:
chismoso (ser un) *adj.* • (lit.): to be a gossip • SEE – **chismoso**, *p. 66.*

SYNONYM -3:
cuentista (ser un) *adj.* • (lit.): to be a story teller.

ADDITIONAL SYNONYMS:
SEE – **blabbermouth**, *p. 208.*

nabo *m.* penis • (lit.): turnip.

NOTE:
The term *nabo* literally means "turip" but is used in slang to mean "penis," so be careful how you use it! For example:

Creo que venden nabos en este mercado.

Common Translation #1:
I think they sell **turnips** in this market.

Common Translation #2:
I think they sell **penises** in this market.

SYNONYMS:
SEE – **penis**, *p. 243.*

nalga de ángel *f. (Mexico)* marijuana • (lit.): buttocks of an angel.

nalgas *f.pl.* • **1.** buttocks • **2.** vagina • (lit.): buttocks.

nalgón *n.* a person with a big buttocks • (lit.): someone with a large buttocks.

example:
Debes parar de mirar la televisión y empezar a hacer ejercicios o te vas a convertir en un **nalgón**.

translation:
You need to stop watching television and start getting some exercise or you're going to turn into a **fat-ass**.

necio/a *n. & adj.* fool; foolish • (lit.): foolish.

example:
La gente que no practica el sexo con precaución es **necia**.

translation:
People who don't practice safe sex are **crazy**.

néctar *m.* semen • (lit.): nectar.

nido *m. (Mexico)* vagina • (lit.): bird's nest or hiding place.

SYNONYMS:
SEE – **vagina**, *p. 263.*

no importar un carajo *exp.* not to give a damn • (lit.): not to mind a penis.

example:
No me importa un carajo lo que dices.

translation:
I **don't give a damn** what you say.

no importar un cojón *exp.* not to give a damn • (lit.): not to care a testicle.

example:
A Beatriz **no le importan un cojón** sus clases. Por eso está reprobando todas sus clases.

translation:
Beatriz **doesn't give a damn** about her school work. That's why she's failing all of her classes.

no importar un huevo *exp.* not to give a damn • (lit.): egg (or "testicle").

example:
A Daniel no le importa un huevo su trabajo. Sinceramente, creo que lo van a echar pronto.

translation:
Daniel doesn't give a damn about his job. Frankly, I think he's going to get fired soon.

no importar un pepino *exp.* not to give a hoot • (lit.): not to care a cucumber.

example:
No me importa un pepino lo que la gente piense de mí.

translation:
I don't give a damn what people think about me.

¡No me jodas! *exp.* Don't bother me! • (lit.): Don't fuck me!

novia *f.* girlfriend • (lit.): bride, fiancée.

example:
¿Esa es tu **novia**? ¡Enhorabuena! ¡Es muy simpática y tan bonita!

translation:
That's your **girlfriend**? Congratulations! She's very nice and so beautiful!

novio *m.* boyfriend • (lit.): bridegroom, fiancé.

example:
¿Conoces a mi **novio**? Creo que nos vamos a casar algún día.

translation:
Did you meet my **boyfriend**? I think we're going to get married someday.

ñema *f. (Santo Domingo)* penis.

ALSO:
macañema *f.* cocksucker (from the verb *mascar* meaning "to chew").

SYNONYMS:
SEE – **penis**, *p. 243.*

obraderas *f.pl. (Mexico)* diarrhea (from the verb *obrar* meaning "to make a bowl movement").

example:
Si bebes agua en ese país, puedes coger **obraderas**.

translation:
If you drink the water in that country, you may get **diarrhea**.

obrar *v.* to defecate • (lit.): to perform or to build.

example:
Si tu perro **obra** en la acera, tienes que limpiarlo.

translation:
If your dog **craps** on the sidewalk, you need to clean it up.

obstáculos *m.pl. (Mexico)* testicles • (lit.): obstacles.

ojal *m.* • vagina (lit.): buttonhole, slit.

SYNONYMS:
SEE – **vagina**, *p. 263.*

ojete *m.* anal sphincter • (lit.): eyelet, eyehole.

NOTE:
In Mexico, this term is also used to describe someone who is a pain in the neck. For example: *Miguel es un ojete;* Miguel is a pain in the neck.

ojitos (hacer) *exp.* to make eyes at someone • (lit.): to make little eyes.

example:
¡Cuidado! Ricardo te está **haciendo ojitos** pero ayer lo vi en el cine con otra.

translation:
Be careful! Ricardo was **making eyes** at you but yesterday I saw him at the movies with another woman.

ojo del culo *m.* anal sphincter • (lit.): eye of the ass.

¡Olé! *interj. (Spain)* Yippee! Alright!

example:
!Olé! Vaya gol que ha metido Alvaro.

translation:
Yippee! What a goal Alvaro just scored!

NOTE:
This expression has its roots in the bullfights. It is still the traditional cheer from the audience when a bullfighter makes a good pass.

ALSO:
¡Y olé! *interj. (Spain).*

SYNONYM:
¡Caramba! *interj. (Mexico).*

NOTE:
¡Caramba! can be used to express either excitement or disappointment depending on the context.

orégano *m. (Mexico)* marijuana • (lit.): oregano.

orégano chino *m. (Mexico)* marijuana • (lit.): Chinese oregano.

orto *m. (Argentina, Uruguay)* ass • (lit.): rise of the sun.

ostentador/a *n. & adj.* show-off; showy • (lit.): one who is ostentatious.

example:
¿Has visto lo que llevaba Claudia puesto? ¡Qué **ostentadora**!

translation:
Did you see what Claudia was wearing? What a **show-off**!

pacaya *f. (El Salvador)* penis • (lit.): elongated vegetable.

SYNONYMS:
SEE – **penis**, *p. 243.*

pachanga *f.* party.

example:
Esta **pachanga** es muy divertida. Todo el mundo se lo está pasando muy bien.

translation:
This **party** is a lot of fun. Everybody is having a good time.

NOTE:
ir de pachanga *exp.* to go out and have a good time.

SYNONYM -1:
fiestón *m. (Puerto Rico)*

SYNONYM -2:
movida *f. (Spain).*

SYNONYM -3:
parranda *f.*

SYNONYM -4:
reventón *m.* • (lit.): bursting, explosion.

padrote *m.* pimp • (lit.): large father.

pagar al contado *exp.* to pay cash on the barrel • (lit.): to pay counted.

example:
Cuando como en un restaurante, siempre intento **pagar al contado** en lugar de con tarjeta de crédito.

translation:
When I eat at a restaurant, I always try to **pay cash** instead of using my credit card.

SYNONYM -1:
pagar a tocateja *exp.*

SYNONYM -2:
pagar con billetes *exp.* • (lit.): to pay with bills.

SYNONYM -3:
pagar con dinero contante y sonante *exp.* • (lit.): to pay with money that you can actually count and hear.

pagar la casa *exp.* to pay rent • (lit.): to pay the house.

example:
No tengo dinero porque ayer **pagué la casa**.

translation:
I don't have any money because yesterday I **paid my rent**.

pahuela *f.* prostitute, whore.

paja *f.* masturbation • (lit.): straw • *hacer una paja;* to jerk off.

SYNONYMS:
SEE – **masburbate**, *p. 239.*

pajarito *m.* penis • (lit.): small bird.

SYNONYMS:
SEE – **penis**, *p. 243.*

pájaro *m.* derogatory for "homosexual" • (lit.): bird.

NOTE:
The term *pájaro* literall means "bird" but is used in slang to mean "homosexual," so be careful how you use it!
For example:

Conozco a ese pájaro.

Translation in Chile, Ecuador, Peru:
I know that **guy**.

Translation in Cuba, Dominican Republic, Puerto Rico:
I know that **homosexual**.

pajero *m.* a person who masturbates.

SYNONYMS:
SEE – **masturbate**, *p. 239*.

palo *m.* penis • (lit.): pole, stick.

NOTE -1:
echar un palo *exp.* to fornicate • (lit.): to throw the stick or "penis."

NOTE -2:
The term *palo* literally means "pole" but is used in slang to mean "penis," so be careful how you use it! For example:

Le echó un palo a su perro.

Common Translation #1:
He **threw** his dog a stick.
Common Translation #2:
He **fucked** his dog.

SYNONYMS:
SEE – **penis**, *p. 243*.

pan *m. (El Salvador)* vagina • (lit.): bread.

SYNONYMS:
SEE – **vagina**, *p. 263*.

pan comido (ser) *exp.* to be easy, a cinch • (lit.): to be eaten bread.
example:
Este examen es **pan comido**.
translation:
This test is **a cinch**.

SYNONYM:
estar tirado/a *adj. (Spain)* • (lit.): to be thrown away • *Este examen está tirado;* This test is so easy.

NOTE:
In Argentina, *estar tirado/a* means "to be exhausted."

pandero *m.* buttocks • (lit.): large tambourine.

panocha *f. (Mexico)* vagina • (lit.): sweetbread.

SYNONYMS:
SEE – **vagina**, *p. 263*.

panuda *f. (El Salvador)* large vagina.

SYNONYMS:
SEE – **vagina**, *p. 263*.

panzón/ona *n. & adj.* fat slob; chubby, fat, pot-bellied (from *panga* meaning "belly").
example:
Cecila estaba tan delgada. Ahora es una **panzona**.
translation:
Cecilia used to be so thin. Now she's a **fat slob**.

panzudo al pedo *adj.* *(Argentina)* extremely fat • (lit.): paunchy to the fart.
example:
Mi tío es **panzudo al pedo**. ¡Le encanta comer!
translation:
My uncle is **fat out to here**. He loves to eat!

papasito *m. & adj.* a hot daddy; sexy • (lit.): little father.
example:
Carlos tiene muchas novias. Es un **papasito**!
translation:
Carlos has a lot of girlfriends. He's such a **hunk**!

papaya *f. (Cuba, Central America, Puerto Rico)* vagina.

NOTE -1:
The term *papayay* is used in Cuba, Puerto Rico, and the Dominican Republic to mean "vagina," so be careful how you use it! For example:

¿Te gusta la papaya?

Common Translation:
Do you like **papaya**?
Translation in Cuba / Puerto Rico / Dominican Republic
Do you like **vagina**?

NOTE -2:
In Cuba, the papaya fruit is called *fruta bomba,* or literally, "bomb fruit" (or "fruit shaped like a bomb").

SYNONYMS:
SEE – **vagina**, *p. 263*.

papayón/ona *n. & adj.* *(Cuba)* asshole, jerk; jerky • (lit.): big vagina (since *papaya* is used to mean "vagina" in Cuba).
example:
¿Has invitado tú a ese **papayón** a la fiesta?
translation:
You invited that **asshole** to your party?

papo/a *n. & adj. (El Salvador)* idiot; crazy.
example:
Jaime es un **papo** si piensa que va ser médico algún día. No es lo suficientemente listo.
translation:
Jaime is a **nut** if he thinks he's going to be a doctor someday. He's not smart enough.

para chuparse los dedos *exp.* said of something delicious • (lit.): to suck or lick one's fingers.
example:
Esta comida está **para chuparse los dedos**.
translation:
This food is **delicious**.

NOTE:
A popular Spanish advertisement talks about a famous family restaurant whose chicken is: "Finger lickin' good!"; *Está para chuparse los dedos!*

SYNONYM:
estar a toda madre *exp.* *(Mexico)* • This popular Mexican expression is used to express enthusiasm about food as well as situations • (lit.): to be like an entire mother.

paracaídas *m.* condom • (lit.): parachute.

paraguas *m.* condom • (lit.): umbrella.

pararse *v.* to get an erection • (lit.): to stand up.

pargo *m.* *(Cuba)* derogatory for "homosexual" • (lit.): red snapper.

parlanchín *m.* blabbermouth • (lit.): talkative.

example:
Juan habla sin parar. Es un **parlanchín**.

translation:
Juan talks nonstop. He's a **blabbermouth**.

SYNONYMS:
SEE – **blabbermouth**, *p. 208*.

parrocha *f.* vagina • (lit.): small pickled sardine.

SYNONYMS:
SEE – **vagina**, *p. 263*.

parte de atrás *m.* buttocks • (lit.): behind part.

parte posterior *m.* buttocks • (lit.): posterior part.

partes *f.pl.* genitals • (lit.): parts.

partes nobles *f.pl.* penis • (lit.): noble parts.

SYNONYMS:
SEE – **penis**, *p. 243*.

partirle el corazón a alguien *exp.* to break someone's heart • (lit.): to break someone's heart.

example:
Parece que Laura **le rompió el corazón a Felipe**.

translation:
It looks like Laura **broke Felipe's heart**.

pasar por alto *exp.* to overlook • (lit.): to overpass.

example:
Yo iba a **pasar por alto** algunas cosas, pero esto es demasiado.

translation:
I was going **to overlook** some things, but this is too much.

pasar por la piedra *exp.* to fornicate • (lit.): to pass by the stone.

pasar por las armas *exp.* to fornicate • (lit.): to pass by the arms.

pasarse de la raya *exp.* to go too far, to overstep one's bounds • (lit.): to cross the line.

example:
Yo creo que Jaime **se pasó de la raya** cuando intentó besar a Isabel.

translation:
I think Jaime **went a little too far** when he tried to kiss Isabel.

NOTE:
This expression is so popular among Spanish-speakers, that often *de la raya* is omitted since it is already understood by the listener. For example: *Te has pasado;* You went too far.

SYNONYM:
írsele la mano a alguien *exp.* • (lit.): to go the hand to someone.

pashpa *f. (El Salvador)* vagina.

SYNONYMS:
SEE – **vagina**, *p. 263*.

pasta *f.* money, "dough" • (lit.): pasta.

example:
Se nota que Javier tiene **pasta**. ¡Mira su coche!

translation:
You can tell Javier is loaded with **money**. Look at his house!

SYNONYMS:
SEE – **lana**, *p. 121*.

pato *m.* derogatory for "homosexual" • (lit.): duck.

pavor (tener) *exp.* to be scared.

example:
Sara **tenía pavor** de ir a la escuela el primer día.

translation:
Sara was **scared** to go to school on the first day.

SYNONYM:
temblando (estar) *adj.* • (lit.): to be trembling.

ALSO:
temblar de miedo *exp.* • (lit.): to shake with fear.

pecho *m.* chest.

VARIATION:
pechos *m.pl.*

NOTE:
pechera f. breasts • *¡Qué pechera!;* What breasts!

pechonalidad *m.* breasts, "tits."

NOTE:
This is a humorous variation of the feminine noun *personalidad* meaning "personality."

pedazo *m. (Uruguay)* penis • (lit.): piece.

SYNONYMS:
SEE – **penis**, *p. 243.*

pedazo de *adj.* great (when used before a noun) • (lit.): piece.

example:
Alberto se acaba de comprar un **pedazo** de coche.

translation:
Alberto just bought a **great** car.

ALSO:
pedazo de pan (ser un) *exp.* to be very kind or easy going • (lit.): to be a piece of bread.

SYNONYM:
pasada de *adj. (Spain)* • (lit.): a passage of.

pedazo de pelotudo *m.* *(Argentina)* jerk, idiot • (lit.): piece of someone with balls.

example:
¡Le dejé mi coche a Jaime y el **pedazo de pelotudo** lo estrelló contra una pared!

translation:
I lent my car to Jaime and that **idiot** crashed it into a wall!

pederse *v.* to fart • (lit.): to fart.

example:
¡No me puedo creer que **te pedas** en mi coche!

translation:
I can't believe **you'd fart** in my car!

pedo *m.* • **1.** fart • **2.** drunkenness • **3.** ugly.

example -1:
Ese chiste es tan gracioso como un **pedo** en un traje espacial.

translation:
That joke is as funny as a **fart** in a spacesuit.

example -2:
Manolo agarró un buen **pedo** en la fiesta.

translation:
Manolo got really **drunk** at the party.

example -3:
Ese tipo es un **pedo**.

translation:
That guy is an **ugly person**.

pedorrera *f.* many farts, a series of farts.

example:
¿Has oído esa **pedorrera**? ¡Qué asco!

translation:
Did you hear **all that farting**? That's disgusting!

pedorrero *m.* one who farts a lot, farter.

example:
Mi tío tiene problemas con el estómago. Es un **pedorrero**.

translation:
My uncle has gastric problems. He's a **farter**.

peerse *v.* to fart • (lit.): to fart

example:
Es de mala educación **peerse** en público.

translation:
It's rude **to fart** in public.

pegarse como una ladilla *exp.* to stick to someone like glue • (lit.): to stick to someone like a crab (as in pubic lice).

example:
Alberto es un pesado. Siempre **se pega como una ladilla**.

translation:
Alberto is a pain. He **sticks to me like glue**.

NOTE:
This expression is considered somewhat crude and should be used with discretion.

pelársela *v.* to masturbate • (lit.): to peel it oneself.

SYNONYMS:
SEE – **masturbate**, *p. 239*.

película equis *f.* dirty movie, X-rated movie • (lit.): an X(-rated) movie.

example:
¡No podemos llevar a los niños a ver eso...es una **película equis**!

translation:
We can't take the children to see that...it's an **X-rated movie**!

pelmazo/a *n.* idiot • (lit.): undigested food.

example:
¡Ese **pelmazo** se ha saltado un semáforo en rojo!

translation:
That **idiot** ran a red light!

pelón/ona *n. & adj.* baldy; bald.

example:
Enrique tiene solamente diez y seis años y ya está **pelón**.

translation:
Enrique is only sixteen years old and he's already **bald**.

pelona *f.* penis.

NOTE:
This is from the adjective *pelón* meaning "bald."

SYNONYMS:
SEE – **penis**, *p. 243*.

pelota *n. & adj.* • **1.** kiss-ass • **2.** idiot; stupid • (lit.): ball (or one who "licks someone's balls or testicles").

example -1:
El único motivo por el que Roberto fue ascendido, es porque es un **pelota**.

translation:
The only reason Roberto got a promotion is because he's a **kiss-ass**.

ALSO:
pelota *adj. (Colombia)* stupid.

example -2:
¡Marco es tan **pelota**! ¡Manejó en la calle en sentido contrario!

translation:
Marco is such an **idiot**! He drove down the street in the wrong direction!

pelotas *n. & adj. (Colombia)* dumbbell, idiot; stupid • (lit.): that which has with balls.

example:
¡Antonio se lavó el pelo con pasta dentrífica! ¡Qué **pelotas**!

translation:
Antonio accidentally washed his hair with toothpaste! What an **idiot**!

NOTE:
tener pelotas *exp.* to have courage • (lit.): to have balls.

pelotas michinadas *f.pl. (Central and South America, Mexico)* blue balls.

pelotudo y boludo *exp. (Argentina)* said of someone who is an extreme asshole with a great deal of nerve (or "balls") • (lit.): balled and balled.

example:
¡Armando ha intentado ligarse a mi novia! ¡Verdaderamente es un **pelotudo y un boludo**!

translation:
Armando just tried to pick up my girlfriend! He **really has nerve**!

pelotudo/a *n. & adj.* idiot; stupid.
example:
Se me ha olvidado mi cita con el médico. ¡Qué **pelotudo**!
translation:
I forgot about my doctor's appointment. What an **idiot**!

NOTE:
This is from the feminine noun *pelota* meaning "ball."

SYNONYM:
boludo *m. (Argentina).*

pendejo/a *n. & adj. (Mexico)* fucker; fucked (said of a contemptible person) • (lit.): pubic hair.
example:
¡Ese **pendejo** acaba de tirar un huevo en mi carro!
translation:
That **fucker** just threw an egg at my car!

pendejo/a de mierda *m. (Argentina, Mexico)* an insult in reference to a trouble-making little child, "piece of shit" • (lit.): pubic hair of shit.

pendona *f.* prostitute, whore • (lit.): despicable person.

pensar para sus adentros *exp.* to think to oneself • (lit.): to think by one's insides.
example:
Estaba yo **pensando para mis adentros** que sería bueno hacer un viaje a Paris este verano.
translation:
I was **thinking to myself** that it would be nice to go on a trip to Paris next summer.

pensar que a uno no le apesta su mierda *exp.* to think one's shit doesn't stink • (lit.): [same].
example:
Olivia es tan vanidosa. Ella **piensa que a ella no le apesta su mierda**.
translation:
Olivia is so conceited. She **thinks her shit doesn't stink**.

pepa *f.* vagina • (lit.): take from the female name *Pepa*.

SYNONYMS:
SEE – **vagina**, *p. 263*.

pepereche *m. (El Salvador)* prostitute, whore.

pepino *m.* penis • (lit.): cucumber.

SYNONYMS:
SEE – **penis**, *p. 243*.

pepita *f.* clitoris • (lit.): nugget.

pera (hacerse una/la) *exp.* to masturbate, to beat off • (lit.): to make oneself a pear.

SYNONYMS:
SEE – **masturbate**, *p. 239.*

perder el habla *exp.* to be speechless • (lit.): to lose one's speech.

example:
Perdí el habla cuando vi a María con ese vestido. ¡Era tan corto!

translation:
I was speechless when I saw Maria wearing that dress. It was so short!

SYNONYM:
quedarse mudo/a *exp.* • (lit.): to remain/become mute.

perder los estribos *exp.* to lose control, to lose one's head, to lose one's temper • (lit.): to lose the stirrups.

example:
Como sigas portándote así, voy a **perder los estribos**.

translation:
If you continue to behave this way, I'm going to **lose my temper**.

SYNONYM -1:
perder la calma *exp.* • (lit.): to lose one's calm.

SYNONYM -2:
perder la paciencia *exp.* • to lose one's patience.

perdida *f.* prostitute • (lit.): lost.

perico *m. (Central and South America, Mexico)* cocaine • (lit.): periwig.

periodo *m.* • (lit.): a woman's period

perra *f.* bitch • (lit.): bitch, female dog.

example:
Esa tipa es una **perra**. Siempre está de mal humor.

translation:
That girl is a **bitch**. She's always in a bad mood.

pesado/a *adj.* dull, tiresome, annoying, irritating, pain in the neck • (lit.): heavy, massive, weighty.

example:
Darío es un **pesado**. Siempre está contando historias aburridas.

translation:
Dario is such a **pain in the neck**. He's always telling boring stories.

SYNONYM -1:
cargante *adj*. • (lit.): loaded.

VARIATION:
cargoso *adj*.

SYNONYM -2:
latoso/a *adj*.

NOTE:
This comes from the expression *dar la lata,* (literally meaning "to give the tin can," is used to mean "to annoy the living daylights out of someone").

ANTONYM -1:
ameno/a *adj*. pleasant, funny • (lit.): amenable.

ANTONYM -2:
chunguero *adj*.

NOTE:
This comes from the term *chunga* meaning "joke" or "jest."

pesquesuda *f*. penis.

SYNONYMS:
SEE – **penis**, *p. 243*.

petardo (ser un) *m*. to be a bore • (lit.): to be a torpedo, firecracker.

example:
No me gusta estar con Miguel. ¡Es tan **petardo**!

translation:
I don't like spending time with Miguel. He's such a **bore**!

petiso de mierda *m*. *(Argentina)* asshole, jerk • (lit.): little shit.

example:
No voy a invitar a ese **petiso de mierda** a mi fiesta de cumpleaños.

translation:
I'm not going to invite that **little shit** to my birthday party.

pez gordo *m*. person of great importance, "big wig" • (lit.): fat fish.

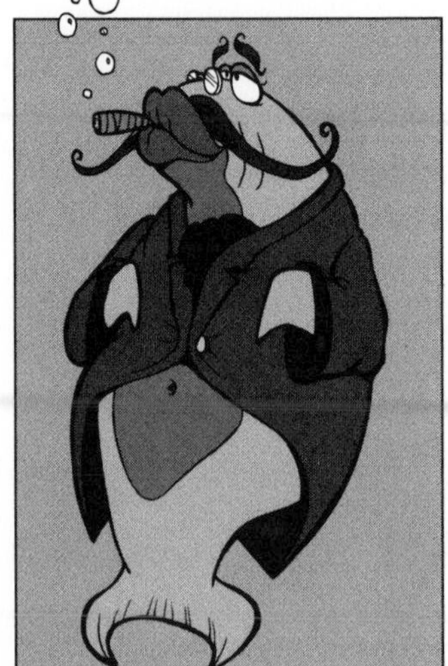

example:
Algún día yo seré el **pez gordo** de esta compañía.

translation:
Someday I'll be the **big wig** in this company.

SYNONYM:
de peso *adj.* • (lit.): of weight, weighty.
example:
Ese señor es una persona **de peso**.
translation:
That man's a **big wig**.

pezón *m.* nipple • (lit.): [same].

picha *(Cuba)* penis.

NOTE -1:
pichada *f.* fornication, screwing • (lit.): urination.

NOTE -2:
pichar *v.* to fornicate, to screw • (lit.): to urinate.

SYNONYMS:
SEE – **penis**, *p. 243*.

pichicato/a *n. & adj.* tightwad; stingy • (lit.): an injection of medicine.
example:
¿Quieres que andemos diez millas? No seas **pichicato**. Vamos a coger un taxi.
translation:
You want us to walk ten miles? Don't be such a **cheapskate**. Let's just get a taxi.

pichicuaca *f. (El Salvador)* penis.

SYNONYMS:
SEE – **penis**, *p. 243*.

pichón *m.* penis • (lit.): squab.

SYNONYMS:
SEE – **penis**, *p. 243*.

NOTE:
The term *pichón* is also used to refer to someone who is very young. For example: *Mario tiene sólo 20 años. Es un pichón;* Mario is only 20 years old. He's a baby.

pichula *f. (Chile)* penis.

NOTE:
This is from the verb *pichulear* meaning "to deceive."

SYNONYMS:
SEE – **penis**, *p. 243*.

pico *m. (Chile)* penis • (lit.): peak.

NOTE -1:
In some parts of South America, *y pico* is used to mean "approximately": *Te veo a las siete y pico;* I'll see you around seven o'clock.

NOTE -2:
The term *pico* literally means "peak" but is used in slang to mean "penis," so be careful how you use it! For example:

¡Qué vista tan bella desde este pico!

Common Translation #1:
What a beautiful view from this **peak**!

Common Translation #2:
What a beautiful view from this **penis**!

SYNONYMS:
SEE – **penis**, *p. 243*.

pijo/a • **1.** *n.* penis *(pija)* • **2.** *adj.* snobby • *¡Qué mujer más pija!;* What a snobby woman! • **3.** *n.* stupid person.

pila *f.* a bunch of, a lot of, a pile of • (lit.): sink, basin.

example:
Estoy muy ocupado. Tengo una **pila** de cosas que hacer.

translation:
I'm very busy. I have **a bunch of** things to do.

SYNONYM:
montón *m.* • (lit.): crowd.

pimiento *m.* penis • (lit.): pimento, pepper.

SYNONYMS:
SEE – **penis**, *p. 243.*

pincharse una llanta *exp.* to get a flat tire • (lit.): to puncture a tire.

example:
Ayer llegué tarde a la escuela porque se me **pinchó una llanta**.

translation:
Yesterday I arrived late to school because I **got a flat tire**.

NOTE:
There are many different synonyms for "tire" depending on the country:

SYNONYM -1:
caucho *m. (Venezuela).*

SYNONYM -2:
cubierta *f. (Argentina, Uruguay).*

SYNONYM -3:
goma *f. (Argentina, Uruguay).*

SYNONYM -4:
llanta *f. (Latin America).*

SYNONYM -5:
neumático *m. (Spain).*

SYNONYM -6:
rueda *f. (Spain).*

pinche *n. & adj.* tightwad; stingy, cheap • (lit.): scullion, kitchen boy.

example:
Diego es un **pinche**. ¡No me invitó ni a un café el día de mi cumpleaños!

translation:
Diego is so **cheap**. He didn't even offer to buy me a cup of coffee for my birthday!

pinchón *m.* sexy girl, hot chick (from the verb *pinchar* meaning "to tease") • (lit.): small bird.

example:
Todos los chavos en la escuela piensan que mi hermana es todo un **pinchón**.

translation:
All the guys in school think my sister is a real **hot chick**.

NOTE:
The masculine noun *chavo* (used in the example above) is a very popular term in Mexico meaning "guy."

pinco *m. (Puerto Rico)* penis • (lit.): penis.

SYNONYMS:
SEE – **penis**, *p. 243*.

pinga *(Cuba, Puerto Rico)* penis • (lit.): shoulder yoke (used for carrying).

SYNONYMS:
SEE – **penis**, *p. 243*.

pingo *m.* prostitute, whore.

pingona *f.* prostitute, whore.

pipa *f.* • **1.** drunkard • **2.** clitoris • (lit.): pipe (for smoking tobacco).

example:
¡Qué lástima! Acabo de descubrir que la madre de Emilio es una **pipa**.

translation:
What a shame! I just found out that Emilio's mother is a **drunkard**.

pipí *m. (child's language)* urine, peepee.

example:
¿Has **hecho pipí** antes de irte a la cama?

translation:
Did you **go peepee** before going to bed?

NOTE:
hacer pipí *exp.* to go peepee.

pipilla *f.* clitoris.

pipote *m. (Southern Spain)* clitoris • (lit.): big sunflower seed.

piropo *m.* compliment.

example:
A Ana siempre le echan muchos **piropos** porque es una mujer muy bella.

translation:
Ana always receives many **compliments** because she's a very beautiful woman.

NOTE:
echar un piropo *exp.* to give a compliment.

piruja *n. & adj.* easy lay; easy • (lit.): vulgar for "slut."

example:
Elvia es una **piruja**. Duerme con todo el mundo.

translation:
Elvia is a **slut**. She has sex with everyone.

pirujo *m.* derogatory for "homosexual" • (lit.): variation of the feminine noun *piruja* meaning "an uninhibited young woman."

pirul *m.* derogatory for "homosexual."

pirulí *m.* penis.

SYNONYMS:
SEE – **penis**, *p. 243*.

pisar a *v.* to fornicate • (lit.): to step on (someone).

pisto/a *adj.* drunk, bombed • (lit.): chicken broth.

example:
Si me tomo media copa de vino, estoy **pista**.

translation:
If I drink half a glass of wine, I get **bombed**.

pistola *f.* penis • (lit.): pistol.

SYNONYMS:
SEE – **penis**, *p. 243*.

pitaya *f.* vagina • (lit.): tropical cactus with an edible fruit.

SYNONYMS:
SEE – **vagina**, *p. 263*.

pitillo *m.* cigarette • (lit.): small whistle.

example:
Pedro tiene mal aliento porque siempre tiene un **pitillo** en la boca.

translation:
Pedro has bad breath because he always has a **cigarette** hanging from his mouth.

SYNONYM -1:
faso *m. (Argentina).*

SYNONYM -2:
pucho *m. (Argentina)* • (lit.): cigarette butt.

pito *m. (Argentina, Spain, Uruguay)* penis • (lit.): horn, whistle.

NOTE:
The term *pito* means literally means "horn" or "whistle" but is used in slang to mean "penis." So be careful how you use it! For example:

¿Soplaste ese pito?

Common Translation #1:
Did you blow that **whistle**?

Common Translation #2:
Did you blow that **penis**?

SYNONYMS:
SEE – **penis**, *p. 243*.

pitón *m. (Puerto Rico)* vagina • (lit.): budding horn.

SYNONYMS:
SEE – **vagina**, *p. 263*.

pitones *m.pl.* breasts, "tits" • (lit.): budding horns (of a bull, deer, goat, etc.).

pizarrín *m.* penis • (lit.): slate pencil.

SYNONYMS:
SEE – **penis**, *p. 243*.

plantar a alguien *exp.* to dump someone • (lit.): to throw someone out.

example:
¿Has oido la noticia? Verónica **dejó plantado** a Pedro porque ¡lo pescó con otra mujer!

translation:
Did you hear the news? Veronica **dumped Pedro** because she caught him with another woman!

plata *f.* money • (lit.): silver.

example:
En los Estados Unidos los jugadores de baloncesto ganan mucha **plata**.

translation:
In the United States, basketball players make a lot of **money**.

SYNONYMS:
SEE – **lana**, *p. 121.*

ALSO:
podrido/a de dinero (estar) *exp.* to be rich • to be rolling in money • (lit.): to be rotten in money.

NOTE:
Any synonym for *dinero* may be substituted.

plátano *m.* penis • (lit.): banana.

SYNONYMS:
SEE – **penis**, *p. 243.*

platicar *v. (Mexico)* to have a little chat, to talk.

example:
Me encanta **platicar** con Darío. ¡Es tan inteligente y simpático!

translation:
I love to **talk** with Darío. He's so smart and nice!

SYNONYM -1:
charlar *v. (Argentina, Cuba, Spain, Uruguay).*

SYNONYM -2:
dar la lata *exp. (Cuba, Puerto Rico).*

plomo/a *n. (Argentina)* annoying (said of a person) • (lit.): lead.

example:
Un amigo mío se queda en mi casa una semana más. Al principio no me molestaba, pero se está convirtiendo en un **plomo**.

translation:
A friend of mine is staying at my house for another week. I didn't mind at first, but he's becoming more and more a **pain in the ass**!

pluma *f.* prostitute • (lit.): feather.

plumero *m. (Puerto Rico)* derogatory for "homosexual" • (lit.): feather duster.

poco a poco *exp.* little by little • (lit.): little to little.

example:
Poco a poco terminé todo el proyecto.

translation:
Little by little I finished the whole project.

poderoso caballero es Don Dinero *exp.* money talks • (lit.): Mr. money is a powerful gentleman.

example:
Me dieron la mejor mesa del restaurante. **Poderoso caballero es Don Dinero**.

translation:
They gave me the best table in the restaurant. **Money makes the world go 'round**.

poli *f.* a popular abbreviation for *policía* meaning "police," or "cops."

example:
¡Corre que viene la **poli**!

translation:
Run! The **cops** are coming!

SYNONYM -1:
cana *f. (Argentina)*.

SYNONYM -2:
chota *f.*

polla *f. (Spain)* penis • (lit.): young hen.

NOTE:
The term *polla* literally means "young hen" but is used in slang to mean "penis," so careful how you use it! For example:

Mi hermana cría pollas.

Common Translation #1:
My sister raises **young hens**.

Common Translation #2:
My sister raises **penises**.

SYNONYMS:
SEE – **penis**, *p. 243*.

polvo (echar un) *exp.* to fornicate • (lit.): to throw a powder.

pompi(s) *m.pl. (children's language)* buttocks.

poner a alguien como un trapo *exp.* to rake someone over the coals, to read someone the riot act • (lit.): to put someone like a rag.

example:
Juan **puso al mesero como un trapo** porque no le trajo la comida a tiempo.

translation:
Juan **raked the waiter over the coals** because he didn't bring him his meal on time.

poner al corriente *exp.* to bring up-to-date, to inform, to give the lowdown • (lit.): to put in the current or in the flow of knowledge.

example:
Te voy a **poner al corriente** de lo que sucedió ayer en la oficina.

translation:
I'm going to **bring you up-to-date** about what happened yesterday at the office.

SYNONYM:
poner al día *exp.* • (lit.): to put to the day.

poner al día *exp.* to bring up-to-date, to inform, to give the lowdown • (lit.): to put to the day.

example:
Pedro, ¡te voy a **poner al día**! Han pasado muchas cosas desde que te fuiste de vacaciones.

translation:
Pedro, I'm going **to bring you up to date**! A lot of things happened while you were on vacation.

SYNONYM:
poner al tanto *exp.* • (lit.): to put one at the point (in a score).

poner el grito al cielo *exp.* to raise the roof, to scream with rage, to hit the ceiling • (lit.): to put a scream to the sky.

example:
Lynda **puso el grito al cielo** cuando vio que la casa estaba muy sucia.

translation:
Lynda **hit the ceiling** when she found out that the house was a mess.

VARIATION:
poner en el grito al cielo *exp.* • (lit.): to make a scandal.

SYNONYM -1:
formar/armar un follón *exp. (Spain).* • (lit.): to make a scandal.

SYNONYM -2:
hacer/formar un escándalo *exp.* • (lit.): to make a scandal.

poner en ridículo *exp.* to make a fool out of someone • (lit.): to put [someone] in ridiculous.

example:
Jorge está **poniendo en ridículo** a su jefe a propósito.

translation:
Jorge is **making a fool out of** his boss on purpose.

poner las cartas sobre la mesa *exp.* to to put one's cards on the table • (lit.): to put the cards on the table.

example:
Si vas a hablar conmigo, **pon las cartas sobre la mesa**.

translation:
If you're going to talk to me, **put all your cards on the table**.

poner[se] colorado/a *exp.* to blush, to turn red • (lit.): to put oneself (to become) red.

example:
Si sigues hablando así me voy a **poner rojo**.

translation:
If you continue to talk like that, I'm going **to turn red**.

VARIATION:
poner[se] rojo/a *exp.* • (lit.): to put oneself (to become) red.

SYNONYM:
acholar[se] *v. (Ecuador, Peru)* • (lit.): to shame (oneself).

SYNONYM -2:
ruborizar[se] *v. (Latin America)* • (lit.): to make oneself blush.

ponerse a flote *exp.* to get back up on one's own two feet again • (lit.): to put oneself afloat.

example:
Después de comenzar su nuevo trabajo, Juan **se puso a flote** otra vez.

translation:
After starting his new job, Juan is **back on his feet**.

SYNONYM:
levantar la cabeza *exp.* • (lit.): to lift the head.

NOTE:
This could be best compared to the American expression, "to hold up one's head" or "to pull oneself back up."

ponerse los pelos de punta *exp.* to have one's hair stand on end • (lit.): to put one's hairs on end.

example:
Se me pusieron los pelos de punta cuando vi al elefante escaparse del zoológico.

translation:
My hair stood on end when I saw the elephant escaping from the zoo.

ponerse duro *exp.* to get an erection • (lit.): to put oneself hard.

popa *f.* buttocks • (lit.): stern (in a ship), poop-deck.

popeta *f. (Puerto Rico)* penis.

SYNONYMS:
SEE – **penis**, *p. 243*.

por fortuna *exp.* fortunately • (lit.): by fortune.

example:
Hoy hubo una gran explosión en la fábrica pero **por fortuna** no hubo heridos.

translation:
There was a big explosion at the factory today but **fortunately** no one was hurt.

por las buenas o por las malas *exp.* whether one likes it or not, one way or another • (lit.): by the goods or by the bads.

example:
Por las buenas o por las malas vas a hacer lo que te digo.

translation:
One way or another you are going to do what I say.

VARIATION:
a las buenas o a las malas *exp.* • (lit.): to the good ones or to the bad ones.

SYNONYM:
de una manera u otra *exp.* • (lit.): one way or another.

por las nubes (estar) *exp.* astronomical, sky high • (lit.): to be by the clouds.

example:
Los precios de esta tienda están **por las nubes**.

translation:
Prices at this store are **astronomical**.

por lo general *exp.* as a general rule, usually • (lit.): generally.

example:
Por lo general no me gusta comer mucha carne roja.

translation:
As a general rule, I don't like to eat too much red meat.

SYNONYM -1:
por lo común *exp.* • (lit.): by the common.

SYNONYM -2:
por lo regular *exp.* • (lit.): by the regular.

por ningún motivo *exp.* under no circumstances • (lit.): by no motive.

example:
Por ningún motivo me hables en ese tono de voz.

translation:
Under no circumstances are you to talk to me using that tone of voice.

SYNONYM:
bajo ningún motivo *exp.* • (lit.): under no motive.

por si acaso *exp.* just in case • (lit.): by if case.

example:
Voy a llevar mi abrigo **por si acaso** hace frío más tarde.

translation:
I'm going to bring my coat with me **just in case** it gets cold later.

porra *f.* penis • (lit.): club, bludgeon.

SYNONYMS:
SEE – **penis**, *p. 243*.

posaderas *f.* buttocks • (lit.): innkeeper.

presa fácil (ser una) *f.* to be an easy lay • (lit.): to be an easy grab.

example:
Estoy seguro de que Inés se acostará contigo; oído decir que es una **presa fácil**.
translation:
I'm sure Inés will have sex with you. She's known as **an easy lay**.

prieta *f.* penis • (lit.): the swarthy one.

SYNONYMS:
SEE – **penis**, *p. 243*.

probar fortuna *exp.* to try one's luck • (lit.): to try fortune.
example:
Cuando voy a Las Vegas me gusta **probar fortuna** en el casino.
translation:
When I go to Las Vegas I enjoy **trying my luck** in the casino.

prostíbulo *m.* whorehouse (from the masculine noun *prostituto* meaning "prostitute").

puñeta (hacer) *exp.* to masturbate, to beat off • (lit.): to make a cuff.

SYNONYMS:
SEE – **masturbate**, *p. 239*.

pupusa *f.* *(El Salvador)* vagina • (lit.): a tortilla filled with cheese.

SYNONYMS:
SEE – **vagina**, *p. 263*.

purgación *f.* menstruation, period • (lit.): purging.

puta *f.* prostitute, whore.

ALSO -1:
de puta madre *exp.* • **1.** said of something excellent • *¡Esa casa es de puta madre!;* That house is excellent! • **2.** to be in excellent shape • *Esa tipa está de puta madre;* That girl is in great shape.

ALSO -2:
ir de putas *exp.* to walk the streets.

ALSO -3:
putada *f.* annoyance, pain in the neck.

NOTE:
The term *puto/a* is commonly used in place of the adjectives *jodido/a* and *chingado/a* both meaning "fucking":
ese jodido/chingado/puto examen; that fucking test.

puta la madre, puta la hija *exp.* like mother, like daughter • (lit.): the mother's a whore, [so] the daughter's a whore.
example:
Angela tiene sexo con un tipo diferente cada noche exactamente como su madre. **Puta la madre, puta la hija**.
translation:
Angela has sex with a different guy every night just like her mother. **Like mother, like daughter**.

puta madre *f. (Mexico)* motherfucker • (lit.): mother.

example:
¡Esa **puta madre** me acaba de dar una patada!

translation:
That **motherfucker** just kicked me!

NOTE:
In Spanish, to talk about someone's mother disparagingly is a prelude to a fight.

ALSO:
me vale madre *exp.* I don't give a fuck • (lit.): it's worth a mother to me.

puta/o de mierda *f.* *(Argentina)* unclean whore • (lit.): whore of shit.

puto *m. & adj.* derogatory for "homosexual" • (lit.): male/female prostitute.

example:
Benito es un **puto**. Le gusta los hombres.

translation:
Benito is a **homosexual**. He likes men.

NOTE:
puta *f. & adj.* prostitute, slut.

putonero/a *n. & adj.* from the feminine noun *puta* meaning "whore" • (lit.): one who likes whores.

example:
Ese tío es un **putonero**, siempre anda con mujerzuelas.

translation:
That guy's a real **whore-hound**. He is always hanging out with easy women.

putonga *f.* prostitute • (lit.): large prostitute, whore.

¡Qué cagada! *interj.* *(Argentina)* Darn! What bad luck! • (lit.): What shit!

example:
¡Me enteré que te robaron el carro! ¡Qué **cagada**!

translation:
I heard that your car was stolen! What **bad luck**!

¡Qué coño! *exp. (Cuba)* What the hell!

MEXICO:
¡Qué carajo! *exp.*

¿Qué coño es esto? *exp.* What the hell is this?

MEXICO:
¿Qué carajo es esto? *exp.*

¿Qué coño quieres? *exp.* What the hell do you want?

MEXICO:
¿Qué carajo quieres? *exp.*

¿Qué hay de nuevo? *exp.* What's new? • (lit.): [same].

example:
¿**Qué hay de nuevo** Sergio? ¡Hace tiempo que no te veo!

translation:
What's new, Sergio? It's been a long time!

NOTE:
de nuevo *adv.* again.

example:
Lo hizo **de nuevo**.

translation:
He/She did it **again**.

SYNONYM -1:
¿Qué haces, papá? *exp.* *(Argentina)* What are you up to, pal? • (lit.): What are you doing, pops?

SYNONYM -2:
¿Qué hubo? *exp. (Cuba)*• (lit.): What was? / What had?

SYNONYM -3:
¿Qué onda? *exp.* • *(Mexico)* (lit.): What wave?

¿Qué mosca te ha picado? *exp.* What's bugging you? • (lit.): What fly has bitten you?

example:
No sé **qué mosca te ha picado** pero no me gusta cuando estás de mal humor.

translation:
I don't know **what's eating you**, but I don't like it when you are in such a bad mood.

SYNONYM:
¿Qué bicho te ha picado? *exp.* • (lit.): What bug has bitten you?

¡Qué te jodas! *interj.* Fuck off! • (lit.): May you fuck yourself!

¡Qué te la mame tu madre! *interj.* Go to hell! • (lit.): May your mother suck it for you!

¡Qué va! *exclam.* Baloney! No way! Get out of here! • (lit.): What goes!

example:
– ¿Tú crees que va a llover hoy?
– **!Qué va!** ¿No ves que hace sol?

translation:
– Do you think it's going to rain today?
– **No way**! Don't you see the sun is out?

NOTE:
This exclamation is not used in Argentina or Uruguay.

SYNONYM -1:
¡Qué bobada! *exclam.* What nonsense!

SYNONYM -2:
¡Qué disparate! *exclam.* What baloney!

SYNONYM -3:
¡Qué tontería! *exclam.* What stupidity!

quebracho *m. (Mexico)* derogatory for "homosexual" • (lit.): quebracho bark.

quebrachón *m. (Mexico)* derogatory for "homosexual" • (lit.): large piece of quebracho bark.

quedar de encargo *exp.* *(Mexico)* to make pregnant, to "knock up" • (lit.): made to order.

quedarse mudo/a *exp.* to be speechless, not to be able to respond, to be flabbergasted • (lit.): to remain mute.

example:
Antonio **se quedó mudo** cuando vio a Luisa con ese vestido anaranjado.

translation:
Antonio **was flabbergasted** when he saw Luisa wearing that orange dress.

SYNONYM -1:
dejar sin habla *exp.* • (lit.): to leave [someone] without speech.

SYNONYM -2:
perder el habla *exp.* • (lit.): to lose the speech.

¿Quién coño viene? *exp.* Who the hell is coming?

MEXICO:
¿Quién carajo viene? *exp.*

quilombo *n. (Argentina, Uruguay)* whorehouse.

NOTE:
This term is commonly used in Argentina and Uruguay as an interjection: *Qué quilombo!;* What a mess!

quinto coño (estar en el) *exp.* to be somewhere very far • (lit.): to be in the fifth vagina.

example:
¿Tu vas a manejar a la casa de Francisco? ¡Es tan lejos! ¡Está **en el quinto coño**!

translation:
You're going to drive to Francisco house? It's so far! It's **in the middle of nowhere**!

NOTE:
The masculine term *coño* is an extremely vulgar slang term for "vagina."

quitarle al mondongo un peso de encima *exp.* *(Mexico)* to defecate • (lit.): to empty out the intestines.
example:
He desayunado tanto que tengo que **quitarle al mondongo un peso de encima**.
translation:
I ate so much breakfast that I think I need **to take a dump**.

quitarse años *exp.* to lie about one's age • (lit.): to take off years.
example:
Teresa siempre **se quita años**.
translation:
Teresa always **lies about her age**.

rabo *m.* penis • (lit.): tail.

SYNONYMS:
SEE – **penis**, *p. 243*.

rabo del ojo (mirar/ver por el) *exp.* to look/to see out of the corner of the eye • (lit.): to look/to see by the tail of the eye.
example:
Miré por el rabo del ojo y vi que todo el mundo se estaba fijando en mí.
translation:
I looked out of the corner of my eye and I saw that everybody was staring at me.

SYNONYM:
mirar/ver de reojo *exp.* • (lit.): to look suspiciously at.

raja *f.* vagina • (lit.): gash.

SYNONYMS:
SEE – **vagina**, *p. 263*.

rajada *f.* vagina • (lit.): gash.

SYNONYMS:
SEE – **vagina**, *p. 263*.

rajita *f.* vagina • (lit.): little slit.

SYNONYMS:
SEE – **vagina**, *p. 263*.

ramera *f.* prostitute • (lit.): prostitute, whore.

raro/a *adj.* weird, strange, peculiar • (lit.): rare.
example:
Los Gonzalez son muy **raros**. Nunca salen de su casa.

translation:
The Gonzalezs are very **weird**. They never leave their house.

ALSO:
rara vez *exp*. seldom • (lit.): rare time.

rascarse el bolsillo *exp*. to cough up money • (lit.): to scratch one's pocket.
example:
Estoy cansado de **rascarme el bolsillo** para pagar la casa cada mes. A lo mejor es hora de que compre una casa.
translation:
I'm tired of **coughing up money** every month on rent. Maybe it's time for me to buy a house.

NOTE:
In Mexico, it is common to hear *pagar la* ***renta*** which is borrowed from English.

rayado/a *n. & adj*. idiot; stupid *(Argentina)* • (lit.): striped one.
example:
Laura no sabe cómo encender su computadora. Es una **rayada**.
translation:
Laura can't figure out how to turn on her computer. She's **stupid**.

reata *f. (Mexico)* penis • (lit.): rope.

SYNONYMS:
SEE – **penis**, *p. 243*.

rechulo/a *adj*. very "cool," neat.
example:
Este libro está **rechulo**.
translation:
This book is really **cool**.

NOTE:
In Spanish, it is very popular to attach the prefix "*re*" to the beginning of certain adjectives for greater emphasis.
For example:
bonito = beautiful...
rebonito = really beautiful;
fuerte = strong...
refuerte = really strong, etc.

SYNONYM -1:
chévere *adj. (Puerto Rico)*.

SYNONYM -2:
¡Qué grande! *interj. (Argentina)*.

SYNONYM -3:
¡Qué guay! *interj. (Spain)*.

regalito *m*. a lousy present or gift (usually used sarcastically) • (lit.): small gift.
example:
¡Vaya **regalito**! ¡Mi papá me dio un dólar de regalo para mi cumpleaños!
translation:
What a **great gift**! My dad gave me one dollar for my birthday!

regarse *v*. to ejaculate, to have an orgasm • (lit.): to wet oneself.

regatear *v. (a popular soccer term)* to hoard • (lit.): to bargain.

example:
Los otros jugadores odian a Maradona porque le gusta **regatear** mucho.

translation:
The other players can't stand Maradona because he likes to **hoard** the ball a lot.

NOTE:
This refers to the act of hoarding the ball in a soccer game.

SYNONYM:
chupar *v.* • (lit.): to suck.

regir *v. (Mexico)* to defecate • (lit.): to rule.

example:
Creo que el niño se ha **regido** otra vez en los pantalones.

translation:
I think the baby **pooped** in his pants again.

regla *f.* woman's period • (lit.): ruler.

remolino del pellejo *exp. (Mexico)* anus • (lit.): the whirlpool of the skin.

renacuajo/a *n.* little kid, small child, shrimp, little runt • (lit.): tadpole.

example:
En la casa de Manuel siempre hay un montón de **renacuajos**.

translation:
There are always a lot of **small kids** at Manuel's house.

SYNONYM -1:
chiquillo/a *n.*

NOTE:
This noun comes from the adjective *chico/a* meaning "small."

SYNONYM -2:
chiquitín/a *n.*

NOTE:
This noun comes from the adjective *chico/a* meaning "small."

SYNONYM -3:
crío/a *m.* • (lit.): a nursing-baby.

SYNONYM -4:
escuincle *m.* little kid, small child.

SYNONYM -5:
gurrumino/a *n.* • (lit.): weak or sickly person, "whimp."

SYNONYM -6:
mocoso/a *n.* • (lit.): snot-nosed person.

SYNONYM -7:
párvulo *m.* • (lit.): tot.

SYNONYM -8:
pequeñajo/a *n.*

NOTE:
This noun comes from the adjective *pequeño/a* meaning "small."

SYNONYM -9:
pituso/a *n.* smurf (from the cartoon characters).

ANTONYM -1:
grandote *m.*

NOTE:
This noun comes from the adjective *grande* meaning "big."

ANTONYM -2:
grandulón/a *n.* big kid.

NOTE:
This noun comes from the adjective *grande* meaning "big."

repisas *f.pl. (Mexico)* breasts, "tits" • (lit.): shelves.

resbalón *m. (Mexico, Guatemala)* whorehouse, brothel.

example:
Siempre hay tantas mujeres en la casa de Laura. A veces me pregunto si ella es la dueña de un **resbalón**.

translation:
There are always lots of women at Laura's house. Sometimes I wonder if she's running a **whorehouse**.

retazo macizo *m. (Mexico)* penis • (lit.): stiff piece.

SYNONYMS:
SEE – **penis**, *p. 243*.

retozona • **1.** *f. (Mexico)* prostitute • **2.** *adj.* frisky.

reventar *v.* • **1.** to annoy, to bug • **2.** to tire someone out • (lit.): to burst.

example (1):
Me **revienta** cuando llegas tarde.

translation:
It **bugs** me when you're late.

example (2):
¡Ernesto come tanto que un día de estos ¡va a **reventar**!

translation:
Pedro eats so much that one of these days he's going to **explode**!

SYNONYM:
matar *v. (Spain)* • (lit.): to kill.

reventón *m.* party • (lit.): bursting, explosion.

example:
Esta noche vamos a ir a un **reventón**.

translation:
Tonight we are going to a **party**.

SYNONYMS:
SEE – **pachanga**, *p. 149*.

revisar los interiores *exp. (Mexico)* to have sex • (lit.): to check on one's insides.

revista equis *f.* dirty magazine • (lit.): an X(-rated) magazine.

example:
¡Encontré una **revista equis** en el cuarto de mi hermano pequeño! Dónde la habrá conseguido?
translation:
I found a **dirty magazine** in my little brother's bedroom! Where'd he get it?

riata *f. (Mexico)* penis.

SYNONYMS:
SEE – **penis**, *p. 243*.

rifle *m. (Mexico)* penis • (lit.): rifle.

NOTE:
This term is borrowed from English.

SYNONYMS:
SEE – **penis**, *p. 243*.

robot *m.* deadhead, person who doesn't show his/her feelings, apathetic person • (lit.): robot.

example:
Julio parece un **robot**. Nunca se ríe.
translation:
Julio look like a **deadhead**. He never laughs.

rodillo *m.* penis • (lit.): rolling pin.

rollo *m.* • **1.** ordeal • **2.** long boring speech or conversation • **3.** boring person or thing • **4.** *(Spain)* movie, story • (lit.): roll, paper roll.

example (1):
¡Qué **rollo**! ¡Ahora se me descompuso mi carro!
translation:
What an **ordeal**! Now my car broke down!

example (2):
El discurso de Augusto es tan **rollo** que me estoy quedando dormido.
translation:
Augusto's speech is so **boring** I'm falling asleep.

example (3):
Ese tipo es un **rollo**. Me estoy quedando dormido al escucharlo hablar.
translation:
That guy is so **boring**. I'm falling asleep just by listening to him talk.

example (4):
Esta noche hay un buen **rollo** en la televisión.
translation:
There's a good **movie** on television tonight.

ALSO -1:
meter un rollo *exp.* to lie, to tell a lie • (lit.): to introduce a roll.

ALSO -2:
¡Qué rollo! *interj.* How boring!

ALSO -3:
soltar el rollo *exp.* to talk a lot • (lit.): to set free or let go a roll.

romper *v. (Mexico)* to deflower a girl • (lit.): to tear, to break down.

VARIATION:
romper el tambor *exp.* • (lit.): to bust open the screen.

romper a *v.* to burst out, to do something suddenly.

example:
Agustín **rompió a** reír cuando se enteró que ganó la lotería.

translation:
Agustin **burst out** laughing when he found out he won the lottery.

SYNONYM -1:
echarse a *v.* • (lit.): to throw oneself to • *echarse a llorar / reír;* to burst out crying / laughing.

SYNONYM -2:
largar *v. (Argentina)* • (lit.): to release.

SYNONYM -3:
ponerse a *v.* • (lit.): to put.

romper el hielo *exp.* to break the ice • (lit.): to break the ice.

example:
Hice una broma para **romper el hielo**.

translation:
I told a joke **to break the ice**.

romperle la crisma a alguien *exp.* to ring someone's neck. • (lit.): to break someone's chrism.

example:
Como no te portes bien, **te voy a romper la crisma**.

translation:
If you don't behave well, I'm **going to ring your neck**.

SYNONYM -1:
romperle el alma a alguien *exp.* • (lit.): to break someone's soul.

SYNONYM -2:
romperle el bautismo a alguien *exp.* • (lit.): to break one's baptism.

SYNONYM -3:
romperle la cara a alguien *exp.* to smash someone's face • (lit.): [same].

SYNONYM -4:
romperle la nariz [a alguien] *exp.* • (lit.): to break someone's nose.

rosco *m.* vagina • (lit.): ring-shaped roll of pastry.

SYNONYMS:
SEE – **vagina**, *p. 263*.

rul *m. (Mexico)* anus.

rulacho *m. (Mexico)* anus.

rule *m. (Mexico)* prostitute.

ruletera *f. (Mexico)* prostitute.

sacar de quicio a alguien *exp.* to drive someone crazy • (lit.): to bring someone to his/her threshold (of tolerance).

example:
¡Los nuevos vecinos hacen tanto ruido! ¡**Me sacan de quicio**!

translation:
The new neighbors are making so much noise! **They're driving me crazy**!

sacatón/ona *n. & adj.* scaredy-cat; scared • (lit.): from the verb *sacar* meaning "to pull away quickly."

example:
Simón no sale por la noche. Es un **sacatón**.

translation:
Simón won't go outside at night. He's a **scaredy-cat**.

sacudírsela *v.* to masturbate • (lit.): to shake it oneself.

SYNONYMS:
SEE – **masturbate**, *p. 239*.

safado/a *n. & adj.* idiot, fool; foolish • (lit.): brazen, bold.

example:
Mi nuevo jefe habla solo todo el tiempo. ¡Está **safado**!

translation:
My new boss keeps talking to himself all the time. He's a **real idiot**!

salame *m. (Argentina)* penis • (lit.): salami.

SYNONYMS:
SEE – **penis**, *p. 243*.

salchicha *f.* penis • (lit.): sausage.

SYNONYMS:
SEE – **penis**, *p. 243*.

salido/a *adj.* horny.

NOTE:
This is a variation of the verb *salir* meaning "to leave."

salir con alguien *exp.* to date someone • (lit.): to go out with someone.

example:
Voy a **salir con** Silvia mañana por la noche. ¿Puedes recomendarme un buen restaurante?

translation:
I'm **going out with** Silvia tomorrow night. Can you suggest a good restaurant?

saltar a la vista *exp.* to be obvious • (lit.): to jump to the sight.

example:
Salta a la vista que Pepe hace ejercicio diariamente.

translation:
It's obvious that Pepe exercises daily.

SYNONYM:
saltar a los ojos *exp.* • (lit.): to jump to the eyes.

seguidillas *f.pl. (Mexico)* diarrhea, "the runs" • (lit.): flamenco song and dance

example:
Me duele el estómago. Creo que voy a tener **seguidillas**.

translation:
My stomach hurts. I think I'm going to have **the runs**.

señorita de compañía *f.* prostitute • (lit.): call-girl.

ser más puta que las gallinas *exp. (Cuba)* (said of a woman) to be as horny as a toad • (lit.): to be as slutty as the hens.

example:
Josefa se muere por los hombres. Esta tipa **es más puta que las gallinas**.

translation:
Josefa is always running after men. That guy **is horny as a toad**.

seta *f.* vagina • (lit.): mushroom.

SYNONYMS:
SEE – **vagina**, *p. 263*.

sexo tribal *m.* gang bang • (lit.): tribal sex.

NOTE:
This act is consensual and therefore not considered rape as is *violación en grupo*.

SIDA *m.* AIDS • (lit.): Sindrome Inmunodeficiencia Adquirida.

sin falta *exp.* without fail • (lit.): without fail.

example:
Mañana voy a comprarme un abrigo nuevo **sin falta**.

translation:
Tomorrow I'm going to buy myself a new coat **without fail**.

sin faltar una coma *exp.* down to the last detail • (lit.): without missing a comma.

example:
Te voy a contar lo que pasó **sin faltar una coma**.

translation:
I'm going to tell you what happened **down to the last detail**.

SYNONYM:
con puntos y comas *exp.* • (lit.): with periods and commas.

singar *v. (Cuba)* to fornicate • (lit.): to pole or propel with an oar.

sobarse la picha *exp. (Costa Rica)* to masturbate • (lit.): to fondle the penis oneself.

VARIATION:
sobársela *v.*

SYNONYMS:
SEE – **masturbate**, *p. 239*.

sobre gustos no hay nada escrito *exp.* to each his own [taste] • (lit.): on tastes, there is nothing written (when it come to tastes, there are no rules).

example:
¡Mira qué zapatos lleva Adolfo! **Sobre gustos no hay nada escrito**.

translation:
Look at the shoes Adolfo is wearing! **To each his own taste**.

SYNONYM:
en gustos se rompen géneros *exp.* • (lit.): in tastes one can break genders.

socotroco/a *n. & adj. (Cuba)* idiot; stupid.

example:
¿Por qué quieres salir con Ernesto? Es todo un **socotroco**. ¡Ni siquiera sabe cuánto son dos más dos!

translation:
Why do you want to go out with Ernesto? He's such an **idiot**. He can't even add two plus two!

¡Sola vaya! *interj. (Cuba)* Good riddance! • (lit.): Just go!

example:
¡No vuelvas aquí nunca! ¡**Sola vaya**!

translation:
Don't ever come back here again! **Good riddance**!

sombrero *m.* condom • (lit.): hat.

example:
¡No olvides ponerte el **sombrero** si vas a acostarte con ella!

translation:
Don't forget to put on your **hat** if you are going to bed with her.

NOTE:
There is a popular merengue song called *Ponte el sombrero* which has the double meaning of "Put on your hat" and "Put on your condom," depending on the context.

sombrero de Panama *exp.* *(Mexico)* condom • (lit.): Panama's hat.

sopladores *m.pl. (Mexico)* testicles • (lit.): ventilators.

soplapollas *m. (Spain)* jackass, jerk • (lit.): cocksucker.

example:
¿Vas a salir con Pablo? ¡Es un **soplapollas**!

translation:
You're going out with Pablo? He's such a **jerk**!

soreco/a *n. & adj.* idiot; stupid *(El Salvador)*.

example:
Soy tan **soreca**. No puedo comprender cómo se arma mi nueva bicicleta.

translation:
I'm so **stupid**. I just can't figure out how to assemble my new bicycle.

subir a la cabeza *exp.* • to go to one's head (said of conceit or alcohol) • (lit.): to go up to one's head.

example:
Parece que a Arturo se le **subió a la cabeza** el hecho de que ahora es supervisor.

translation:
It seems that the fact that Arturo is now a supervisor **went to his head**.

subir al guayabo *exp.* *(Mexico)* to have sex • (lit.): to go up to the jelly.

sudar la gota gorda *exp.* to sweat blood, to make a superhuman effort • (lit.): to sweat the fat drop.

example:
Cuando voy al gimnasio siempre **sudo la gota gorda**.

translation:
When I go to the gym, I always **sweat bullets**.

SYNONYM:
sudar petróleo *exp.* • (lit.): to sweat petroleum.

suertudo/a *adj.* lucky person.

example:
Paco es un **suertudo**. Ya ha ganado la lotería dos veces.

translation:
Paco is such a **lucky person**. He won the lottery twice already.

sunfiate *m. (El Salvador)* anus.

supercontento/a *adj.* ultra happy.

example:
Ernesto está **supercontento** con su motocicleta nueva.

translation:
Ernesto is **ultra happy** with his new motorcycle.

ALSO:
pegando saltos (estar) *exp.* to be jumping for joy • (lit.): to be jumping.

taconera *f. (Mexico)* prostitute.

NOTE:
This comes from the verb *taconear* meaning "to tap one's heels."

tacuche de filiberto *m. (Mexico)* condom • (lit.): clothing of the filbert (since *filiberto* is used to mean "penis" in slang).

talego *m.* jail, prison.

example:
¡Si sigues portándote así vas a acabar en el **talego**!

translation:
If you continue to behave that way, you're going to end up in **jail**!

SYNONYM -1:
bote *m.* • (lit.): rowboat.

SYNONYM -2:
cana *f. (Argentina)* • **1.** prison, "slammer" • **2.** police.

SYNONYM -3:
fondo *m. (Puerto Rico)* • (lit.): the bottom.

NOTE:
acabar en el talego/bote *exp.* to end up in jail, in the "slammer."

talonera *f.* prostitute • (lit.): someone who walks very quickly.

tamale *m.* vagina • (lit.): tamale.

SYNONYMS:
SEE – **vagina**, *p. 263*.

tan claro como el agua (estar) *exp.* to be as plain as the nose on one's face • (lit.): to be as clear as water.

example:
¡Está **tan claro como el agua** que Guillermo odia su trabajo.

translation:
It's **as plain as day** that Guillermo hates his job.

SYNONYM:
tan claro como que yo me llamo [fill in your own name] *exp.* • (lit.): it's as clear as my name is [fill in your own name].

tana *f. (Mexico)* prostitute.

tanates *m.pl. (Mexico)* testicles • (lit.): bundle, parcel.

tanto pedo para cagar aguado *exp.* much ado about nothing • (lit.): so much farting for such watery shit.

tapado/a *n. & adj.* idiot; stupid • (lit.): covered-up.

example:
Mi nueva vecina sale a la calle en traje de baño en pleno invierno. Creo que está un poco **tapada**.

translation:
My new neighbor wears bathing suits outside during the winter. I think she's a little **nuts**.

tarado/a *n. & adj.* idiot; stupid. • (lit.): defective, damaged.

example:
Si te crees que me voy a levantar tan temprano para llevarte al aeropuerto, ¡estás **tarado**! Vete en taxi.

translation:
If you think I'm going to get up that early to drive you to the airport, you're **nuts**! Just take a taxi.

tarugo/a *n. & adj.* *(Guatemala, Mexico)* idiot; stupid • (lit.): wooden peg.

example:
Creía que mi novio era normal. Pero después de unos meses me dí cuenta de que es un **tarugo**.

translation:
I thought my boyfriend was so normal. But after a few months, I realized that he's really a **crackpot**!

tecolote *m.* drunkard • (lit.): owl.

example:
Mira a ese **tecolote** allí. ¡Creo que es mi profesor de biología!

translation:
Look at that **drunkard** over there. I think that's my biology teacher!

tener algo en la punta de la lengua *exp.* to have something on the tip of the tongue • (lit.): [same].

example:
No me acuerdo de cómo se llama ese tipo, pero lo **tengo en la punta de la lengua**.

translation:
I don't remember that guy's name but **it's on the tip of my tongue**.

tener don de gentes *exp.* to have a way with people • (lit.): to have a gift of people.

example:
Estefanía **tiene don de gentes**.

translation:
Estefania **has a way with people**.

tener fama de *exp.* to have a reputation for • (lit.): to have fame for.

example:
Ese restaurante **tiene fama de** servir buena comida.

translation:
That restaurant **has a reputation for** good food.

tener la mecha puesta *exp. (Cuba)* to be menstruating, to be "on the rag" • (lit.): to have the fire on.

tener los huesos molidos *exp.* to be wiped out, exhausted, ready to collapse • (lit.): to have ground up bones.

example:
He trabajado todo el día. **Tengo los huesos molidos**.

translation:
I've worked all day long. **I'm wiped out**.

SYNONYM -1:
estar hecho/a polvo *exp. (Spain)* • (lit.): to be made of dust.

SYNONYM -2:
estar hecho/a un trapo *exp.* to be made of rag.

SYNONYM -3:
estar reventado/a *adj.* • (lit.): to be smashed.

tener los mangos bajitos *exp. (Cuba)* to have sagging breasts • (lit.): to have low-hanging mangos.

example:
Es difícil creer que ese mujer fue una modelo hermosa. Ahora ella tiene noventa-seis años y ¡**tiene los mangos bajitos**!

translation:
It's hard to believe that woman used to be a beautiful model. Now she's ninety-six years old and **has low-hanging tits**!

tener madera para *exp.* to have what it takes, to be cut out for [something] • (lit.): to have the wood for [something].

example:
Augusto no **tiene madera para** ser bombero.

translation:
Augusto doesn't **have what it takes** to be a firefighter.

SYNONYM:
estar hecho/a para *exp.* • (lit.): to be made for.

tener malas pulgas *exp.* to be irritable, ill-tempered • (lit.): to have bad fleas.

example:
José siempre **tiene malas pulgas**.

translation:
Jose is always so **irritable**.

SYNONYM -1:
tener mal humor *exp.* • (lit.): to have bad humor or mood.

SYNONYM -2:
tener un humor de perros *exp.* • (lit.): to have a mood of dogs.

tener pájaros en la cabeza *exp.* to be crazy, to have a screw lose • (lit.): to have birds in the head.

example:
Daniel **tiene pájaros en la cabeza**.

translation:
Daniel **has a screw lose**.

SYNONYM -1:
estar loco/a como una cabra *exp.* • (lit.): to be like a goat.

SYNONYM -2:
estar loco/a de remate *exp.* • (lit.): to be crazy in the end.

SYNONYM -3:
estar tocado/a *exp.* *(Spain)* • (lit.): to be touched.

SYNONYM -4:
faltarle un tornillo *exp.* (lit.): to have a screw missing.

tener una boda por todo lo alto *exp.* to have a huge wedding • (lit.): to have a wedding for all the high.

example:
Cuando me case, voy a **tener una boda por todo lo alto**.

translation:
When I get married, I'm going **to have a huge wedding**.

tener una vena *exp.* said to describe a homosexual • (lit.): to have one vein.

tenerla dura *exp.* to get an erection • (lit.): to have it hard.

tenerla tiesa *exp.* to get an erection • (lit.): to have it stiff.

teresas *f.pl.* breasts, "tits" • (lit.): Theresas.

tertulia *f.* social gathering, "get-together."

example:
Todos los sábados por la noche tenemos una **tertulia** en casa de Ramón.

translation:
Every Saturday night, we have a **get-together** at Ramon's house.

ALSO:
tertulia (estar de) *exp.* to talk, to chat.

SYNONYM -1:
charla *f.* (from the verb *charlar* meaning "to chat").

SYNONYM -2:
movida *f. (Spain).*

testarudo *adj.* stubborn, headstrong.

example:
¡Javier es un **testarudo**! Cuando se le mete una idea en la cabeza, nunca cambia de opinión.

translation:
Javier is so **stubborn**! When he gets an idea in his head, he never changes his mind.

NOTE:
This comes from the feminine latin word *testa* meaning "head."

SYNONYM -1:
cabezón *adj.* • **1.** headstrong • **2.** big-headed.

NOTE:
This term comes from the feminine noun *cabeza* meaning "head."

SYNONYM -2:
terco *adj.* • (lit.): obstinate, stubborn.

SYNONYM -3:
tozudo *adj.* • (lit.): obstinate, stubborn.

tetas *f.pl.* breasts, "tits" • (lit.): [same].

tetona *f.* woman with large breasts (from the feminine plural noun *tetas* meaning "breasts").

tetorras *m.pl.* breasts, "tits" • (lit.): large breasts, large tits (from the feminine plural noun *tetas* meaning "breasts").

tía *f. (Cuba, Spain)* girl, "chick" • (lit.): aunt.

example:
¡Mira a esa **tía**! ¡Me gusta su minifalda!

translation:
Look at that **chick**! I like her miniskirt!

SYNONYM -1:
tipa *f.* • (lit.): type.

SYNONYM -2:
mina *f. (Argentina)*

ANTONYM -1:
tío *m. (Cuba, Spain)* guy, "dude" • (lit.): uncle.

ANTONYM -2:
tipo *m.* • (lit.): type.

tía buena *f. (Spain)* hot chick • (lit.): good aunt.

example:
Tu hermana pequeña se ha convertido en una verdadera **tía buena**.

translation:
Your little sister has really turned into a **hot chick**.

NOTE:
The feminine noun *tía* is commonly used in Spain to mean "woman" or "girl."

tiempo de perros *exp.* lousy weather • (lit.): weather of dogs.

example:
Hoy hace un **tiempo de perros**.

translation:
Today we're having **lousy weather**.

timbón/ona *n. & adj. (Mexico)* fatso; extremely fat.

example:
Es un vestido muy bonito, pero estoy **timbona** para ponérmelo.

translation:
What a beautiful dress. But I'm **too fat** to fit into it.

tío *m. (Cuba, Spain)* guy, "dude" • (lit.): uncle.

example:
Conozco a ese **tío**. Solía ir a mi escuela.

translation:
I know that **guy**. He used to go to my school.

NOTE:
tía *f.* girl, "chick" • (lit.): aunt.

SYNONYM:
tipo *m. (Mexico, Puerto Rico, Argentina)* guy, "dude" • (lit.): type.

ALSO:
tipa *f.* girl, "chick" • (lit.): type.

tipo *m.* guy, "dude" • (lit.): type.

example:
¡Ese **tipo** está loco!

translation:
That **guy** is crazy!

SYNONYM:
tío *m. (Spain)* • (lit.): uncle.

ANTONYM:
tipa *f.* girl, "chick."

tirar *v. (Chile, Colombia, Ecuador, Peru, Venezuela)* to fornicate • (lit.): to throw away.

tirarse *v.* to fornicate • (lit.): to throw oneself.

tirarse a mamar *exp.* to give a blow job • (lit.): to pull oneself a sucking.

tirarse/jalarse de los pelos *exp.* to squabble, to have a fight (either verbally or physically) • (lit.): to pull from one's hairs.

example:
Verónica y Luis se estaban **tirando de los pelos**.

translation:
Veronica and Luis were **having a big fight**.

NOTE:
The verb *jalarse* is used primarily in Mexico.

tocar la trompeta *exp.* to give a blow job • (lit.): to play the trumpet.

tocársela *v.* to masturbate • (lit.): to touch it oneself.

SYNONYMS:
SEE – **masturbate**, *p. 239*.

todo oídos (ser) *exp.* to be all ears • (lit.): to be all ears.

example:
Dime lo que pasó. **Soy todo oídos**.

translation:
Tell me what happened. **I'm all ears**.

tolete *m. (Cuba)* penis • (lit.): club.

SYNONYMS:
SEE – **penis**, *p. 243*.

tomar a broma *exp.* to take lightly • (lit.): to take like a joke.

example:
¡**No te lo tomes a broma**! Estoy hablado en serio.

translation:
Don't take it lightly! I'm serious.

ANTONYM:
tomar en serio *exp.* to take it seriously • (lit.): to take it seriously.

tomarle el pelo a alguien *exp.* to pull someone's leg • (lit.): to take someone's hair.

example:
Creo que me estás **tomando el pelo**.

translation:
I think you're **pulling my leg**.

SYNONYM:
hacerle guaje a uno *exp. (Mexico)* • (lit.): to make a fool of someone.

ALSO:
venir al pelo *exp.* to come in very handy • (lit.): to come to the hair • *Este reloj que me regalaron me viene al pelo;* This watch they gave me comes in handy.

tomar mujer *exp.* to get married to a woman • (lit.): to take a woman.

example:
¿David ha **tomado mujer**? Creí que le gustaba ser un solterón.

translation:
David **got married**? I thought he enjoyed being a bachelor.

ALSO:
tomar hombre *exp.* to get married to a man • (lit.): to take a man.

tomar un poco de aire fresco *exp.* to get some fresh air • (lit.): to take a little fresh air.

example:
Me duele la cabeza. Voy a **tomar un poco de aire fresco**.

translation:
I have a headache. I'm going **to get some fresh air**.

SYNONYM:
tomar el fresco *exp.* • (lit.): to take some fresh (air).

tomarle la palabra a alguien *exp.* to take someone at his/her word • (lit.): to take the word to someone.

example:
Está bien. Voy a **tomarte la palabra**.

translation:
Okay. I'm going **to take you at your word**.

tompeates *m.pl. (Mexico)* testicles.

tonterías *f.pl.* nonsense, "B.S."

example:
Ese artículo dice un montón de **tonterías**.

translation:
That article is a lot of "**bull**."

tonto *m.* vagina • (lit.): silly, foolish.

SYNONYMS:
SEE – **vagina**, *p. 263*.

torcer el brazo de alguien *exp.* to convince someone to do something, to twist someone's arm • (lit.): to twist one's arm.

example:
Bueno, **me has torcido el brazo**. Mañana te ayudo a limpiar la casa.

translation:
Well, **you twisted my arm**. Tomorrow I'll help you do some housecleaning.

tornillo *m.* penis • (lit.): screw.

SYNONYMS:
SEE – **penis**, *p. 243*.

torta *f. (El Salvador)* vagina • (lit.): cake, torte.

SYNONYMS:
SEE – **vagina**, *p. 263*.

tortera *f.* a derogatory term for "lesbian" • (lit.): tortilla maker.

tortillera *f.* a derogatory term for "lesbian" • (lit.): one who sells tortillas.

NOTE:
The term *tortillera* literally means "one who sells tortillas" but is used in slang to mean "lesbian," so be careful how you use it! For example:

Es mi tortillera favorita.

Common Translation #1:
She's my favorite **tortilla vendor**.

Common Translation #2:
She's my favorite **lesbian**.

tostón *m.* said of someone or something boring • (lit.): anything overtoasted (and therefore unwanted).

example:
Nuestro nuevo profesor de biología es un **tostón**. Me es difícil mantenerme despierto en su clase.

translation:
Our new biology teacher is such a **bore**. I have trouble staying awake in his class.

totoreco/a *n. & adj. (El Salvador)* idiot; stupid • (lit.): stunned, confused, bewildered.

example:
¡Quítate la pantalla de la lámpara de la cabeza! ¡La gente va a pensar que estás **totoreco**!

translation:
Take that lamp shade off your head! People are going to think you're **crazy**!

traer por los pelos *exp.* to be farfetched • (lit.): to be carried by the hairs.

example:
Me parece que su cuento está **traído por los pelos**.

translation:
I think his story is a little **farfetched**.

tragar *v.* • **1.** to eat • **2.** to drink • (lit.): to swallow.

example:
¿Tienes hambre? ¿Quieres algo de **tragar**?

translation:
Are you hungry? Do you want something to **eat**?

SYNONYM -1:
embuchar *v.* to eat • (lit.): to cram food into the beak of a bird.

SYNONYM -2:
jalar *v. (Spain).*

SYNONYM -3:
jamar *v.*

SYNONYM -4:
morfar *v. (Argentina).*

SYNONYM -5:
papear *v. (Spain).*

SYNONYM -6:
zampar *v.* • (lit.): to stuff or cram (food) down, to gobble down.

tragar el anzuelo *exp.* to swallow it hook, line, and sinker • (lit.): to swallow the hook.

example:
Alberto **se tragó el anzuelo**. No se dio cuenta de que lo que le dije es mentira.

translation:
Alberto **swallowed it hook, line, and sinker**. He didn't realize what I told him is a lie.

tranca *f. (Cuba, Puerto Rico)* penis • (lit.): club, thick stick.

SYNONYMS:
SEE – **penis**, *p. 243*.

trapos *m.* clothes • (lit.): rags.

example:
Ana tiene unos **trapos** muy bonitos.

translation:
Ana has very nice **clothes**.

SYNONYM -1:
paños *m.* • (lit.): rags.

SYNONYM -2:
pilchas *f.pl. (Argentina).*

SYNONYM -3:
ropaje *m.* • (lit.): robes.

ALSO -1:
poner a uno como un trapo *exp.* to give someone a severe reprimand • (lit.): to put oneself like an old rug.

ALSO -2:
sacar los trapos a relucir *exp.* to air one's dirty laundry in public • (lit.): to take one's dirty laundry to shine.

traque *m.* loud fart • (lit.): loud bang.

example:
¿Has oído ese **traque**? ¡Sonó como si alguien hubiera explotado!

translation:
Did you hear that **loud fart**? It sounded like someone exploded!

trasero *m.* anus • (lit.): rear.

trastero *m. (Mexico)* anus or asshole • (lit.): storeroom.

trasto *m.* penis • (lit.): old piece of furniture, piece of lumber.

SYNONYMS:
SEE – **penis**, *p. 243*.

trastornado/a (estar) *adj.* to be furious, angry.

example:
El jefe está **trastornado** porque Pepe no terminó el trabajo.

translation:
The boss is **furious** because Pepe didn't finish his job.

SYNONYM -1:
cabreado/a *adj.* (to be) all worked up over something.

ALSO:
agarrar/pillar un cabreo *exp.* to fly off the handle.

SYNONYM -2:
ponerse loco/a *exp. (Puerto Rico)* to cause to go crazy (with anger).

SYNONYM -3:
rabioso/a *adj.* • (lit.): rabid (or full of rabies).

tratar(se) + de *exp.* to be about, to pertain to • (lit.): to treat oneself of.

example (1):
Esta obra de teatro **trata de** Don Quijote.

translation:
This play **is about** Don Quixote.

example (2):
¿De qué **se trata**?

translation:
What **is this about**?

trato hecho *exp.* it's a deal • (lit.): deal done.

example:
Trato hecho. Te compro la motocicleta.

translation:
It's a deal. I'll buy your motorcycle.

triángulo *m. (Puerto Rico)* derogatory for "homosexual" • (lit.): triangle.

trío *m.* threesome • (lit.): trio.

trompa *f.* penis • (lit.): horn.

SYNONYMS:
SEE – **penis**, *p. 243*.

trompudo/a *n. & adj.* big-mouthed person, loud-mouth.

example:
Alejandro no para de hablar. Es un **trompudo**.

translation:
Alejandro never stops talking. He's such a **big-mouth**.

NOTE:
This is from the feminine noun *trompa* meaning "elephant's trunk" or the musical instrument the "horn."

tronado/a *adj. (El Salvador)* drunk, bombed • (lit.): spoiled.

example:
¿Cómo te has podido beber todo el vaso de Vodka? ¡Yo estaría totalmente **tronado**!

translation:
How did you drink that entire glass of Vodka? I'd be totally **bombed**!

troncho/a *n. & adj. (El Salvador)* fatso; fat • (lit.): stalk, stem.

example:
Me voy a poner **troncho** como no me ponga a dieta.

translation:
I'm going to get **fat** if I don't go on a diet.

tronco *m. (Puerto Rico)* penis • (lit.): trunk.

SYNONYMS:
SEE – **penis**, *p. 243*.

tropezar con alguien *exp.* to bump into someone • (lit.): to trip or stumble with someone.

example:
Ayer **tropecé con** Martha en la calle y lo encontré muy delgada.

translation:
Yesterday I **bumped into** Martha in the street and she looked really thin to me.

SYNONYM -1:
chocarme con alguien *exp. (Argentina)* • (lit.): to collide oneself with someone.

SYNONYM -2:
toparse con alguien *exp. (Cuba, Puerto Rico, Spain)* • (lit.): to bump oneself with someone.

truño *n.* shit.

example:
Ten cuidado de no pisar un **truño**. Hay muchos perros en este barrio.

translation:
Be careful not to walk in any **shit**. There are a lot of dogs in this neighborhood.

trupe *f.* group of friends or family members, (the whole) gang.

example:
Me encanta ir de vacaciones con toda la **trupe**.

translation:
I love going on vacation with the whole **gang**.

VARIATION:
tropa *f.*

SYNONYM -1:
ganga *f. (Puerto Rico)* applies to a whole family or group.

SYNONYM -2:
peña *f. (Spain)*.

¡Tu madre tiene un pene! *exp. (an insult of contempt)* • (lit.): Your mother has a penis!

NOTE:
Any insult involving the other person's mother will most likely lead to a fight!

¡Tu madre! *interj.* Go to hell! • (lit.): Your mother!

NOTE:
Any insult involving the other person's mother will most likely lead to a fight!

¡Tu puta madre! *interj.* Go to hell! • (lit.): Your whore of a mother!

NOTE:
Any insult involving the other person's mother will most likely lead to a fight!

tubar *v.* to fornicate • (lit.): to knock down.

tunco/a *n. & adj. (El Salvador)* fatso; very fat • (lit.): *(Honduras, Mexico)* hog, pig.

example:
Daniela era **tunca**, pero después de estar a régimen seis meses, está guapísima.

translation:
Daniela used to be **fat**, but after dieting for six months, she's beautiful.

un buen meneo *exp.* a good lay • (lit.): a good move.

example:
La verdad es que sabes que Carla es un **buen meneo** y no te interesa conocer su personalidad.

translation:
The truth is that you know Carla is a **good lay** and you're not interested in knowing her personality.

un buen revolcón *m.* a good lay • (lit.): a good rolling about.

un hueso duro de roer (ser) *exp.* to be a tough nut to crack • (lit.): to be a hard bone to chew.

example:
Juana es un **hueso duro** de roer. Es muy difícil llegar a conocerla.
translation:
Juana is a **tough nut to crack**. She's very difficult to get to know.

un vómito *m. (Argentina)* said of anything disgusting • (lit.): a vomit.
example:
No me voy a comer eso. ¡Parece **un vómito**!
translation:
I'm not eating that food. It looks **disgusting**!

una buena cogida *f.* a good lay • (lit.): a good fuck.
NOTE:
This expression applies to both men and women.

una buena tranca *f.* a good lay • (lit.): a good thick stick.

una mierda *f. (Argentina)* said of something unpleasant or worthless • (lit.): a shit.

uña y carne (ser como) *exp.* to be inseparable, to be hand in glove, to be as thick as thieves • (lit.): to be fingernail and flesh.
example:
Oscar y Elena son **como uña y carne**.
translation:
Oscar and Elena are **insepa-rable**.

SYNONYM -1:
como carne y hueso *exp. (Argentina)* • (lit.): like flesh and bone.

SYNONYM -2:
como uña y dedo *exp. (Argentina)* • (lit.): like nail and finger.

SYNONYM -3:
como uña y mugre *exp. (Mexico)* • (lit.): like a finger-nail and its dirt.

ANTONYM:
llevarse como perro y gato *exp.* to fight like cats and dogs • (lit.): to get along like dog and cat.

vaca *f.* fatso (applies only to a woman) • (lit.): cow.
example:
¡Este vestido me hace parecer una **vaca**!
translation:
This dress makes me look like a **fat cow**!

vacilar *v.* • **1.** to joke around, to clown around, to tease • **2.** to have a good time • **3.** to show off.

example -1:
A Manuel le gusta **vacilar**.

translation:
Manuel loves to **joke around**.

example -2:
Me encanta **vacilar** con mis amigos los sábados por la noche.

translation:
I love **having a good time** with my friends on Saturday nights.

example (3):
Me gusta mucho **vacilar** con mi moto nueva.

translation:
I love **showing off** my new motorcycle.

ALSO:
vacilón *m.* • **1.** spree, party, shindig • **2.** something funny, cool, neat.

SYNONYM -1:
bromear *v. (Spain)* (from the feminine noun *broma* meaning "joke").

SYNONYM -2:
chirigotear *v.* to clown around.

SYNONYM -3:
pitorrearse *v.* • **1.** to clown around • **2.** to make fun of someone.

vale *interj.* okay, "you got a deal" • (lit.): worth.

example:
– ¿Quieres ir al cine conmigo?
– ¡**Vale**!

translation:
– Do you want to go to the movies with me?
– **Okay**!

NOTE:
This interjection comes from the verb *valer* meaning "to have worth."

ALSO:
¡**Sí, vale**! *interj.* Why, yes!

SYNONYM -1:
genial *adj. (Argentina)*.

SYNONYM -2:
OK *interj.*

NOTE:
This interjection has been borrowed from English and is becoming increasingly popular throughout the Spanish-speaking countries.

vara *f.* penis • (lit.): stick.

SYNONYMS:
SEE – **penis**, *p. 243*.

¡Vaya! *interj.* • **1.** *(used to indicate surprise or amazement)* Well! How about that! • **2.** *(commonly used to modify a noun)* What an amazing... • **3.** *(used to modify a statement)* Really! • (lit.): Go!

example (1):
¡**Vaya**! Parece que va a empezar a llover.

translation:
How about that! It looks like it's going to start raining.

example (2):
¡**Vaya** equipo! • !**Vaya** calor!

translation:
What a team! • **What** heat!

example (3):
Es un buen tipo, ¡**vaya**!

translation:
What a good guy. **Really**!

SYNONYM -1:
¡Che! *interj. (Argentina)* • *¡Che, no me digas!;* You're telling me! • *(extremely popular) ¡Hola, che!;* Hi there!

SYNONYM -2:
¡Vamos! *interj.* • (lit.): Let's go!

NOTE -1:
Vamos may also be used within a sentence to indicate that the speaker has just changed his/her mind or is making a clarification. In this case, *vamos* is translated as "well."

example:
Es guapa. **Vamos**, no es fea.

translation:
She's pretty. **Well**, she's not ugly.

NOTE -2:
Both *vaya* and *vamos* are extremely popular and both come from the verb *ir* meaning "to go."

velga *f. (Puerto Rico)* penis (from *verga* meaning "broomstick").

NOTE:
In Puerto Rico, it is common to pronounce the "R" as an "L" when it occurs within a word. Even the country itself is often pronounced *Puelto Rico* by the natives.

SYNONYMS:
SEE – **penis**, *p. 243*.

venirse *v. (Mexico)* to ejaculate • (lit.): to come.

venirse a menos *exp.* • (lit.): to come back to less • **1.** said of something that has deteriorated, "to go to the dogs" • **2.** said of someone who is not as important as before.

example -1:
Esta cuidad se ha **venido a menos**.

translation:
This city has **gone to the dogs**.

example -2:
Antes Miguel era muy importante pero ahora se ha **venido a menos**.

translation:
Miguel used to be very important but now **his popularity is slipping**.

verde *f.* marijuana • (lit.): green.

example:
¿Has oído decir que arrestaron a Estéban por manejar bajo los efectos de la **verde**?

translation:
Did you hear that Stephan got arrested for driving under the influence of **marijuana**?

veregallo *m. (Mexico)* masturbation.

SYNONYMS:
SEE – **masturbation**, *p. 239*.

verga *f.* • **1.** penis • **2.** stupid person ("dick-head") (lit.): broomstick.

SYNONYMS:
SEE – **penis**, *p. 243*.

vergallito *m. (Mexico)* masturbation • (lit.): small penis.

SYNONYMS:
SEE – **masturbation**, *p. 239*.

verse con alguien *exp.* to meet someone • (lit.): to see oneself with someone.

example:
Mañana voy a **ver con** mi primo. Tenemos mucho que hablar.

translation:
Tomorrow I'm going to **meet with** my cousin. We have a lot to talk about.

ALSO:
quedar con alguien *exp.* to make an appointment with someone • (lit.): to remain with someone.

¡Vete a hacer puñetas! *exp. (Spain)* Fuck off! • (lit.): Go beat off!

¡Vete a joder por ahí! *interj.* Fuck off! • (lit.): Go fuck over there!

¡Vete a la [mismísima] mierda! *exp.* Go to hell! • (lit.): Go to the [very same] shit!

¡Vete a la reverenda mierda! *interj. (Cuba)* Go to hell! • (lit.): Go to holy shit!

¡Vete al carajo! *interj.* Go to hell! • (lit.): Go to the asshole's house!

¡Vete al coño de tu madre! *interj.* Go to hell! • (lit.): Go to your mother's vagina!

MEXICO:
¡Vete al carajo de tu madre! *interj.*

NOTE:
The masculine term *coño* is an extremely vulgar slang term for "vagina."

¡Vete al diablo! *interj.* Go to hell! • (lit.): Go to the devil!

¡Vete por ahí a que te la den por el culo! *interj.* Go to hell! • (lit.): Go where you'll get it up the ass!

víbora *f.* penis • (lit.): viper.

SYNONYMS:
SEE – **penis**, *p. 243*.

vieja conchuda *f.* *(Argentina)* old woman • (lit.): old one with a vagina (from the feminine noun *concha*, literally "seashell," which is a vulgar term for "vagina").

example:
Nuestra profesora de matemáticas es una **vieja conchuda** que lleva enseñando miles de años.

translation:
Our math teacher is an **old relic** who's been teaching for a thousand years.

vieja tetuda *f. (Argentina)* old woman • (lit.): old one with tits.

example:
Espero que esa **vieja tetuda** no sea la nueva jefa.

translation:
I hope that **old lady** isn't our new boss.

viejo boludo *m. (Argentina)* stupid old fart • (lit.): old one with balls.

example:
Mi médico es un **viejo boludo**. Voy a buscarme otro.

translation:
My doctor is an **stupid old fart**. I'm going to find someone else.

viejo pelotudo *m.* *(Argentina)* old codger • (lit.): old one with balls.

example:
¡No me puedo creer que dejen a un **viejo pelotudo** como ese detrás del volante!

translation:
I can't believe that they let an **old codger** like that behind the wheel!

viejo [rabo] verde *m.* dirty old man • (lit.): old green tail.

example:
¡Ese hombre está saliendo con una mujer veinte años más joven que él! Yo creo que es un **viejo [rabo] verde**.

translation:
That man is dating a girl twenty years younger than he is! I think he's just a **dirty old man**.

viejo/a de mierda *n.* "old fart" • (lit.): old person of shit.

example:
¿Conociste al nuevo jefe? Es un **viejo de mierda** y creo que va a ser muy estricto.
translation:
Did you meet the new boss yet? He's an **old fart** and I think he's going to be very strict.

viejos *m.pl.* parents, folks • (lit.): the old ones.
example:
Me encanta ir a casa de mis **viejos** porque siempre hay algo bueno de comer.
translation:
I love going to my **folks** because there is always something good to eat.

NOTE -1:
viejo *m.* • **1.** father • **2.** husband • (lit.): old man.

NOTE -2:
vieja *f.* • **1.** mother • **2.** wife • (lit.): old woman.

violación en grupo *f.* gang bang • (lit.): group violation.

NOTE:
This act is nonconsensual and considered rape as opposed to *sexo tribal*, meaning "group sex."

vivir al día *exp.* to live day to day, to live from hand to mouth • (lit.): to live to the day.
example:
Mucha gente en este país **vive al día**.
translation:
Many people in this country **live day to day**.

vivo *adj. (Argentina, Uruguay, Spain)* smart, clever, bright • (lit.): alive.
example:
Alvaro es un **vivo**. Siempre se sale con la suya.
translation:
Alvaro is so **smart**. Everything always goes his way.

SYNONYM -1:
despabilado/a *adj.*

SYNONYM -2:
despierto/a *adj.* • (lit.): awaken.

SYNONYM -3:
espabilado/a *adj. (Spain).*

SYNONYM -4:
listillo/a *adj.*

NOTE:
This comes from the adjective *listo* meaning "clear" or "smart."

SYNONYM -5:
pillo *adj.* • (lit.): roguish, mischievous.

ANTONYM -1:
adoquín *adj.* • (lit.): paving block.

ANTONYM -2:
bruto/a *adj.* • (lit.): stupid, crude.

ANTONYM -3:
cabezota *adj.* • (lit.): big-headed.

NOTE:
This comes from the feminine noun *cabeza* meaning "head."

ANTONYM -4:
zopenco/a *adj.* • (lit.): dull, stupid.

volteado *m.* derogatory for "homosexual" • (lit.): turned around.

volver loco/a a alguien *exp.* to drive someone crazy • (lit.): to turn someone crazy.

example:
El tráfico de esta ciudad me está **volviendo loco**.

translation:
All the traffic in this city is **making me crazy**.

vomitar hasta la primera papilla *exp.* to vomit, to barf one's guts up • (lit.): to vomit even one's first soft food.

example:
Estuve tan enfermo la semana pasada, que **vomité hasta la primera papilla**.

translation:
I was so sick last week that **I barfed my guts up**.

vomitar hasta las tripas *exp.* to vomit, to barf one's guts up • (lit.): to vomit up to one's guts.

example:
Creo que anoche algo me sentó mal. Estuve **vomitando hasta las tripas** durante tres horas.

translation:
I think I had food poisoning last night. I was **vomiting my guts up** for three hours.

y por si fuera poco *exp.* and if that wasn't enough, and to top it off • (lit.): and by a little out.

example:
Hoy me robaron la cartera, **y por si fuera poco**, tuve un accidente.

translation:
Today my wallet was stolen, **and to top it off**, I was in an accident.

¡[Y una] mierda! *exp.* Bullshit! • (lit.): And a shit!
example:
¿Manuel te dijo que es rico? ¿**[Y una] mierda**! ¿Qué mentiroso!
translation:
Manuel told you he's rich? **Bullshit**! He's such a liar!

yiyi *m. (Puerto Rico)* derogatory for "homosexual."

yoyo *m. (Mexico)* vagina.

SYNONYMS:
SEE – **vagina**, *p. 263*.

yuca *f. (El Salvador)* penis • (lit.): yucca plant.

SYNONYMS:
SEE – **penis**, *p. 243*.

Z

zacate inglés *m. (Mexico and Central America)* marijuana • (lit.): English hay.

zanahoria *f.* penis • (lit.): carrot.

SYNONYMS:
SEE – **penis**, *p. 243*.

zapato *m. (Argentina)* idiot, jerk • (lit.): shoe.
example:
¿Has visto el sombrero que lleva Miguel? ¡Parece un **zapato** con é!
translation:
Did you see the hat Miguel is wearing? It makes him look like a **jerk**!

zonas (las) *f.pl.* red-light districts in Mexico and Colombia • (lit.): the areas.
example:
Juan va todos los días a **las zonas** a la hora del almuerzo. A él le debe gustar mucho el sexo.
translation:
Juan goes every day to **the red-light district** during lunch. He must really love sex.

zoofilia *m.* bestiality.

zopenco/a *n. & adj.* jerk; stupid • (lit.): dull, stupid.
example:
¡Nunca saldría con Jorge! ¡Es un **zopenco**!
translation:
I'd never go out with Jorge! He's such a **jerk**!

zorra *f.* bitch • (lit.): fox.

example:
¿Has conocido ya a la nueva jefa? ¡Es una **zorra**!
translation:
Did you meet the new boss? She's such a **bitch**!

zullarse *v.* to fart • (lit.): to fart.
example:
La próxima vez que tengas que **zullarte**, por favor levántate de la mesa.
translation:
The next time you have **to fart**, please leave the table.

zullón *m.* fart • (lit.): fart.
example:
¡Hay un **zullón** que ha estado pululando por esta habitación durante una hora!
translation:
There's a **fart** that's been lingering in this room for an hour!

zurrar *v.* to defecate • (lit.): to reprimand, to hit.
example:
Si tienes que **zurrar**, usa el otro baño. Este está roto.
translation:
If you need **to take a dump**, use the other toilet. This one isn't working.

NOTE -1:
In Argentina, this verb means "to fart silently."

NOTE -2:
zurullo/zurullón *m.* turd • (lit.): hard lump.

zurullo *m.* turd • (lit.): hard lump.
example:
Cuidado donde juegas. Hay muchos **zurullos** en este parque.
translation:
Be careful where you play. There are **turds** all over this park.

NOTE:
The term *zurullo* literally means "hard lump" but is used in slang to mean "turd," so be careful how you use it! For example:

Esta sopa tiene muchos zurullos.

Common Translation #1:
This soup has a lot of **lumps** in it.
Common Translation #2:
This soup has a lot of **turds** in it.

zurullón *m.* turd • (lit.): hard lump.
example:
¡Ay, no! ¡He pisado un **zurullón** y he estropeado mis zapatos nuevos!
translation:
Oh, no! I stepped in a **turd** and ruined my new shoes!

STREET SPANISH THESAURUS

Part 2

(Obscenities, Vulgarities, Vulgar and Non-vulgar Insults, Bodily Functions & Sounds, Sexual Slang, Offensive Language, etc.)

A GOOD LAY

un buen meneo *exp.* a good lay • (lit.): a good move.

un buen revolcón *m.* a good lay • (lit.): a good rolling about.

una buena cogida *f.* a good lay • (lit.): a good fuck.

NOTE:
This expression applies to both men and women.

una buena tranca *f.* a good lay • (lit.): a good thick stick.

AIDS

SIDA *m.* Sindrome Inmunodeficiencia Adquirida.

BALD

calco *m.* • (lit.): tracing (drawing).

example:
¿Conoces a Ernesto? ¡Es **calco** y sólo tiene diecisiete años!

translation:
Do you know Ernesto? He's **bald** and he's only seventeen years old!

calvito *adj.*

example:
Me temo que voy a ser **calvito**, porque mi padre perdió todo el pelo en su veintena.

translation:
I'm afraid I'm going to be **bald** because my father lost all of his hair when he was in his twenties.

NOTE:
This is from the adjective *calvo* meaning "bald."

pelón/ona *n. & adj.* baldy; bald.

example:
Enrique tiene solamente diez y seis años y él ya está **pelón**.

translation:
Enrique is only sixteen years old and he's already **bald**.

BLABBERMOUTH / GOSSIP

bocón/ona *n. & adj.* blabbermouth; gossipy • (lit.): big-mouthed.

example:
Estuve hablando por teléfono con Susana más de una hora. ¡Es una **bocona**!

translation:
I was on the telephone with Susana for an hour. She's such a **blabbermouth**!

NOTE:
This is from the feminine noun *boca* meaning "mouth."

chismolero/a *n. & adj.* one who spreads gossip or *chismes*; gossipy.
example:
No te creas nada de lo que dice Ana. ¡Qué **chismolera**!
translation:
Don't believe anything Ana says. What a **gossip**!

chismoso/a *n.* one who spreads gossip or chismes.
example:
No le cuentes a Jorge nada personal. Es un **chismoso**.
translation:
Don't tell anything personal to Jorge. He's a **gossip**.

comadrera *f.* blabbermouth.
example:
¿Cómo sabías que me iba a casar?¿Te lo dijo la **comadrera** de Cristina?
translation:
How did you know I was getting married? Did that **blabbermouth** Christina tell you?

NOTE:
This is from the feminine noun *comadre* meaning "gossip."

cotorra *f.* • (lit.): parrot.
example:
¡Le conté un secreto a Ana y se lo contó a todo el mundo! Se me había olvidado lo **cotorra** que es.
translation:
I told a secret to Ana and she told everyone! I forgot what a **blabbermouth** she is.

cuentero/a *n. & adj.* *(Argentina)* a gossip; gossipy • (lit.): one who tells tales.
example:
¿Le contaste un secreto a Antonio? No fue buena idea. Es un **cuentero**.
translation:
You told Antonio a secret? That wasn't a good idea. He's such a **blabbermouth**.

enredador/a *n. (Spain)* a gossip • (lit.): meddler.
example:
Le conté a Armando todos mis problemas personales y se los contó a todos sus amigos. ¡Nunca volveré a confiar en ese **enredador**!
translation:
I told Armando all about my personal problems and he told all of his friends. I'll never trust that **blabbermouth** again!

enredoso/a *n. & adj. (Chile, Mexico)* a gossip; gossipy • (lit.): fraught with difficulties.

example:
A Mateo le encanta expandir rumores. Es un **enredoso**.
translation:
Mateo likes to spread rumors. He's a **gossip**.

farandulero/a *n. & adj.* a gossip; gossipy • (lit.): actor, strolling player.
example:
Benito y yo éramos buenos amigos hasta que descubrí que era un **farandulero**. No puedo volver a confiar en él.
translation:
Benito and I used to be good friends until I discovered that he was a **gossip**. I can never trust him again.

gritón/ona *n. & adj.* loudmouth; gossipy.
example:
Habla bajo. Esto es una biblioteca. ¡Eres un **gritón**!
translation:
Keep your voice down. This is a library. You're such a **loudmouth**!
NOTE:
This is from the verb *gritar* meaning "to shout."

hablador/a *n. & adj.* blabbermouth; gossipy.
example:
¿Le contaste a Jesús mi secreto? ¡Qué **hablador**!
translation:
You told Jesús my secret? What a **blabbermouth**!
NOTE:
This is from the verb *hablar* meaning "to speak."

hocicón/ona *n. & adj.* loudmouth; gossipy • (lit.): mouthy (since this term comes from the masculine noun *hocico* meaning "snout").
example:
No quiero invitar a Anita a mi fiesta porque no la soporto. ¡Es tan **hocicona**!
translation:
I don't want to invite Anita to my party because I can't stand her. She's such a **loudmouth**!

lengua larga (tener) *exp. (Argentina)* • (lit.): to have a long tongue.
example:
A Angel le encanta chismear. **Tiene la lengua larga**.
translation:
Angel loves to gossip about people. **He's a blabbermouth**.

lenguasuelta *n. & adj. (Mexico)* a gossip; gossipy • (lit.): loose tongue.
example:
¡Para de ser **lenguasuelta**! Ésas no son más que mentiras.

translation:
Stop being a **gossip**! Those are nothing but lies.

lenguatuda *f. (Argentina)* • (lit.): one with a long tongue (used for blabbing).
example:
Consuelo no puede guardar un secreto. Es una **lenguatuda**.
translation:
Consuelo can't keep a secret. She's such a **blabbermouth**.

mitotero/a *n. & adj.* a gossip; gossipy • (lit.): rowdy, noisy person.
example:
Te lo advierto, Margarita es una verdadera **mitotera**. No le cuentes nada personal.
translation:
I'm warning you. Margarita is a real **gossip**. Don't tell her anything personal.

parlanchín *m.* blabbermouth • (lit.): talkative.
example:
Armando habla sin parar. Es un **parlanchín**.
translation:
Armando talks nonstop. He's a **blabbermouth**.

trompudo/a *n. & adj.* big-mouthed person.
example:
Alejandro no para de hablar. Es un **trompudo**.
translation:
Alejandro never stops talking. He's such a **big-mouth**.

NOTE:
This is from the feminine noun *trompa* meaning "elephant's trunk" or the musical instrument the "horn."

BORING (TO BE)

pesado/a *n. & adj.* a bore; boring • (lit.): heavy.
example:
El discurso de David fue **pesado**.
translation:
David's lecture was **boring**.

petardo (ser un) *m.* • (lit.): to be a torpedo, firecracker.
example:
No me gusta estar con Miguel. ¡Es tan **petardo**!
translation:
I don't like spending time with Miguel. He's such a **bore**!

tostón *m.* • (lit.): anything overtoasted (and therefore unwanted).
example:
Nuestro nuevo profesor de biología es un **tostón**. Me es difícil mantenerme despierto en su clase.

translation:
Our new biology teacher is such a **bore**. I have trouble staying awake in his class.

BROWN-NOSE (TO) / BROWN-NOSER

hacer la barba *exp.*
• (lit.): to do the beard.

example:
La razón por la que Ricardo ha conseguido un ascenso es porque siempre está **haciendo la barba**.

translation:
The reason Ricardo got a promotion is because he's such a **brown-noser**.

hacer la pelotilla *exp.*
• (lit.): to do the testicle or "lick someone's balls" (since *pelotilla*, literally meaning "small balls," is used in Spanish slang to mean "small testicles").

example:
David ha debido **hacer la pelotilla** para conseguir que le subieran el sueldo.

translation:
David must have **brown-nosed** to get a raise.

lameculo[s] *m. & adj.*
• (lit.): butt-licker.

example:
¿Has oído cómo le hablaba Ana al jefe? Nunca supe que fuera tan **lameculo[s]**.

translation:
Did you hear how Ana was talking to the boss? I never knew she was such a **kiss-ass**.

lamesuelas *m. & adj.*
• (lit.): leather licker.

example:
La razón por la que al jefe le gusta tanto Victor es porque éste es un **lamesuelas**.

translation:
The reason the boss likes Victor so much is because he's such a **kiss-ass**.

pelota *n. & adj.* • (lit.): ball (or one who "licks someone's balls or testicles").

example:
El único motivo por el que Roberto fue ascendido, es porque es un **pelota**.

translation:
The only reason Roberto got a promotion is because he's a **kiss-ass**.

ALSO:
pelota *adj.* (Colombia) stupid.

BURP (TO)

echarse/largarse un erupto *exp.* to burp • (lit.): to throw an eruption.

example:
¡Luis **se echó un erupto** en medio de la clase!

translation:
Luis **burped** in the middle of class!

COCAINE

basuco *m. (Mexico, Central and South America)* crack cocaine.

lina *f. (Mexico)* line of cocaine • (lit.): line.

llello *m. (Mexico, Puerto Rico)* cocaine, crack.

perico *m. (Mexico, Central and South America)* cocaine • (lit.): periwig.

CRAZY (TO BE)

enfermo mental (ser un) *exp.* • (lit.): to be a mentally corrupt person.

example:
No me puedo creer que Cynthia vaya a ser madre. ¡Es una **enferma mental**!

translation:
I can't believe Cynthia is going to be a mother. She's such a **mental case**!

faltar un tornillo *exp.* • (lit.): to be missing a screw.

example:
Mi psiquiatra habla solo todo el tiempo. Yo creo que **le falta un tornillo**.

translation:
My psychiatrist talks to himself all the time. I think **he has a screw loose**.

loco/a como una cabra (estar) *exp.* • (lit.): to be as crazy as a nanny goat.

example:
Si yo fuera tú no confiaría en él. ¡Está **loco como una cabra**!

translation:
I wouldn't trust him if I were you. He's **out of his mind**!

loco/a de remate (estar) *exp.* • (lit.): to be crazy to the end.

example:
Si piensas que voy a salir con Manuel, ¡es que estás **loco de remate**!

translation:
If you think I'm going to go out with Manuel, you're **nuts**!

DEFECATE (TO)

bosta *f.* turd, cow dung • (lit.): cow dung.

example:
Cuidado por donde andas. El pasto está lleno de **bosta**.

translation:
Be careful where you walk. The grass is full of **turds**.

cagadero *m.* bathroom, "shithouse" (from the verb *cagar* meaning "to shit").

example:
Antes de salir, tengo que ir al **cagadero**.

translation:
Before we leave, I need to go to the **shithouse**.

cagar *v.* to defecate • (lit.): to shit.

example:
¡Ese niño está **cagando** en la acera!

translation:
That little kid is **shitting** on the sidewalk!

cerote *m. (Nicaragua)* turd • (lit.): large zero.

example:
Algo huele fatal. ¿Has pisado un **cerote**?

translation:
Something smells terrible. Did you step in a **turd**?

churro *m.* • **1.** turd • **2.** penis • (lit.): long fritter (*churro;* a long, straight fried pastry).

example:
¡Ese perro acaba de largarse grandísimo **churro**!

translation:
That dog just laid the biggest **turd**!

NOTE -1:
The noun *churro* is also used to refer to a failure. For example: *La película fue un churro;* The movie was a bomb.

NOTE -2:
In Argentina and Colombia, a *churro* means "a sexy guy."

desocupar *v.* to defecate • (lit.): to empty.

example:
¡Huele como si alguien hubiera **desocupado** dentro del tren!

translation:
It smells like people **crapped** in this train!

jiñar *v.* • **1.** to defecate • **2.** to urinate.

example:
Es ilegal **jiñar** en la acera.

translation:
It's illegal **to crap** on the sidewalk.

obrar *v.* to defecate • (lit.): to perform or to build.

example:
Si tu perro **obra** en la acera, tienes que limpiarlo.

translation:
If your dog **craps** on the sidewalk, you need to clean it up.

quitarle al mondongo un peso de encima *exp.* *(Mexico)* to defecate • (lit.): to empty out the intestines.

example:
He desayunado tanto que tengo que **quitarle al mondongo un peso de encima**.

translation:
I ate so much breakfast that I need **to take a dump**.

regir *v.* *(Mexico)* to defecate • (lit.): to rule.

example:
Creo que el niño se ha **regido** otra vez en los pantalones.

translation:
I think the baby **pooped** in his pants again.

zurrar *v.* to defecate • (lit.): to reprimand, to hit.

example:
Si tienes que **zurrar**, usa el otro baño. Éste está roto.

translation:
If you need **to take a dump**, use the other toilet. This one isn't working.

NOTE -1:
In Argentina, this verb means "to fart silently."

NOTE -2:
zurullo/zurullón *m.* turd • (lit.): hard lump.

zurullo *m.* turd • (lit.): hard lump.

example:
Cuidado donde juegas. Hay muchos **zurullos** en este parque.

translation:
Be careful where you play. There are **turds** all over this park.

zurullón *m.* turd • (lit.): hard lump.

example:
¡Ah, no! ¡He pisado un **zurullón** y he estropeado mis zapatos nuevos!

translation:
Oh, no! I stepped in a **turd** and ruined my new shoes!

DIARRHEA

andar con el estómago flojo *exp. (Mexican)* to have diarrhea • (lit.): to walk around with a loose stomach.
example:
No puedo ir contigo al cine; **ando con el estómago flojo**.
translation:
I can't go with you to the movies. **I have diarrhea**.

andar con mal tapón *exp. (Mexico)* to be constipated • (lit.): to walk around with a defective cork.
example:
No me encuentro bien. **Ando con mal tapón**.
translation:
I don't feel well. **I'm constipated**.

obraderas *f.*pl. *(Mexico)* diarrhea (from the verb *obrar* meaning "to make a bowel movement").
example:
Si bebes agua en ese país, puedes coger **obraderas**.
translation:
If you drink the water in that country, you may get **diarrhea**.

seguidillas *f.*pl. *(Mexico)* diarrhea, "the runs" • (lit.): flamenco song and dance
example:
Me duele el estómago. Creo que voy a tener **seguidillas**.
translation:
My stomach hurts. I think I'm going to have **the runs**.

DRIVE SOMEONE CRAZY (TO)

sacar de quicio a alguien *exp.* • (lit.): to bring someone to his/her threshold (of tolerance).
example:
¡Los nuevos vecinos hacen tanto ruido! **¡Me sacan de quicio**!
translation:
The new neighbors are making so much noise! **They're driving me crazy**!

volver loco/a a alguien *exp.* to drive someone crazy • (lit.): to turn someone crazy.
example:
El tráfico de esta ciudad me está **volviendo loco**.
translation:
All the traffic in this city is **making me crazy**.

DRUNK(ARD)

bolo *m. (El Salvador, Nicaragua)* • (lit.): skittle.

example:
Eduardo tiene un problema con la bebida. Creo que es un **bolo**.

translation:
Eduardo has a problem with alcohol. I think he's a **drunk**.

borrachal *m.* (from the adjective *borracho/a* meaning "drunk").

example:
David no puede encontrar trabajo porque todo el mundo sabe que es un **borrachal**.

translation:
David can't get a job because everyone knows he's a **drunk**.

borrachón/ona *f. & adj. (Argentina)* • (lit.): big drunkard.

example:
Como siempre, Marco bebió demasiado en mi fiesta. ¡Es un **borrachón**!

translation:
As usual, Marco had too much to drink at my party. He's such a **drunk**!

bufa *f. (Cuba)* • (lit.): jest, piece of buffoonery.

example:
Yo no sabía que Antonio era un **bufa**. Ayer se presentó al trabajo con una botella de vino en la mano.

translation:
I didn't know Antonio was such a **drunk**. Yesterday he showed up at work holding a wine bottle.

chupandín *m. (Argentina)* • (lit.): big sucker (from the verb *chupar* meaning "to suck").

example:
¿Viste cuánto alcohol bebió Jack ayer por la noche? ¡No tenía idea de que fuera tan **chupandín**!

translation:
Did you see how much alcohol Jack drank last night? I had no idea he was such a **lush**!

codo empinado *m.*
• (lit.): tilted elbow.

example:
¡Nunca me había dado cuenta de que Francisco era un **codo empinado**! ¿Has visto cuánto vino tomó durante la cena?

translation:
I never realized what a **drunk** Francisco was! Did you see how much wine he drank during dinner?

cuete (ponerse) *adj.* to get drunk • (lit.): slice of rump (of beef).

example:
Benito nunca parece demasiado sano. Yo creo que **se pone cuete** todo el tiempo.

translation:
Benito never looks very healthy. I think he **gets drunk** all the time.

engazado/a *adj.* • (lit.): gassed up.
example:
Ricardo se puso **engazado** en mi fiesta.
translation:
Ricardo got **plastered** at my party.

manudo/a *n. (El Salvador)* drunkard.
example:
No pienso volver a invitar al **manudo** de Rafael a mi casa nunca más. ¡Fue tan vergonzoso!
translation:
I'm never inviting that **drunkard** Rafael to my house again. He was so embarrassing!

pipa *f.* • (lit.): pipe (for smoking tobacco).
example:
¡Qué lástima! Acabo de descubrir que la madre de Emilio es una **pipa**.
translation:
What a shame! I just found out that Emilio's mother is a **drunkard**.

pisto/a *adj.* drunk, bombed • (lit.): chicken broth.
example:
Si me tomo media copa de vino, estoy **pista**.
translation:
If I drink half a glass of wine, I get **bombed**.

tecolote *m.* • (lit.): owl.
example:
Mira a ese **tecolote** de allí. ¡Creo que es mi profesor de biología!
translation:
Look at that **drunkard** over there. I think that's my biology teacher!

tronado/a *adj.* (El Salvador) • (lit.): spoiled.
example:
¿Cómo te has podido beber todo el vaso de Vodka? ¡Yo estaría totalmente **tronado**!
translation:
How did you drink that entire glass of Vodka? I'd be totally **bombed**!

EJACULATE

acabar *v. (Argentina)* to ejaculate, to have an orgasm • (lit.): to finish • *¡Estoy por acabar!;* I'm going to ejaculate!

correrse *v.* to ejaculate, to have an orgasm.

NOTE:
The intransitive form of this verb *correr* literally means "to run." However, in the reflexive form, it carries a sexual connotation.

expulsar *v.* to ejaculate • (lit.): to expel, eject.

gozar *v.* to ejaculate • (lit.): to enjoy.

irse *v.* to ejaculate • (lit.): to leave, go away.

irse a la gloria *exp.* to ejaculate • (lit.): to go to the glory.

irse de la varilla *exp.* to ejaculate • (lit.): to go from the stick.

lanzar *v.* to ejaculate • (lit.): to throw.

regarse *v.* to ejaculate, to have an orgasm • (lit.): to wet one-self.

venirse *v.* *(Mexico)* to ejaculate • (lit.): to come.

ERECTION

armado (estar) *adj.* to get an erection • (lit.): to be armed.

empalmado (estar) *adj.* to get an erection • (lit.): to be connected.

empalmarse *v.* to get an erection • (lit.): to connect, to join.

enrucado (estar) *adj.* to get an erection.

pararse *v.* to get an erection • (lit.): to stand up.

ponerse duro *exp.* to get an erection • (lit.): to put oneself hard.

tenerla dura *exp.* to get an erection • (lit.): to have it hard.

tenerla tiesa *exp.* to get an erection • (lit.): to have it stiff.

FART (TO)

bufa *f.* fart • (lit.): jest, piece of buffoonery.

example:
¡Qué olor! Huele a **bufa**.

translation:
What's that odor? It smells like a **fart**.

carapedo *m.* stupid, fart-face • (lit.): fart-face.

example:
¡**Carapedo**! ¡Déjame en paz!

translation:
Stupid! Leave me alone!

cuesco *m.* fart • (lit.): stone, punch.

example:
¡Acabo de oír al vecino tirarse un **cuesco**!

translation:
I just heard the next door neighbor **fart**!

de pedo *adv.* by luck • (lit.): by fart (something that happens as easily as a fart).

example:
Gané el concurso **de pedo**.

translation:
I won the contest **by luck**.

discreto/a como pedo de monja *exp.* to be indiscrete • (lit.): as discrete as a nun's fart.

example:
Puedes confiar en él y contarle todos tus problemas porque él es tan **discreto como pedo de monja**.

translation: You can confide in him and tell him all your problems because he's **very discrete**.

follar *v.* • **1.** to fart silently • **2.** to have sex.

example -1:
Algo huele mal. Creo que el niño se ha **follado**.

translation:
Something smells funny. I think the baby **farted**.

example -2:
Verónica es una mujer muy bella. Me encantaría **follármela**.

translation:
Veronica is a beautiful woman. I would love **to have sex with her**.

NOTE:
follón *m.* a silent fart, an SBD ("silent but deadly"). See next entry.

VARIATION -1:
follarse *v.*

VARIATION -2:
follonarse *v.*

follón *m.* • **1.** silent fart, an SBD ("silent but deadly") • **2.** jam, mess.

example -1:
¡Creo que el niño se ha tirado un **follón**!

translation:
I think the baby let lose an **SBD**!

example -2:
¡Carlos se metió en un **follón**!

translation:
Carlos got himself into a **real jam**!

follonarse *v.* to fart silently.

example:
Después de comerme toda esa comida picante, creo que voy a **follonarme**.

translation:
After eating all that spicy food, I think I'm going **to fart**.

NOTE:
This is a variation of the term **follar**.

mal aire *m.* fart • (lit.): bad air.

example:
¡Qué asco! ¡Creo que huelo un **mal aire**!

translation:
Yuck! I think I smell a **fart**!

pederse *v.* to fart • (lit.): to fart.

example:
¡No me puedo creer que **te pedas** en mi coche!

translation:
I can't believe **you'd fart** in my car!

pedo *m.* • **1.** fart • **2.** drunkenness • **3.** ugly.

example -1:
Ese chiste es tan gracioso como un **pedo** en un traje espacial.

translation:
That joke is as funny as a **fart** in a spacesuit.

example -2:
Manolo agarró un buen **pedo** en la fiesta.

translation:
Manolo got really **drunk** at the party.

example -3:
Ese tipo es un **pedo**.

translation:
That guy is an **ugly person**.

pedorrera *f.* many farts, a series of farts.

example:
¿Has oído esa **pedorrera**? ¡Qué asco!

translation:
Did you hear **all that farting**? That's disgusting!

pedorrero *m.* one who farts a lot, farter.

example:
Mi tío tiene problemas de estómago. Es un **pedorrero**.

translation:
My uncle has gastric problems. He's a **farter**.

peerse *v.* to fart • (lit.): to fart

example:
Es de mala educación **peerse** en público.

translation:
It's rude **to fart** in public.

traque *m.* loud fart • (lit.): loud bang.

example:
¿Has oído ese **traque**? ¡Sonó como si alguien hubera explotado!

translation:
Did you hear that **loud fart**? It sounded like someone exploded!

zullarse *v.* to fart • (lit.): to fart.

example:
La próxima vez que tengas que **zullarte**, por favor levántate de la mesa.

translation:
The next time you have **to fart**, please leave the table.

zullón *m.* fart • (lit.): fart.

example:
¡Hay un **zullón** que ha estado pululando por esta habitación durante una hora!

translation:
There's a **fart** that's been lingering in this room for an hour!

FAT SLOB

botija *n. & adj.* fat slob; chunky, fat • (lit.): short-necked earthen jug.

example:
A mí me daría vergüenza salir con esa **botija**.

translation:
I would be embarrassed to go out with that **fat slob**.

chancho *m.* • (lit.): fat pig.

example:
Ese **chancho** se acaba de comer siete hamburguesas. No me sorprende que esté así.

translation:
That **fat slob** just ate seven hamburgers. It doesn't surprise me he looks like that.

¡Che gordo, te vas a reventar! *exp. (Argentina)* in response to seeing someone very fat • (lit.): Hey fatso, you're going to explode!

example:
¡**Che gordo, te vas a reventar**! ¡Deja de comerte esa tarta!

translation:
Hey fatso, you're going to explode! Stop eating that cake!

NOTE:
Although this is a masculine noun, it can be applied to a woman as well.

comilón/ona *n. & adj.* one who eats a lot, pig; piggy.

example:
¿Has visto todo lo que se ha comido Alfonso para almorzar? ¡Qué **comilón**!

translation:
Did you see how much food Alfonso ate during lunch? What a **pig**!

NOTE:
This is from the verb *comer* meaning "to eat."

cuchi *m.* • (lit.): variation of cochino meaning "filthy."

example:
Como te comas todo eso, te vas a poner **cuchi**.

translation:
If you eat all that, you're going to become a **fat pig**.

elefante *m. & adj.* fatso; fat • (lit.): elephant.

example:
Después de comer tanto dulce, me siento como un **elefante**.

translation:
After eating so much dessert, I feel like a **fat pig**.

foca *f. (Spain)* • (lit.): seal.

example:
No pienso ponerme ese traje de baño. ¡Parezco una **foca**!

translation:
I'm not going to wear that bathing suit. It makes me look like a **fat cow**!

gordinflón/ona *n. & adj.* fatso; fat.

example:
Solía ser un **gordinflón**, pero después de mucha dieta y ejercicio, finalmente estoy en forma.

translation:
I used to be a **fat pig**, but after a lot of dieting and exercising, I'm finally in perfect shape.

NOTE:
This is from the adjective *gordo* meaning "fat."

gordo/a chancho *n. & adj.* *(Argentina)* fatso; fat • (lit.): fat hog-like person.

example:
Nuestro jefe es un **gordo chancho**. No sé por qué no se pone a dieta.

translation:
Our new boss is a **fat pig**. I don't know why he doesn't go on a diet.

gordo/a de mierda *n.* *(Argentina)* an insult for "fatso" • (lit.): fat one of shit.
example:
¡Ese **gordo de mierda** me estafó!
translation:
That **fat pig** ripped me off!

jamón/ona *n. & adj.* fatso; fat • (lit.): ham.
example:
¡Vaya **jamona**! ¡Debe pesar una tonelada!
translation:
What a **fatso**! She must weigh a ton!

panzón/ona *n. & adj.* fat slob; chubby, fat.
example:
Cecila estaba tan delgada. Ahora es una **panzona**.
translation:
Cecilia used to be so thin. Now she's a **fat slob**.

panzudo al pedo *adj.* *(Argentina)* extremely fat • (lit.): paunchy to the fart.
example:
Mi tío es **panzudo al pedo**. ¡Le encanta comer!
translation:
My uncle is **fat out to here**. He loves to eat!

puerco/a *n. & adj. (Argentina)* • (lit.): pig.
example:
¿Te has comido la tarta entera? ¡Qué **puerco**!
translation:
You ate that entire cake? What a **pig**!

troncho/a *n. & adj.* *(El Salvador)* fatso; fat • (lit.): stalk, stem.
example:
Me voy a poner **troncho** como no me ponga a dieta.
translation:
I'm going to get **fat** if I don't go on a diet.

tunco/a *n. & adj. (El Salvador)* fatso; fat • (lit.): *(Honduras, Mexico)* hog, pig.
example:
Daniela era **tunca**, pero después de estar a régimen seis meses, está guapísima.
translation:
Daniela used to be **fat**, but after dieting for six months, she's beautiful.

vaca *f.* fatso (applies only to a woman) • (lit.): cow.
example:
¡Este vestido me hace parecer una **vaca**!

translation:
This dress makes me look like a **fat cow**!

HEROIN

caballo *m.* heroin • (lit.): horse.

chinaloa *f. (Mexico)* opium, heroin.

chocolate de fu man chu *m. (Mexico)* opium, heroin • (lit.): chocolate of fu manchu.

gumersinda *f.* heroin or opium.

HOMOSEXUAL

afeminado *m.* homosexual • (lit.): an effeminate [man].

amaricado • **1.** *m.* derogatory for "homosexual" • **2.** *adj.* effeminate.

amaricarse *v.* to become homosexual (from the masculine noun *maricón* which is derogatory for "homosexual").

bijirita *f. (Cuba)* derogatory for "homosexual."

bufo *m.* derogatory for "homosexual" • (lit.): clownish, comic.

bujarrón *m.* derogatory for "homosexual" • (lit.): sodomite.

champe *m. (Cuba)* derogatory for "homosexual."

NOTE:
This is a variation of the masculine noun *champí* meaning "a tiny insect."

chuparosa *f.* derogatory for "homosexual."

NOTE:
This is a variation of the masculine noun *chupaflor* meaning "humming bird."

ciendango *m. (Cuba)* derogatory for "homosexual."

cochón *m.* derogatory for "homosexual."

comilón *m. (Argentina)* derogatory for "homosexual" • (lit.): big eater (of penis).

cua-cua *m. (Puerto Rico)* derogatory for "homosexual."

NOTE: This is the sound a duck makes and is applied to homosexuals who walk with fast little steps much like a duck.

cuarenta y uno *m. (Mexico)* derogatory for "homosexual" • (lit.): forty-one.

NOTE: This expression may have originated since some people think that if a person is over forty and not married, it may be a sign of homosexuality.

culastrón *m. (Argentina)* derogatory for "homosexual."

NOTE: This is a variation of the masculine noun *culo* meaning "ass."

culero *m.* derogatory for "homosexual" (from the masculine noun *culo* meaning "buttocks," or closer, "ass").

cundango *m.* derogatory for "homosexual."

de la acera de enfrente *exp.* derogatory for "homosexual" • (lit.): (someone) from the other side of the street.

de la cáscara amarga *exp.* derogatory for "homosexual" • (lit.): (someone) from the bitter peel (of fruit)

de la otra acera *exp.* somewhat derogatory for "homosexual" • (lit.): (someone) from the other side of the street.

de los otros *m.* somewhat derogatory for "homosexual" • (lit.): one of them.

fresco *m.* derogatory for "homosexual" • (lit.): fresh.

gay *adj.* widely accepted term for "homosexual" • (lit.): homosexual, gay.

invertido *adj.* derogatory for "homosexual" • (lit.): inverted.

jardinera *f.* derogatory for "homosexual" • (lit.): female gardener.

joto *m. (Mexico)* derogatory for "homosexual" • (lit.): effeminate.

loca *m. (Venezuela)* derogatory for "homosexual" • (lit.): crazy woman.

mamplora *f. (El Salvador)* derogatory for "homosexual."

marchatrás *m. (Argentina)* derogatory for "homosexual" • (lit.): one who goes backward.

marica *m.* derogatory for "homosexual" • (lit.): magpie.

maricón *m. (very common)* derogatory for "homosexual."

maricona *f.* derogatory for "homosexual."

mariposa *f. (Mexico)* derogatory for "homosexual" • (lit.): butterfly.

mariquita *f.* derogatory for "homosexual" • (lit.): ladybird.

mesero sin charola *m.* derogatory for "homosexual" • (lit.): waiter without a tray (since the hand is in an effeminate position with the palm facing upward).

pargo *m. (Cuba)* derogatory for "homosexual" • (lit.): red snapper.

pato *m.* derogatory for "homosexual" • (lit.): duck.

NOTE: This term is applied to homosexuals who walk with fast little steps much like a duck.

pirujo *m.* • (lit.): variation of the feminine noun *piruja* meaning "an uninhibited young woman."

pirul *m.* derogatory for "homosexual."

plumero *m. (Puerto Rico)* derogatory for "homosexual" • (lit.): feather duster.

puto *m.* derogatory for "homosexual" • (lit.): sodomite.

quebracho *m. (Mexico)* derogatory for "homosexual" • (lit.): quebracho bark.

quebrachón *m. (Mexico)* derogatory for "homosexual" • (lit.): large piece of quebracho bark.

tener una vena *exp.* said to describe a homosexual • (lit.): to have one vein.

triángulo *m. (Puerto Rico)* derogatory for "homosexual" • (lit.): triangle.

volteado *m.* derogatory for "homosexual" • (lit.): turned around.

yiyi *m. (Puerto Rico)* derogatory for "homosexual."

HORNY

arrecho *adj. (Ecuador, Peru)* horny • (lit.): sexually excited.

calentorro/a *adj.* horny.

NOTE: This is a variation of the adjective *caliente* meaning "hot."

caliente *adj.* horny, sexually hot • (lit.): hot.

salido/a *adj.* horny.

NOTE:
This is a variation of the verb *salir* meaning "to leave."

ser más puta que las gallinas *exp. (Cuba)* (said of a woman) to be as horny as a toad • (lit.): to be as slutty as the hens.

JERK / IDIOT • CRAZY / STUPID

adoquín *adj. (Cuba)* • (lit.): paving stone.

example:
Carlos es un **adoquín**. Echó agua accidentalmente en el depósito de gasolina y ¡estropeó su coche!

translation:
Carlos is such an **idiot**. He accidentally put water in his gas tank and ruined his car!

baboso/a *n. & adj.* • idiot; stupid • (lit.): one who dribbles a lot.

example:
Víctor llegó tarde su primer día de trabajo porque se le olvidó la dirección. ¡Qué **baboso**!

translation:
Victor was late his first day on the job because he forgot the address. What an **idiot**!

bereco/a *n. & adj. (El Salvador)* idiot; stupid.

example:
Angélica es tan **bereca**. Echó sal en el café pensando que era azúcar.

translation:
Angelica is so **stupid**. She put salt in her coffee thinking it was sugar.

bobo/a *n. & adj.* idiot; stupid • (lit.): foolish.

example:
Luis es **bobo** si piensa que le voy a prestar más dinero.

translation:
Luis is **stupid** if he thinks he can borrow more money from me!

bofa *n. (Cuba)*.

example:
Mira a esa **bofa**. Está hablando sola.

translation:
Look at that **crazy woman**. She's talking to herself.

NOTE:
This is from the verb *bofarse* meaning "to sag."

bonachón/na *n. & adj.* sucker, simpleton; gullible • (lit.): someone who is too nice and good (from the adjective *bueno* meaning "good").
example:
Enrique se cree todo lo que le dices. ¡Es un **bonachón**!
translation:
Enrique believes everything you tell him. What a **sucker**!

buche *n. & adj. (Cuba)* idiot; crazy • (lit.): mouthful.
example:
Si fuera tú, no me fiaría de él. Francamente, creo que está un poco **buche**.
translation:
I wouldn't trust him if I were you. Frankly, I think he's a little **crazy**.

buey *n. & adj.* idiot; stupid • (lit.): ox, bullock.
example:
A Juan se le olvidó ponerse los pantalones para salir. ¡Qué **buey**!
translation:
Juan forgot to put on his pants when he went outside. What a **geek**!

burro/a *n. & adj.* jerk; crazy. • (lit.): donkey.
example:
¡Nunca saldría con un **burro** como ése!
translation:
I'd never go out with a **jerk** like that!

NOTE:
In Mexico, the term **burro/a** is also used to mean "a bad student."

cebollín *m. (Cuba)* stupid person • (lit.): small onion.
example:
Me pregunto cómo un **cebollín** como Oscar ha podido sacar una A en el examen de matemáticas.
translation:
I wonder how an **idiot** like Oscar got an A on the math test!

cebollón *m. (Cuba)* stupid person • (lit.): large onion.
example:
Todo el mundo piensa que Marcelo es un **cebollón**, pero la verdad es que es un genio.
translation:
Everyone thinks that Marcelo is an **idiot**, but he's actually a genius.

chiflado/a *n. & adj.* crackpot; crazy, nuts • (lit.): whistled (from the verb *chiflar* meaning "to whistle").

example:
Si crees que puedes conducir de San Francisco a Los Angeles en sólo tres horas, ¡estás **chiflado**!
translation:
If you think you can drive to Los Angeles from San Francisco in only three hours, you're **nuts**!

chirusa *f. (Argentina)* idiotic little girl • (lit.): ignorant young woman.
example:
¿Conociste a la hija de Marcela? ¡Qué **chirusa**!
translation:
Did you meet Marcela's daughter? What a little **geek**!

comebasura *n. & adj.* idiot; stupid • (lit.): garbage-eater.
example:
Alfredo es un verdadero **comebasura**. Le dice a todo el mundo que pertenece a la realeza.
translation:
Alfredo is a real **idiot**. He tells everyone that he is royalty.

corto/a de mate *adj. (Argentina)* touched in the head, nuts • (lit.): short in the gourd.
example:
Creo que nuestra profesora es un poco **corta de mate**. En sus clases se empieza a reir sin motivo.
translation:
I think our new teacher is a little **touched in the head**. During her lectures, she starts laughing for no reason.

cretinita *f. & adj. (Argentina)* idiotic little girl; jerky • (lit.): little cretin.
example:
¡Esa **cretinita** me ha robado el bolígrafo!
translation:
That **little cretin** stole my pen!

cretino *m. & adj.* jerk; jerky • (lit.): cretin.
example:
El hermano de Steve es un pequeño **cretino**. No para de desatarme los cordones de mis zapatos.
translation:
Steve's brother is a little **cretin**. He keeps untying my shoes.

guabina *f. (Cuba)*.
example:
¡Qué **guabina**! Paula está todo el día tirada viendo la televisión.
translation:
What an **idiot**! Paula just sits around and watches television all day.

guaje *m. & adj. (El Salvador, Mexico)* idiot; stupid.

jerk / idiot • crazy / stupid

example:
Con ese sombrero Pancho parece un **guaje**.
translation:
With that hat Pancho is wearing he looks like a **jerk**.

hecho polvo *n. (Spain)* • jerk, geek • (lit.): made of dust.
example:
Arnaldo parece un **hecho polvo** con sus gafas nuevas.
translation:
Arnaldo looks like a **geek** in his new glasses.

NOTE -1:
In Argentina and Mexico, this expression is used to mean "to ache." For example: *Mis pies están hechos polvo;* My feet are aching.

NOTE -2:
In Argentina, *hecho/a polvo* may also be used to mean "exhausted" • *Estoy hecho polvo hoy;* I'm exhausted today.

latoso/a *n. & adj.* jerk, pain in the neck; jerky. • (lit.): made of tin can.
example:
Simón es un **latoso**. Me sigue a todas partes.
translation:
Simón is an **annoying little jerk**. He follows me around everywhere.

locote *n.* big idiot.
example:
Mi hermana es psiquiatra y trabaja con **locotes** todo el día.
translation:
My sister is a psychiatrist who works with **crazy people** all day long.

NOTE:
This is from the adjective *loco/a* meaning "crazy."

lurio/a *adj. (Mexico)* • (lit.): mad, crazy.
example:
Estás **lurio** si te crees que te puedes comer esa tarta entera.
translation:
You're **crazy** if you think you can eat that entire cake.

VARIATION:
lurias *adj.*

maje *adj.* crazy.
example:
Tú estás **maje** si crees que el jefe te va a conceder un ascenso.
translation:
You're **out of your mind** if you think the boss is going to give you a raise.

NOTE:
This is from the verb *majar* meaning "to crush, pound, mash."

menso/a *(Mexico) n. & adj.* idiot; jerky • (lit.): foolish, stupid.

jerk / idiot • crazy / stupid

example:
Acabo de enterarme de que Carla está en un hospital psiquiátrico. No sabía que estaba **mensa**.
translation:
I just heard that Carla is in a mental hospital. I didn't know she was **nuts**.

necio/a *n. & adj.* fool; foolish • (lit.): foolish.
example:
La gente que no practica el sexo con precaución es **necia**.
translation:
People who don't practice safe sex are **crazy**.

papo/a *n. & adj. (El Salvador)* idiot; crazy.
example:
Jaime es un **papo** si piensa que va ser a médico algún día. No es lo suficientemente listo.
translation:
Jaime is a **nut** if he thinks he's going to be a doctor someday. He's not smart enough.

pelmazo/a *n.* • (lit.): undigested food.
example:
¡Ese **pelmazo** se ha saltado una luz roja!
translation:
That **idiot** ran a red light!

pelota *n. & adj.* idiot; stupid.
example:
¡Marco es tan **pelota**! ¡Manejó en la calle en sentido contrario!
translation:
Marco is such an **idiot**! He drove down the street in the wrong direction!

pelotudo/a *n. & adj.* idiot; stupid.
example:
Se me ha olvidado mi cita con el médico. ¡Qué **pelotudo**!
translation:
I forgot about my doctor's appointment. What an **idiot**!

NOTE:
This is from the feminine noun *pelota* meaning "ball."

rayado/a *n. & adj. (Argentina)* idiot; stupid • (lit.): striped one.
example:
Laura no sabe cómo encender su computadora. Está **raya-da**.
translation:
Laura can't figure out how to turn on her computer. She's **stupid**.

safado/a *n. & adj.* idiot, fool; foolish • (lit.): brazen, bold.
example:
Mi nuevo jefe habla solo todo el tiempo. ¡Está **safado**!

translation:
My new boss keeps talking to himself all the time. He's a **real idiot**!

socotroco/a *n. & adj. (Cuba)* idiot; stupid.

example:
¿Por qué quieres salir con Ernesto? Es todo un **socotroco**. ¡Ni siquiera sabe cuánto son dos más dos!

translation:
Why do you want to go out with Ernesto? He's such an **idiot**. He can't even add two plus two!

soreco/a *n. & adj.* idiot; stupid *(El Salvador)*.

example:
Soy tan **soreca**. No puedo comprender cómo se arma mi nueva bicicleta.

translation:
I'm so **stupid**. I just can't figure out how to assemble my new bicycle.

tapado/a *n. & adj.* idiot; stupid • (lit.): covered up.

example:
Mi nueva vecina sale a la calle en traje de baño en pleno invierno. Creo que está un poco **tapada**.

translation:
My new neighbor wears bathing suits outside during the winter. I think she's a little **nuts**.

tarado/a *n. & adj.* idiot; stupid. • (lit.): defective, damaged.

example:
Si te crees que me voy a levantar tan temprano para llevarte al aeropuerto, ¡estás **tarado**! Vete en taxi.

translation:
If you think I'm going to get up that early to drive you to the airport, you're **nuts**! Just take a taxi.

tarugo/a *n. & adj. (Guatemala, Mexico)* idiot; stupid • (lit.): wooden peg.

example:
Creía que mi novio era normal. Pero después de unos meses me dí cuenta de que es un **tarugo**.

translation:
I thought my boyfriend was so normal. But after a few months, I realized that he's really a **crackpot**!

totoreco/a *n. & adj. (El Salvador)* idiot; stupid • (lit.): stunned, confused, bewildered.

example:
¡Quítate la pantalla de la lámpara de la cabeza! ¡La gente va a pensar que estás **totoreco**!

translation:
Take that lamp shade off your head! People are you going to think you're **crazy**!

zopenco/a *n. & adj.* jerk; stupid • (lit.): dull, stupid.
example:
¡Nunca saldría con Jorge! ¡Es un **zopenco**!
translation:
I'd never go out with Jorge! He's such a **jerk**!

KISS

besar con la lengua *exp.* to give a French kiss • (lit.): to kiss with the tongue.

beso *m.* • (lit.): kiss.

beso francés *m.* French kiss • (lit.): [same].

beso negro *m.* a kiss that is applied with the tongue up someone's rectum • (lit.): black kiss.

morder *v.* to give a French kiss • (lit.): to bite.

morreo *m.* French kiss.
NOTE:
This is a variation of the masculine noun *morro* meaning "snout."

muerdo *m.* a French kiss, a kiss with the tongue.
NOTE:
This comes from the verb *morder* meaning "to bite."

LAZY

aplomado/a *n. & adj.* lazy bum; lazy • (lit.): said of something that refuses to move.
example:
Miguel nunca se ofrecerá a ayudarte. Es demasiado **aplomado**.
translation:
Miguel will never volunteer to help you. He's so **lazy**.
NOTE:
The adjective *aplomado/a* may also be used to mean "self-assured."

arrastrado/a *n. & adj.* lazy bum; lazy. • (lit.): wretched, miserable.
example:
Angela y yo hicimos una gran fiesta, pero no me ayudó nada. ¡Es tan **arrastrada**!
translation:
Angela and I threw a big party, but she didn't help me at all. She's so **lazy**!

bacán *m. (Argentina, Uruguay)* lazy bum.
example:
¡Eres un **bacán**! ¡Levántate del sofá y ponte a trabajar!
translation:
You're such a **lazy bum**! Get off the couch and do some work!

¡Che dejá de dormir, fiaca de mierda, movete un poco! *exp. (Argentina)* used in response to seeing a lazy person • (lit.): Hey, stop sleeping, you lazy piece of shit, and move around a little!
example:
¡**Che dejá de dormir, fiaca de mierda, movete un poco**! ¡Tenemos mucho trabajo que hacer!
translation:
Hey, stop sleeping, you lazy piece of shit, and move around a little! We have a lot of work to do!

conchudo/a *n. & adj.* lazy bum; lazy.
example:
Mi hermano es un **conchudo**. No hace nada todo el día.
translation:
My brother is a **lazy bum**. He doesn't do a thing all day.

dormilón/ona *n. & adj.* lazy bum; lazy • (lit.): one who sleeps a lot (from the verb *dormir* meaning "to sleep").
example:
El tío de Enrique es un **dormilón**. Está todo el día durmiendo.
translation:
Enrique's uncle is such a **lazy bum**. All he does is sleep all day.

empollón/ona *n. & adj.* lazy bum; lazy • (lit.): grind.
example:
Mi jefe es tan **empollón**, que al final termino haciendo yo todo el trabajo.
translation:
My boss is so **lazy** that I end up doing all of his work!

flojo/a . & adj. lazy bum; lazy • (lit.): loose, weak.
example:
Eres demasiado **flojo**. Tienes que intentar motivarte.
translation:
You're so **lazy**. You need to try to get motivated.

follón/ona *n. & adj.* lazy bum; lazy.
example:
Tienes que dejar de ser un **follón** o nunca encontrarás trabajo.
translation:
You've got to stop being such a **lazy bum** or you'll never find a job.

gafitas *m. (Spain)* • (lit.): small eyeglasses.

example:
He decidido echar a Adolfo. Es buen chico pero es un **gafitas**.

translation:
I've decided to fire Adolfo. He's a very good guy but he's a **lazy bum**.

gandul/a *n. & adj.* lazy bum; lazy.

example:
La razón por la que se está hundiendo esta compañía es porque hay demasiados **gandules** en ella.

translation:
The reason this company isn't surviving is because there are too many **lazy people** in it.

grandote boludo *m. (Argentina)* idiot, jerk • (lit.): big-balled (testicles) one.

example:
¿Has visto el sombrero que lleva Miguel? ¡Parece un **grandote boludo**!

translation:
Have you seen the hat Miguel is wearing? He looks like an **idiot**!

haragán *n. & adj.* lazy bum; lazy.

example:
Nunca he conocido a nadie tan **haragán** como Pedro. Está durmiendo todo el día.

translation:
I've never met anyone as **lazy** as Pedro. All he does is sleep all day.

holgazán/ana *n. & adj.* lazy bum; lazy • (lit.): lazy, indolent.

example:
Pedro es un **holgazán**. No le gusta trabajar.

translation:
Pedro is such a **geek**. He doesn't like to work.

huevón/ona (ser un) *n. & adj.* lazy bum; lazy • (lit.): to be like a testicle (since *huevón* comes from the term *huevo* which literally means "egg" but it used in slang to mean "testicle").

example:
Mi hermano y yo somos completamente opuestos. Yo soy muy activo y él es un **huevón**.

translation:
My brother and I are totally opposite. I'm very motivated and he's a **lazy bum**.

LESBIAN

bollaca *f.* a derogatory term for "lesbian."

bollera *f.* a derogatory term for "lesbian" • (lit.): baker.

cachapera *f. (Puerto Rico)* a derogatory term for "lesbian."

cachapera *f. (Venezuela)* a derogatory term for "lesbian."

NOTE:
This comes from the feminine term *cachapa* which is a thin pancake, usually served stacked. Therefore, a stack of *cachapas* conjures up the image of several vaginas stacked one on top of the other.

NOTE:
cachapear *v.* to engage in lesbian sex • *Ellas se estaban cachapeando;* They're having lesbian sex.

macha *f. & adj.* a somewhat derogatory term for "lesbian" • (lit.): the feminine form of *macho* meaning "very masculine."

VARIATION:
machona *f. (Argentina).*

machorra *f.* a somewhat derogatory term for "lesbian."

NOTE:
This is a variation of the masculine noun *macho* meaning "manly."

marimacha *f.* a derogatory term for "lesbian."

NOTE:
This is a variation of the feminine noun *marica* meaning "sissy" and the adjective *macho* meaning "manly."

tortera *f.* a derogatory term for "lesbian" • (lit.): tortilla maker.

tortillera *f.* a derogatory term for "lesbian" • (lit.): one who sells tortillas.

MADAME

(pertaining to a bordello)

madama *f. (Mexico)* madame of a brothel.

madre superiora *f. (Mexico)* a madame of a brothel • (lit.): mother superior.

madrina *f. (Mexico)* a madame of a brothel • (lit.): godmother.

madrota *f. (Mexico)* a madame of a brothel.

NOTE:
This is a variation of the feminine noun *madrona* meaning "pampering mother."

mariscala *f. (Mexico)* a madame of a brothel.

MARIJUANA

acostarse con rosemaria *exp. (Mexico)* to smoke marijuana • (lit.): to go to bed with Rosemary.

aracata *f. (Mexico)* marijuana.

atizar coliflor tostada *exp. (Mexico)* to smoke marijuana • (lit.): to smoke toasted cauliflower.

atizar mota *exp. (Mexico)* to smoke marijuana • (lit.): to stir powder.

chora *f. (Mexico)* marijuana.

grifear *v. (Mexico)* to smoke marijuana.

grilla *f. (Mexico, Central and South America)* marijuana (lit.): female cricket.

hierba *f. (Mexico)* marijuana • (lit.): grass or herb.

NOTE:
Also spelled: *yerba*.

malva *f. (Mexico)* marijuana • (lit.): mallow.

mary *f. (Mexico)* marijuana.

mastuerzo *m. (Mexico)* marijuana.

moravia *f. (Mexico)* marijuana.

morisqueta *f. (Mexico)* marijuana • (lit.): speck.

motivosa *f. (Mexico)* marijuana.

NOTE:
This is a variation of the masculine noun *motivo* meaning "motive" or "reason."

motocicleta *f. (Mexico)* marijuana • (lit.): motorcycle.

motor de chorro *m. (Mexico)* marijuana • (lit.): jet engine.

motorizar *v. (Mexico, Central and South America)* to smoke marijuana • (lit.): to motorize.

nalga de ángel *f. (Mexico)* marijuana • (lit.): buttocks of an angel.

orégano *m. (Mexico)* marijuana • (lit.): oregano.

orégano chino *m. (Mexico)* marijuana • (lit.): Chinese oregano.

verde *f.* marijuana • (lit.): green.

zacate inglés *m. (Mexico and Central America)* marijuana • (lit.): English hay.

MASTURBATE

acariciarse *v.* to masturbate • (lit.): to fondle oneself.

botarse la cantúa *exp. (Cuba)* to masturbate • (lit.): to throw the *cantúa* (a candy made of sweet potato, coconut, sesame, and sugar).

botarse la puñeta *exp. (Cuba)* to masturbate • (lit.): to throw the cuff.

botarse la yuca *exp. (Cuba)* to masturbate • (lit.): to throw the yucca plant.

botarse una paja *exp. (Cuba)* to masturbate • (lit.): to toss a straw.

casado con la viuda de los cinco hijos (estar) *exp. (Cuba)* to masturbate • (lit.): to be married to the widow of the five children.

chaquetear *v.* to masturbate.

VARIATION: **hacer una chaqueta** *exp.* to make a jacket.

hacer una cubana *exp. (Spain)* (said of a man) to reach orgasm by rubbing the penis between a woman's breasts • (lit.): to do it Cuban-style

hacer una paja *exp.* to masturbate (someone else).

VARIATION: **hacerse una paja** *exp.* to masturbate oneself • (lit.): to make a straw.

hacerse las puñetas *exp.* to masturbate • (lit.): to make oneself cuffs.

hacerse un pajote *exp.* to masturbate • (lit.): to make a large straw.

hacerse un solitario *exp.* to masturbate • (lit.): to do a solitary.

hacerse una bartola xp. to masturbate • (lit.): to do a careless act.

hacerse una canuta *exp.* to masturbate • (lit.): to make a tubular container.

hacerse una carlota *exp.* to masturbate • (lit.): to do a Carlota (a woman's name).

hacerse una chaqueta *exp. (Mexico)* to masturbate • (lit.): to make a jacket.

hacerse una gallarda *exp.* to masturbate • (lit.): to make a galliard (a type of French dance).

hacerse una magnolia *exp.* to masturbate • (lit.): to make a magnolia.

hacerse una paja *exp.* to masturbate • (lit.): to make a straw.

hacerse una pera *exp.* to masturbate • (lit.): to make a pear.

hacerse una sombrillita *exp.* to masturbate • (lit.): to make a little umbrella.

meneársela *v.* to masturbate, to beat off • (lit.): to shake it for oneself.

paja *f.* masturbation • (lit.): straw • *hacer una paja;* to jerk off.

pajero *m.* a person who masturbates.

pelársela *v.* to masturbate • (lit.): to peel it oneself.

pera (hacerse una/la) *exp.* to masturbate, to beat off • (lit.): to make oneself a pear.

puñeta (hacer) *exp.* to masturbate, to beat off • (lit.): to make a cuff.

sacudírsela *v.* to masturbate • (lit.): to shake it oneself.

sobarse la picha *exp. (Costa Rica)* to masturbate • (lit.): to fondle the penis oneself.

VARIATION:
sobársela *v.*

tocársela *v.* to masturbate • (lit.): to touch it oneself.

veregallo *m. (Mexico)* masturbation.

vergallito *m. (Mexico)* masturbation • (lit.): small penis.

MENSTRUATE

bandera roja *f.* menstruation • (lit.): red flag.

mala semana *f.* menstruation • (lit.): bad week.

periodo *m.* • (lit.): a woman's period.

purgación *f.* menstruation, period • (lit.): purging.

regla *f.* • (lit.): a woman's period.

tener la mecha puesta *exp. (Cuba)* to be menstruating, to be "on the rag" • (lit.): to have the fire on.

NOT TO GIVE A DAMN

no importar un carajo *exp.* not to give a damn • (lit.): not to mind a penis.
example:
No me importa un carajo lo que dices.
translation:
I **don't give a damn** what you say.

no importar un cojón *exp.* not to give a damn • (lit.): not to care a testicle.
example:
A Beatriz **no le importan un cojón** sus clases. Por eso está reprobando todas sus clases.
translation:
Beatriz **doesn't give a damn** about her school work. That's why she's failing all of her classes.

no importar un huevo *exp.* • (lit.): egg (or "testicle").
example:
A Daniel no le importa un huevo su trabajo. Sinceramente, creo que lo van a echar pronto.

translation:
Daniel doesn't give a damn about his job. Frankly, I think he's going to get fired soon.

no importar un pepino *exp.* • (lit.): not to care a cucumber.
example:
No me importa un pepino lo que la gente piense de mí.
translation:
I don't give a damn what people think about me.

ORAL SEX

chupar/mamar la pinga *exp.* to perform oral sex • (lit.): to suck the "dick."

NOTE: Any slang synonym for "penis" can be used here.

SEE: **penis**, *p. 243.*

dar una mamada *exp.* to give a blow job • (lit.): to give a sucking.

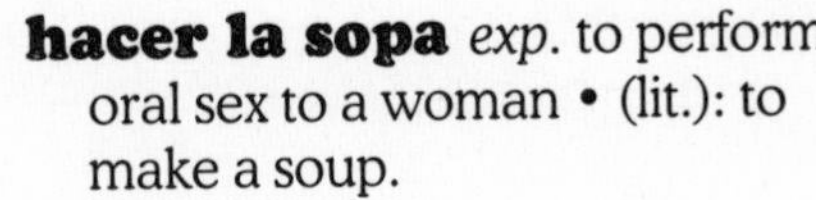

hacer la sopa *exp.* to perform oral sex to a woman • (lit.): to make a soup.

mamada *f.* blow job • (lit.): sucking.

tirarse a mamar *exp.* to give a blow job • (lit.): to pull oneself a sucking.

tocar la trompeta *exp.* to give a blow job • (lit.): to play the trumpet.

PAIN IN THE NECK / ANNOYING PERSON

corcho *m. (El Salvador)* annoying person or idiot • (lit.): cork.
example:
Guillermo me sigue a todas partes. ¡Es un **corcho**!
translation:
Guillermo follows me everywhere. He's such a **pain in the neck**!

estorbo *m.* • (lit.): obstacle.

example:
Cada vez que doy mi opinión sobre algo, Oscar discute conmigo. Es un **estorbo**.

translation:
Every time I give an opinion about something, Oscar argues with me. He's such a **pain in the neck**!

fregado/a *n. & adj.* annoying person, pain in the neck; annoying • (lit.): scrubbing.

example:
Jaime es un **fregado**. ¡Me llama por teléfono cinco veces al día!

translation:
Jaime is such a **pain in the neck**. He calls me on the telephone five times a day!

fregón/ona *n. & adj.* pain in the neck; annoying • (lit.): one who scrubs.

example:
Victor es un **fregón**. Cada vez que hablamos no hace más que contarme sus problemas.

translation:
Victor is a **pain in the neck**. Every time we talk, he does nothing but tell me about his problems.

NOTE:
This term is also commonly used to describe someone who is extremely impressive and "cool."

hinchapelotas *m.* pain in the neck • (lit.): one who makes someone's testicles swell.

example:
No puedo aguantar a Marco. Es un **hinchapelotas**. ¡Siempre me anda molestando con preguntas estupidas!

translation:
I can't stand Marco. He's a **pain in the neck**. He always bugs me with stupid questions!

NOTE:
pelotas *f.pl.* testicles • (lit.): balls (in a game).

latoso/a *n. & adj.* pain in the neck; annoying person • (lit.): made of tin can.

example:
Diana es una **latosa**. No hace más que pedirme favores.

translation:
Diana is a **pain in the neck**. All she ever does is ask me for favors.

PENIS

aparato *m. (Mexico)* penis • (lit.): apparatus.

arma *f.* penis • (lit.): weapon.

¡A la verga! *intjer.* Fuck it! • (lit.): To the penis!

berenjenal *f.* penis • (lit.): eggplant.

biberón *m.* penis • (lit.): baby bottle, feeding bottle.

bicho *m.* penis • (lit.): bug.

broca *f.* penis • (lit.): the bit of a drill.

butifarra *f.* penis • (lit.): pork sausage.

cacho *m. (El Salvador)* penis • (lit.): small piece, chunk.

camote *m.* penis • (lit.): sweet potato.

canario *m.* penis • (lit.): canary.

caoba *f. (Cuba)* penis • (lit.): mahogany tree.

carajo *m.* penis • (lit.): penis.

carallo *m.* penis.

NOTE:
This is a variation of the masculine noun *carajo* meaning "penis."

cipote *m.* penis • (lit.): silly, foolish.

cola *m.* penis • (lit.): tail.

cosita *f.* penis • (lit.): little thing.

curo *m. (Cuba)* penis • (lit.): leather strap.

chaira *f.* penis • (lit.): cobbler's knife.

chiflo *m.* penis • (lit.): whistle.

chile *m. (Mexico)* penis • (lit.): chile, hot pepper.

chilito *m. (Mexico, Spain)* an insulting term for a little penis • (lit.): small chile, small hot pepper.

choncha *f.* penis.

chora *f.* **1.** penis • **2.** *(Mexico)* marijuana • (lit.): female thief.

chorizo *m.* penis • (lit.): pork sausage.

NOTE:
The term *chorizo* literally means "pork sausage" but is used in slang to mean "penis," so be careful how you use it!

chorrico *m.* penis • (lit.): constant flow or stream.

chufle *f.* penis.

chuperson *m. (Mexico)* penis.

churro *m.* • **1.** turd • **2.** penis • (lit.): long fritter (*churro;* a long, straight fried pastry).

NOTE:
The term *churro* means "fritter" but is used in slang to mean "turd" or "penis," so be careful how you use it!

daga *f. (Puerto Rico)* penis • (lit.): dagger.

diablito *m.* penis • (lit.): little devil.

elbi *m. (Puerto Rico)* penis.

elote *m.* penis • (lit.): corn on the cob.

explorador *m.* penis • (lit.): the explorer.

falo *m.* penis • (lit.): phallus, penis.

fierro *m. (Mexico)* penis • (lit.): iron.

galleta *f. (Costa Rica)* penis • (lit.): cracker, cookie.

garrote *m.* penis • (lit.): club or stick.

hermano pequeño *m.* penis • (lit.): little brother.

hierro *m. (Puerto Rico)* penis • (lit.): iron.

hueso *m.* penis • (lit.): bone.

inga *f. (Cuba)* penis • (lit.): inga plant.

instrumento *m.* penis • (lit.): instrument.

lechero *m.* penis.

NOTE:
This is from *leche* literally meaning "milk" but used in slang to mean "semen."

leña *f. (Cuba)* penis • (lit.): firewood.

longaniza *f.* penis • (lit.): pork sausage.

macana *f.* penis • (lit.): heavy wooden club.

machaca *f.* penis • (lit.): crusher, pounder.

machete *m.* penis • (lit.): machete.

mandarria *f. (Cuba)* penis • (lit.): sledge hammer.

manguera *f.* penis • (lit.): water hose.

manolo *m.* penis.

mazo *m.* penis • (lit.): mallet.

mecasala *f. (El Salvador)* penis.

miembrillo *m. (Mexico)* penis • (lit.): small member.

minga *f.* penis • (lit.): communal work.

minina *f. (child's language)* penis, "peepee" • (lit.): kitty cat.

mirasol *m.* penis • (lit.): sunflower.

mitra *f. (Puerto Rico)* penis • (lit.): mitre.

mocongó *m. (Puerto Rico)* penis.

mona *f. (El Salvador)* penis • (lit.): female monkey.

morcilla *f.* penis • (lit.): blood sausage.

morronga *f. (Central America)* penis • (lit.): a female cat.

morrongo *m. (Mexico)* penis • (lit.): male cat.

nabo *m.* penis • (lit.): turnip.

NOTE:
The term *nabo* literally means "turip" but is used in slang to mean "penis," so be careful how you use it!

ñema *f. (Santo Domingo)* penis.

pacaya *f. (El Salvador)* penis • (lit.): elongated vegetable.

pajarito *m.* penis • (lit.): small bird.

palo *m.* penis • (lit.): pole, stick.

NOTE -1:
echar un palo *exp.* to fornicate • (lit.): to throw the stick or "penis."

NOTE -2:
The term *palo* literally means "pole" but is used in slang to mean "penis," so be careful how you use it!

partes nobles *f.pl.* penis • (lit.): noble parts.

pedazo *m. (Uruguay)* penis • (lit.): piece.

pelona *f.* penis.

NOTE:
This is from the adjective *pelón* meaning "bald."

pepino *m.* penis • (lit.): cucumber.

pesquesuda *f.* penis.

picha *(Cuba)* penis.

NOTE -1:
pichada *f.* fornication, screwing.

NOTE -2:
pichar *v.* to fornicate, to screw.

pichicuaca *f. (El Salvador)* penis.

pichón *m.* penis • (lit.): squab.

pichula *f. (Chile)* penis.

NOTE:
This is from the verb *pichulear* meaning "to deceive."

pico *m. (Chile)* penis • (lit.): beak.

NOTE -1:
In some parts of South America, *y pico* is used to mean "approximately": *Te veo a las siete y pico;* I'll see you around seven o'clock.

NOTE -2:
The term *pico* literally means "beak" but is used in slang to mean "penis," so be careful how you use it!

pijo/a • **1.** *n.* penis • **2.** *adj.* snobby • *¡Qué mujer más pija!;* What a snobby woman! • **3.** *n.* stupid person.

pimiento *m.* penis • (lit.): pimento, pepper.

pinco *m. (Puerto Rico)* penis • (lit.): penis.

pinga *(Cuba, Puerto Rico)* penis • (lit.): shoulder yoke (used for carrying).

pirulí *m.* penis.

pistola *f.* penis • (lit.): pistol.

pito *m. (Spain, Uruguay)* penis • (lit.): horn, whistle.

NOTE:
The term *pito* literally means "horn" or "whistle" but is used in slang to mean "penis," so be careful how you use it!

pizarrín *m.* penis • (lit.): slate pencil.

plátano *m.* penis • (lit.): banana.

polla *f. (Spain)* penis • (lit.): young hen.

NOTE:
The term *polla* literally means "young hen" but is used in slang to mean "penis," so be careful how you use it!

popeta *f. (Puerto Rico)* penis.

porra *f.* penis • (lit.): club, bludgeon.

prieta *f.* penis • (lit.): the swarthy one.

rabo *m.* penis • (lit.): tail.

reata *f. (Mexico)* penis • (lit.): rope.

retazo macizo *m. (Mexico)* penis • (lit.): stiff piece.

riata *f. (Mexico)* penis.

rifle *m. (Mexico)* penis • (lit.): rifle.

rodillo *m.* penis • (lit.): rolling pin.

salame *m. (Argentina)* penis • (lit.): salami.

salchicha *f.* penis • (lit.): sausage.

sobarse la picha *exp. (Costa Rica)* to masturbate • (lit.): to fondle the penis oneself.

tolete *m. (Cuba)* penis • (lit.): club.

tornillo *m.* penis • (lit.): screw.

tranca *f. (Cuba, Puerto Rico)* penis • (lit.): club, thick stick.

trasto *m.* penis • (lit.): old piece of furniture, piece of lumber.

trompa *f.* penis • (lit.): horn.

tronco *m. (Puerto Rico)* penis • (lit.): trunk.

vara *f.* penis • (lit.): stick.

velga *f. (Puerto Rico)* penis (from *verga* meaning "broomstick").

verga *f.* • **1.** penis • **2.** stupid person ("dick-head") (lit.): broomstick.

víbora *f.* penis • (lit.): viper.

yuca *f. (El Salvador)* penis • (lit.): yucca plant.

zanahoria *f.* penis • (lit.): carrot.

PIMP

abadesa *f. (Mexico)* pimp • (lit.): head of the house.

alcahuete *m.* pimp • (lit.): wild artichoke.

alcaucil *m.* pimp • (lit.): wild artichoke.

cafiche *m.* (Chile) pimp.

caficio *m. (Argentina)* pimp.

chivo *m.* pimp • (lit.): goat.

cholo *m. (Mexico, Puerto Rico)* • **1.** pimp • **2.** half-breed (the product of a mixed marriage).

chulo *m.* pimp • (lit.): **1.** pimp **2.** cool-looking, flashy.

cortejo *m. (Puerto Rico)* pimp • (lit.): escort.

fundillero *m.* pimp.

gancho *m.* pimp • (lit.): hook.

jebo *m. (Puerto Rico)* pimp.

padrote *m.* pimp • (lit.): large father.

PREGNANT

embarazada *f.* • (lit.): pregnant.

preñada *f.* • (lit.): pregnant.

NOTE:
This term is not used in Spain.

quedar de encargo *exp. (Mexico)* to make pregnant, to "knock up" • (lit.): made to order.

PROSTITUTE

ardilla prostitute *f. (Puerto Rico)* • (lit.): squirrel.

bruja *f.* whore • (lit.): witch.

buscona *f.* prostitute • (lit.): one who searches (from the verb *buscar* meaning "to search").

calienta culos *f.* prostitute • (lit.): ass warmer.

callejera (una) *f.* prostitute • (lit.): pertaining to the street.

chapero *m. (Spain)* male prostitute.

chica de alterne *f.* prostitute • (lit.): alternating girl.

cobo *m. (Puerto Rico)* old whore • (lit.): gigantic snail.

congalera *f.* prostitute, "whore" • (lit.): someone who works at a bordello.

corbejo *m. (Puerto Rico)* old whore.

cualquiera *f.* prostitute • (lit.): anyone.

cuero *m. (Puerto Rico)* prostitute who is into leather • (lit.): leather.

cusca *f.* prostitute, slut • (lit.): prostitute.

del rejue *exp. (Guatemala, Mexico)* prostitute.

del rejuego *exp. (Guatemala, Mexico)* prostitute.

NOTE:
This is a variation of: *del rejue*.

fulana *f.* prostitute • (lit.): so-and-so (anyone).

furcia *f.* prostitute • (lit.): doll, chick.

garraleta *f.* cheap whore.

golfa *f.* prostitute • (lit.): prostitute.

gorrona *f.* prostitute • (lit.): libertine.

guerrillera *f. (Puerto Rico)* prostitute, whore • (lit.): guerrilla, partisan.

jaina *f.* prostitute.

jeba *f. (Puerto Rico)* prostitute, whore.

NOTE:
This is a variation of the masculine noun *jebe* meaning "alum."

josiadora *f. (Puerto Rico)* prostitute, whore.

lagarta *f.* • **1.** prostitute, whore • **2.** bitch • (lit.): lizard.

maleta *f.* prostitute, whore • (lit.): suitcase.

muchachas putierrez *f.pl. (Guatemala, Mexico)* prostitutes • (lit.): Putierrez girls.

NOTE:
The feminine noun *putierrez* is a variation of the term *puta* meaning "prostitute" and is used here in jest as the girls' last name.

mujer de la calle *f.* prostitute • (lit.): a woman of the street.

mujer de la vida galante *f.* prostitute • (lit.): woman of luxurious lifestyle.

mujer fatal *f.* prostitute • (lit.): wicked woman.

pahuela *f.* prostitute, whore.

pendona *f.* prostitute, whore • (lit.): despicable person.

pepereche *m. (El Salvador)* prostitute, whore.

perdida *f.* prostitute • (lit.): lost.

pingo *m.* prostitute, whore.

pingona *f.* prostitute, whore.

pluma *f.* prostitute • (lit.): feather.

puta *f.* prostitute, whore.

ALSO -1:
de puta madre *exp.* • **1.** said of something excellent • *Esa casa es de puta madre;* That house is excellent • **2.** to be in excellent shape • *Esa tipa está de puta madre;* That girl is in great shape.

ALSO -2:
ir de putas *exp.* to walk the streets.

ALSO -3:
putada *f.* annoyance, pain in the neck.

NOTE:
The term *puto/a* is commonly used in place of the adjectives *jodido/a* and *chingado/a* both meaning "fucking": *ese jodido/chingado/puto examen;* that fucking test.

puta de mierda *f.* *(Argentina)* unclean whore • (lit.): whore of shit.

putonga *f.* prostitute • (lit.): large prostitute, whore.

ramera *f.* prostitute • (lit.): prostitute, whore.

retozona • **1.** *f. (Mexico)* prostitute • **2.** *adj.* frisky.

rule *m. (Mexico)* prostitute.

ruletera *f. (Mexico)* prostitute.

señorita de compañía *f.* prostitute • (lit.): call-girl.

taconera *f. (Mexico)* prostitute.

NOTE:
This comes from the verb *taconear* meaning "to tap one's heels."

talonera *f.* prostitute • (lit.): someone who walks very quickly.

tana *f.* *(Mexico)* prostitute.

QUICKLY

a toda prisa *exp.* at full speed, as quickly as possible • (lit.): at all speed.
example:
Voy a la escuela **a toda prisa** porque me levanté tarde.
translation:
I'm **darting off** to school because I woke up late.

a toda vela *exp.* • (lit.): at all sail.

a todo meter *exp.* *(Southern Spain)* • (lit.): at all introduce.

en un abrir y cerrar de ojos *exp.* in the twinkling of an eye • (lit.): in the opening and closing of an eye.

en un avemaría *exp.* • (lit.): in one Hail Mary.

en un chiflido *exp.* • (lit.): in one whistle.

en un credo *exp.* • (lit.): in one creed.

en un decir Jesús *exp.* • (lit.): in one saying of Jesus.

en un dos por tres *exp.* • (lit.): in a two by three.

en un improviso *exp.* *(Colombia, Mexico, Venezuela)* • (lit.): in one sudden action.

en un menos de lo que canta un gallo *exp.* • (lit.): in less time that it takes a rooster to sing (or crow).

en un salto *exp.* • (lit.): in one leap.

en un soplo *exp.* • (lit.): in a gust or blow.

RED-LIGHT DISTRICT

zonas (las) *f.pl.* red-light districts in Mexico and Colombia • (lit.): areas (the).

RUNT

chaparro/a *n. & adj.* runt; runty.
example:
¡Hey **chaparro**! ¡Muévete!
translation:
Hey, **shorty**! Move it!

corchito *m. (Argentina)* • (lit.): little cork.
example:
El **corchito** de Joseph me pidió salir el sábado por la noche.
translation:
That **little runt** Joseph asked me out on Saturday night.

enano/a *n. & adj.* runt; runty. • (lit.): dwarf.
example:
John se cree que es un tipo fuerte, pero no es más que un **enano**.
translation:
John thinks he's so tough but he's nothing but a **little runt**.

inspector de zócalo *m. (Argentina)* • (lit.): baseboard inspector.
example:
¿Le pediste a Enrique que te ayudara a mover el piano? ¡Pero si es un **inspector de zócalo**!
translation:
You asked Enrique to help you move your piano? But he's such a **little runt**!

mierdecilla *f.* • (lit.) small shit.
example:
Ese **mierdecilla** es tan presuntuoso que nadie gusta de él.
translation:
That **little runt** acts so conceited but no one even likes him.

petiso de mierda *m. (Argentina)* • (lit.): little shit.
example:
No voy a invitar a ese **petiso de mierda** a mi fiesta de cumpleaños.
translation:
I'm not going to invite that **little shit** to my birthday party.

SCAREDY-CAT / COWARD

coyón/na *n. & adj.* scaredy-cat; scared.
example:
¡Soy demasiado **coyón** para tirarme en paracaídas!

translation:
I'm too much of a **scaredy-cat** to try parachuting!

sacatón/ona *n. & adj.* scaredy-cat; scared • (lit.): from the verb *sacar* meaning "to pull away quickly."

example:
Simón no sale por la noche. Es un **sacatón**.

translation:
Simón won't go outside at night. He's a **scaredy-cat**.

SEMEN

crema *f.* semen • (lit.): cream.

jugo *m.* semen • (lit.): juice.

leche *f.* semen • (lit.): milk.

NOTE: This term may also be used as an expletive: *¡Leche!;* Damn!

ALSO -1: **de mala leche** *adj.* said of someone who is mean • (lit.): of bad semen.

ALSO -2: **hay mucha mala leche entre ellos** *exp.* there are a lot of bad feelings between them • (lit.): there's a lot of bad semen between them.

ALSO -3: **tener mala leche** *exp.* to be in a bad mood • (lit.): to have bad semen.

licor *m.* semen • (lit.): liquor.

mermelada de membrillo *f. (Mexico)* semen • (lit.): marmalade of the smaller limb (quince jam).

NOTE: **dulce de membrillo** *f. (Argentina).*

néctar *m.* semen • (lit.): nectar.

SEX (TO HAVE)

cachar *v. (Peru)* to have sex, to fornicate • (lit.): to break into pieces.

casquete (echar un) *exp.* to have a fuck • (lit.): to throw a helmet.

cepillar *v.* to fornicate • (lit.): to brush.

VARIATION: **cepillarse a** *v.*

chingar *v.* to fornicate • (lit.): to fuck.

clavar *v.* to fornicate • (lit.): to nail.

coger *v.* to fornicate • (lit.): to get, to catch.

NOTE:
This verb leads to many embarrassing moments for natives of Spain who travel to other Spanish-speaking countries. In Spain, the verb *coger* simply means "to catch." It would not be unusual for a Spaniard to travel to Argentina, for example, and ask where he could "catch" the bus by using the phrase: *¿Donde puedo coger el autobús?* translated in Argentina (and many other Spanish-speaking countries) as: "Where can I fuck the bus?"

comer *v. (Chile, Colombia, Ecuador, Peru, Venezuela)* to fornicate • (lit.): to eat.

culear *v.* to fornicate.

NOTE:
This comes from the masculine noun *culo* meaning "ass."

dar candela por el culo *exp. (Cuba)* to perform anal sex • (lit.): to give fire from one's ass.

encalomar *v.* to fornicate • (lit.): to become overheated.

enjaretarse a *v.* to fornicate • (lit.): to do (something) in a rush.

entabicar *v.* to fornicate • (lit.): to board up, to wall up.

fachar *v. (Venezuela)* to fuck a woman.

follar *v.* • **1.** to fornicate, to fuck • **2.** to fart silently • (lit.): to blow with bellows.

foquin *adj. (Puerto Rico)* fucking.

NOTE:
This is a Puerto Rican adaptation of the English adjective "fucking."

hacer un favor *exp.* to fornicate • (lit.): to do a favor.

hocicar *v.* to fornicate • (lit.): to root, nuzzle, grub around in.

ir a desgastar el petate *exp. (Mexico)* to have sex • (lit.): to go wear down the bedding.

ir a desvencigar la cama *exp. (Mexico)* to have sex • (lit.): to go break the bed.

ir a hacer de las aguas *exp. (Mexico)* to have sex • (lit.): to go make some water.

ir a la junta de conciliación *exp. (Mexico)* to have sex • (lit.): to go to a meeting.

ir a la lucha super libre a calzón *exp. (Mexico)* to have sex • (lit.): to go see wrestling wearing nothing but underwear.

ir a percudir el cochón *exp. (Mexico)* to have sex • (lit.): to tarnish the mattress.

ir a rechinar la cama *exp. (Mexico)* to have sex • (lit.): to make the bed squeak.

ir a un entierro *exp. (Mexico)* to have sex • (lit.): to go to a funeral.

joder *v.* • **1.** to fornicate, to fuck • **2.** to bother the fuck out of someone.

joder como desesperados *exp.* to fornicate • (lit.): to fuck like desperate people.

joder como locos *exp.* to fornicate • (lit.): to fuck like crazy people.

joderse vivos *exp.* to fornicate • (lit.): to fuck alive.

limpiar el sable *exp.* to fornicate • (lit.): to clean the saber.

meterla hasta la empuñadura *exp.* to fornicate • (lit.): to put in up to the sword hilt.

meterla hasta las cachas *exp.* to fornicate • (lit.): to put it up to the buttocks.

meterla hasta los huevos *exp.* to fornicate • (lit.): to put it up to the balls (testicles).

meterla hasta los puños *exp.* to fornicate • (lit.): to put it up to the fists.

metersela a alguien *exp.* to fornicate • (lit.): to put it in someone.

mojar [el churro] *exp.* to fornicate • (lit.): to wet [the long fritter].

NOTE: **churro** *m.* a long, straight fried pastry.

montar *v.* to fornicate • (lit.): to climb up (on someone).

palo (echar un) *exp.* to fornicate • (lit.): to throw a stick or "penis."

NOTE:
palo *m.* penis • (lit.): stick, pole.

pasar por la piedra *exp.* to fornicate • (lit.): to pass by the stone.

pasar por las armas *exp.* to fornicate • (lit.): to pass by the arms.

pisar a *v.* to fornicate • (lit.): to step on (someone).

polvo (echar un) *exp.* to fornicate • (lit.): to throw a powder.

revisar los interiores *exp.* *(Mexico)* to have sex • (lit.): to check on one's insides.

romper *v.* *(Mexico)* to deflower a girl • (lit.): to tear, to break down.

VARIATION:
romper el tambor *exp.* • (lit.): to bust open the screen.

singar *v.* *(Cuba)* to fornicate • (lit.): to pole or propel with an oar.

subir al guayabo *exp.* *(Mexico)* to have sex • (lit.): to go up to the jelly.

tirar *v.* *(Chile, Colombia, Ecuador, Peru, Venezuela)* to fornicate • (lit.): to throw away.

tirarse *v.* to fornicate • (lit.): to throw oneself.

tragar *v.* to fornicate.

tubar *v.* to fornicate • (lit.): to knock down.

SHIT

cagada *f.* shit (from the verb *cagar* meaning "to shit").
example:
Los fertilizantes están realmente hechos de **cagadas**.
translation:
Fertilizer is actually made of **shit**.

mierda • **1.** *interj.* shit (used to express surprise, anger, disappointment) • **2.** filth • (lit.): shit.

truño *n.* shit.
example:
Ten cuidado de no pisar un **truño**. Hay muchos perros en este barrio.

translation:
Be careful not to walk in any **shit**. There are a lot of dogs in this neighborhood.

SHOW-OFF (TO BE A)

farolero/a (ser un/a) *n. & adj.* show-off; showy • (lit.): lantern maker.

example:
Nancy es una **farolera**. Yo creo que le gusta llamar la atención.

translation:
Nancy is such a **show-off**. I think she likes a lot of attention.

ostentador/a *n. & adj.* show-off; showy • (lit.): one who is ostentatious.

example:
¿Has visto lo que llevaba Claudia puesto? ¡Qué **ostentadora**!

translation:
Did you see what Claudia was wearing? What a **show-off**!

SHUT UP!

¡Cállate! *interj.* • (lit.): Shut yourself!

example:
¡**Cállate**! ¡Hablas demasiado!

translation:
Shut up! You talk too much!

¡Cállate/Cierra el hocico! *interj.* • (lit.): Shut your mouth!

example:
¡**Cállate/Cierra el hocico**! ¡Es mentira!

translation:
Shut up! That's a lie!

NOTE:
hocico *m.* • (lit.): the mouth of an animal (and derogatory when used in reference to a person).

¡Cállate/Cierra el pico! *exp.* Shut your trap! • (lit.): Shut your beak!

example:
¡**Cállate/Cierra el pico**! ¡Lo que estás diciendo es mentira!

translation:
Shut your trap! What you're saying is a lie!

¡Cállate/Cierra la boca! *exp.* • (lit.): Close your mouth!

example:
¡**Cállate/Cierra la boca**! ¡Deja de hablar de ella de ese modo!

translation:
Shut your mouth! Stop talking about her that way!

SNOB(BY)

alzado/a *n. & adj.* snob; stuck up • (lit.): from the verb *alzar* meaning "to lift" which refers to a snobby person's nose in the air.

example:
¡Diana es tan **alzada**! Sólo va a restaurantes caros.

translation:
Diana is so **snobby**! She only goes to expensive restaurants.

ampuloso/a *n. & adj.* snob; stuck up • (lit.): verbose, pompous, full of redundancies.

example:
Laura es una **ampulosa**. Sólo invita a gente rica a sus fiestas.

translation:
Laura is a **snob**. She only invites rich people to her parties.

cuello duro *m. & adj.* snob; stuck up • (lit.): hard or stiff neck (from keeping one's nose in the air).

example:
Miguel es un **cuello duro**. Sólo viaja en primera clase.

translation:
Miguel is a **snob**. He'll only travel first class.

fufú *m. & adj.* snob; stuck up • (lit.): Cuban dish made of plantain & pork rind.

example:
Desde que Arnaldo se hizo rico, se ha convertido en un **fufú**.

translation:
Ever since Arnaldo became rich, he's become a **snob**.

fufurufu *n. & adj.* snob; stuck up.

example:
Mi tio es millonario pero no es un **fufurufu** para nada. Tiene los pies en la tierra.

translation:
My uncle is a millionaire but he's not a **snob** at all. He's very down-to-earth.

lleno/a de humos *adj.* *(Argentina)* • (lit.): full of smoke.

example:
La tía de David está **llena de humos**. Se niega a hablar con la gente que no es rica.

translation:
David's aunt is **very snobby**. She refuses to speak to people who aren't rich.

SPIT (TO)

escupir *v.* to spit • (lit.): to spit.

example:
Es ilegal **escupir** en el tren.

translation:
It's illegal **to spit** in the train.

STINGY

aceite *n. & adj. (Cuba)* tightwad; stingy • (lit.): oil.

example:
Eres tan **aceite**. Nunca te ofreces a pagar la cena.

translation:
You're so **stingy**. You never offer to pay for dinner.

agarrado/a *n. & adj.* tightwad; stingy • (lit.): held.

example:
Antonio es muy **agarrado**. Nunca le compra regalos a nadie.

translation:
Antonio is very **stingy**. He never buys people gifts.

apretado/a *n. & adj. (Mexico)* tightwad; stingy • (lit.): squashed, tightly-packed.

example:
Angela solía ser muy **apretada**. Pero desde que le ha tocado la lotería, se ha vuelto muy generosa.

translation:
Angela used to be very **stingy**. But now that she won the lottery, she's become very generous.

codo *m. & adj.* tightwad; stingy • (lit.): elbow.

example:
La razón por la que mi tío es tan rico es porque es un **codo**. Nunca gasta dinero en nada.

translation:
The reason my uncle is so rich is because he's a **tightwad**. He never spends money on anything.

mendigo/a *n. & adj.* tightwad; stingy • (lit.): beggar.

example:
¿Viste el regalo tan barato que me hizo Geraldo para mi cumpleaños? ¡Qué **mendigo**!

translation:
Can you believe the inexpensive gift Geraldo gave me for my birthday? What a **cheapskate**!

pichicato/a *n. & adj.* tightwad; stingy.

example:
¿Quieres que andemos diez millas? No seas **pichicato**. Vamos a coger un taxi.

translation:
You want us to walk ten miles? Don't be such a **cheapskate**. Let's just get a taxi.

translation:
This perfume shop **stinks to high heaven**!

ALSO:
peste *f.* stink, foul smell • (lit.): plague, epidemic disease • *¡Qué peste!;* What a horrible smell!

UGLY / UGLY PERSON

cáncamo *m. (Cuba)* • (lit.): louse.

example:
¡Qué **cáncamo**! Me pregunto cómo puede tener una hermana tan guapa.

translation:
What an **ugly man**! I wonder how he could have such a beautiful sister!

casco *m.* ugly woman • (lit.): helmet.

example:
Paula era un **casco**, pero despues de la cirujía estética, está guapísima.

translation:
Paula used to be a **real ugly woman**, but after her plastic surgery, she's beautiful.

URINATE (TO)

cambiarle el agua al canario *exp.* to urinate • (lit.): to change the canary's water.

example:
Antes de salir de viaje, tengo que **cambiarle el agua al canario**.

translation:
Before we leave on our trip, I need **to take a leak**.

chis *m. (Mexico – children's language)* urine, piss.

example:
Huele a **chis** en este baño.

translation:
It smells of **urine** in this bathroom.

NOTE:
As an interjection, *chis* may be used to mean "shhh!" or "pst!"

cuartito *m.* bathroom, the "john" • (lit.): small room

example:
Necesito ir al **cuartito**.

translation:
I need to visit the **bathroom**.

desbeber *v.* to urinate • (lit.): to "un-drink."

example:
Después de beber toda esa agua, de verdad necesito **desbeber**.

translation:
After drinking all that water, I really need **to take a leak**.

diligencia (hacer una) *exp.* to go to the bathroom (urinate or defecate) • (lit.): to do an errand.

example:
Antes de salir a trabajar, siempre hago una **diligencia** primero.
translation:
Before I leave for work, I always go to the **bathroom** first.

hacer pipí *exp.* to urinate • (lit.): to make peepee.
example:
No te olvides de **hacer pipí** antes de irte a la cama.
translation:
Don't forget **to go peepee** before you go to bed.

ir a botar el agua al canario *exp. (Cuba)* to go take a leak • (lit.): to go to throw away the canary's water.
example:
Creo que he bebido demasiado café; necesito **ir a botar el agua al canario** otra vez.
translation:
I think I drank too much coffee. I need **to take a leak** again.

jiñar *v.* • **1.** to urinate • **2.** to defecate.
example:
¡Tengo que encontrar un sitio donde **jiñar**!
translation:
I need to find somewhere **to relieve myself**!

meadero *m.* urinal (from the verb *mear* meaning "to piss").
example:
El **meadero** en este baño está muy limpio.
translation:
The **urinal** in this bathroom is very clean.

meado[s] *m.*pl. urine, piss (from the verb *mear* meaning "to piss").
example:
El olor a **meado** me pone enfermo.
translation:
The smell of **urine** makes me sick.

mear *v.* to urinate, to piss.
example:
Creo que tengo que llevar a mi hija al baño. Parece que necesita **mear**.
translation:
I think I need to take my daughter to the bathroom. She looks like she needs **to take a leak**.

NOTE:
mearse de risa *exp.* to laugh so hard as to urinate in one's pants • (lit.): [same].

meón *n.* baby, "little pisher" (from the verb *mear* meaning "to piss").
example:
¡Roberto es un **meón**!

translation:
Robert is a **baby**!

pipí *m. (child's language)* urine, peepee.

example:
¿Has **hecho pipí** antes de irte a la cama?

translation:
Did you **go peepee** before going to bed?

NOTE:
hacer pipí *exp.* to go peepee.

VAGINA

almeja *f.* an extremely vulgar term for "vagina" • (lit.): clam.

VARIATION:
almejilla *f.* • (lit.): small clam.

NOTE:
The term *almeja* literally means "clam" but is used in slang to mean "vagina," so be careful how you use it!

argolla *f.* vagina • (lit.): ring, hoop, band.

bacalao *m. (Mexico)* vagina • (lit.): codfish.

bigote *m.* vagina • (lit.): mustache.

bizcocho *m.* vagina • (lit.): sweet bread or sponge cake.

bollo *m.* vagina • (lit.): a type of bread.

CAUTION:
In western Venezuela, the expression *tremendo bollo* means "nice vagina." However, in other parts of the same country, the expression translates as "big mess" or "fine pickle."

NOTE:
The term *bollo* literally means "a type of bread" but is used in slang to mean "vagina," so be careful how you use it!

bruquena *f.* vagina.

cajeta *f. (Argentina)* vagina • (lit.): a type of sweet pudding.

casita de paja *f. (Puerto Rico)* vagina • (lit.): small house of straw.

cepillo *m.* vagina • (lit.): brush.

cocho *m. (El Salvador, Mexico)* vagina • (lit.): dirty, filthy.

coña *f.* • **1.** vagina • **2.** joking.

NOTE:
This is a variation of the masculine noun *coño* which is a vulgar slang term for "vagina."

ALSO -1:
¡No me des la coña! *interj.* Fuck off! • (lit.): Don't give me the vagina!

ALSO -2:
de coña *exp. (Spain)* by pure luck • *Conseguí este trabajo de coña;* I got this job by pure luck.

concha *f. (Argentina, Central America, Cuba, Uruguay,)* vagina • (lit.): seashell.

ALSO:
¡La concha de tu madre! *interj.* an extremely vulgar insult literally meaning "Your mother's vagina!"

VARIATION:
concho *m.*

NOTE:
The term *concha* literally means "seashell" but is used in slang to mean "vagina," so be careful how you use it!

conejo *m.* a vulgar term for "vagina" • (lit.): rabbit.

NOTE:
The term *conejo* literally means "rabbit" but is used in slang to mean "vagina," so be careful how you use it!

coño *m.* an extremely vulgar term for "vagina."

NOTE:
This term is commonly used in many Spanish-speaking countries (with the exception of Mexico) as an interjection denoting surprise, anger, or annoyance. For example: *¡Coño! ¡No sabía que iba a llover!;* Damn! I didn't know it was supposed to rain!

crica *f. (Puerto Rico)* vagina • (lit.): vagina.

cuca *f. (Venezuela, El Salvador)* vagina • (lit.): clever, smart.

cuevita *f.* vagina • (lit.): little cave.

chacón *f. (Argentina)* vagina • (lit.): an inversion of the feminine term *concha* meaning "seashell."

chango *m.* vagina • (lit.): monkey.

chimba *f. (Colombia)* vagina.

chocha *f. (Cuba)* vagina • (lit.): woodcock (a type of game bird).

chocho *m. (Mexico, Spain)* vagina • (lit.): floppy.

chucha *f.* vagina • (lit.): bitch dog *(Chile)*.

NOTE:
The term *chucha* literally means "bitch dog" but is used in slang to mean "vagina," so be careful how you use it!

chumino *m.* vagina.

dona *f.* vagina • (lit.): doughnut.

finquita *f. (Puerto Rico)* vagina • (lit.): small piece of property.

gata *f.* vagina • (lit.): female cat.

grieta *f.* vagina • (lit.): crack.

hediondito *m.* vagina • (lit.): the little smelly one.

higo *m.* vagina • (lit.): fig (fruit).

hoyo *m. (Puerto Rico)* vagina • (lit.): hole.

lacho *m. (Puerto Rico)* vagina.

mico/a *n. (Central America)* vagina • (lit.): car jack.

minino *m. (child's language)* vagina • (lit.): kitty cat.

muñeco *m. (Mexico)* vagina • (lit.): doll, puppet.

nalgas *f.pl.* • **1.** buttocks • **2.** vagina • (lit.): buttocks.

nido *m. (Mexico)* vagina • (lit.): bird's nest or hiding place.

ojal *m.* • vagina • (lit.): button-hole, slit.

pan *m. (El Salvador)* vagina • (lit.): bread.

panocha *f. (Mexico)* vagina • (lit.): sweetbread.

panuda *f. (El Salvador)* large vagina.

papaya *f. (Central America, Cuba, Puerto Rico)* vagina.

NOTE:
The term *papaya* is used in Cuba, Puerto Rico, and the Dominican Republic to mean "penis," so be careful how you use it!

parrocha *f.* vagina • (lit.): small pickled sardine.

pashpa *f. (El Salvador)* vagina.

pepa *f.* vagina • (lit.): take from the female name "Pepa."

pitaya *f.* vagina • (lit.): tropical cactus with an edible fruit.

pitón *m. (Puerto Rico)* vagina • (lit.): budding horn.

pupusa *f. (El Salvador)* vagina • (lit.): a tortilla filled with cheese.

raja *f.* vagina • (lit.): gash.

rajada *f.* vagina • (lit.): gash.

rajita *f.* vagina • (lit.): little slit.

rosco *m.* vagina • (lit.): ring-shaped roll of pastry.

seta *f.* vagina • (lit.): mushroom.

tamale *m.* vagina • (lit.): tamale.

tonto *m.* vagina • (lit.): silly, foolish.

torta *f. (El Salvador)* vagina • (lit.): cake, torte.

yoyo
m. (Mexico) vagina.

VOMIT

un vómito *m. (Argentina)* said of anything disgusting • (lit.): a vomit.

example:
No me voy a comer eso. ¡Parece **un vómito**!

translation:
I'm not eating that food. It looks **disgusting**!

vomitar hasta la primera papilla *exp.* to vomit, to barf one's guts up • (lit.): to vomit even one's first soft-food.

example:
Estuve tan enfermo la semana pasada, que **vomité hasta la primera papilla**.

translation:
I was so sick last week that **I barfed my guts up**.

vomitar hasta las tripas *exp.* to vomit, to barf one's guts up • (lit.): to vomit up to one's guts.

example:
Creo que anoche me sentó algo mal. Estuve **vomitando hasta las tripas** durante tres horas.

translation:
I think I had food poisoning last night. I was **vomiting my guts up** for three hours.

WHOREHOUSE

aduana *f. (Mexico)* whorehouse • (lit.): Customs.

berreadero *m. (Mexico)* whorehouse • (lit.): a place where one can listen to animals bleat.

casa de citas *f.* whorehouse • (lit.): a house where one can have a date.

casa de putas *f.* whorehouse • (lit.): house of whores.

prostíbulo *m.* whorehouse (from the masculine noun *prostituto* meaning "prostitute").

quilombo *n. (Argentina, Uruguay)* whorehouse.

NOTE: This term is commonly used in Argentina and Uruguay as an interjection: *Qué quilombo!;* What a mess!

resbalón *m. (Guatemala, Mexico)* whorehouse, brothel.

ORDER FORM

SLANGMAN PUBLISHING

12206 Hillslope Street
'udio City, CA 91604 • USA

INTERNATIONAL:
1-818-769-1914

TOLL FREE (US/Canada):
1-877-SLANGMAN
(1-877-752-6462)

Worldwide FAX:
1-413-647-1589

' the latest products, preview
'pters, and shop online at:

WW.SLANGMAN.COM

SHIPPING

—Domestic Orders—

JRFACE MAIL
elivery time 5-7 days).
d $4 shipping/handling
' the first item, $1 for
ch additional item.

JSH SERVICE
ailable at extra charge.
ase telephone us for
tails.

International Orders—

/ERSEAS SURFACE
livery time 6-8 weeks).
d $5 shipping/handling
the first item, $2 for
ch additional item.

/ERSEAS AIRMAIL
ilable at extra charge.
ase phone for details.

PRODUCT	TYPE	PRICE
AMERICAN SLANG & IDIOMS		
STREET SPEAK 1: *The Complete Course in American Slang & Idioms*	Book	$18.95
	Audio CDs (2 per set)	$35
	Audio Cassettes (2 per set)	$25
SAVE $6.95!	Book + Audio CDs	$50
SAVE $3.95!	Book + Audio Cassettes	$40
STREET SPEAK 2: *The Complete Course in American Slang & Idioms*	Book	$21.95
	Audio CDs (2 per set)	$35
	Audio Cassettes (2 per set)	$25
SAVE $6.95!	Book + Audio CDs	$50
SAVE $3.95!	Book + Audio Cassettes	$40
STREET SPEAK 3: *The Complete Course in American Slang & Idioms*	Book	$21.95
	Audio CDs (2 per set)	$35
	Audio Cassettes (2 per set)	$25
SAVE $6.95!	Book + Audio CDs	$50
SAVE $3.95!	Book + Audio Cassettes	$40
BIZ SPEAK 1: *Slang, Idioms & Jargon Used in Business English*	Book	$21.95
	Audio CDs (2 per set)	$35
	Audio Cassettes (2 per set)	$25
SAVE $6.95!	Book + Audio CDs	$50
SAVE $3.95!	Book + Audio Cassettes	$40
BIZ SPEAK 2: *Slang, Idioms & Jargon Used in Business English*	Book	$21.95
	Audio CDs (2 per set)	$35
	Audio Cassettes (2 per set)	$25
SAVE $6.95!	Book + Audio CDs	$50
SAVE $3.95!	Book + Audio Cassettes	$40
BIZ SPEAK 3: *Slang, Idioms & Jargon Used in Business English*	Book	$21.95
	Audio CDs (2 per set)	$35
	Audio Cassettes (2 per set)	$25
SAVE $6.95!	Book + Audio CDs	$50
SAVE $3.95!	Book + Audio Cassettes	$40
SPANISH SLANG & IDIOMS		
STREET SPANISH 1: *The Best of Spanish Slang*	Book	$16.95
	Cassette	$12.50
STREET SPANISH 2: *The Best of Spanish Idioms*	Book	$16.95
	Cassette	$12.50
STREET SPANISH 3: *The Best of Naughty Spanish*	Book	$16.95
	Cassette	$12.50
STREET SPANISH DICT. & THESAURUS	Book	$16.95
FRENCH SLANG & IDIOMS		
STREET FRENCH 1: *The Best of French Slang*	Book	$16.95
	Cassette	$12.50
STREET FRENCH 2: *The Best of French Idioms*	Book	$16.95
	Cassette	$12.50
STREET FRENCH 3: *The Best of Naughty French*	Book	$16.95
	Cassette	$12.50
STREET FRENCH DICT. & THESAURUS	Book	$16.95
ITALIAN SLANG & IDIOMS		
STREET ITALIAN 1: *The Best of Italian Slang*	Book	$16.95
	Cassette	$12.50
STREET ITALIAN 2: *The Best of Naughty Italian*	Book	$16.95
	Cassette	$12.50

ORDER FORM

SLANGMAN PUBLISHING

-PAGE 2-

See the latest products, preview chapters, and shop online at:

WWW.SLANGMAN.COM

QUANTITY	TITLE	PRICE	TOTAL

Total for Merchandise	
Sales Tax *(California Residents Only add applicable sales tax)*	
Shipping *(see other side of form)*	
ORDER TOTAL	

prices/availability subject to change

Name ____________________

(School/Company) ____________________

Street Address ____________________

City ____________ State/Province ____________ Postal Code ____________

Country ____________ Phone ____________ Email ____________

METHOD OF PAYMENT (CHECK ONE)

☐ Personal Check or Money Order *(Must be in U.S. funds and drawn on a U.S. bank.)*

☐ VISA ☐ Master Card ☐ Discover

Credit Card Number

Expiration Date

Signature *(important!)*